THE INTELLECTUALISM OF
SAINT THOMAS

THE INTELLECTUALISM OF SAINT THOMAS

By
PIERRE ROUSSELOT, S.J.

Translated with a Foreword by

FATHER JAMES E. O'MAHONY
O.M.Cap., M.A., Ph.D., D.Litt.

Agrégé en Philosophie à l'Université Catholique
de Louvain.

LONDON
SHEED & WARD
MCMXXXV

PRINTED IN GREAT BRITAIN
BY THE WHITEFRIARS PRESS LTD.
LONDON AND TONBRIDGE
FOR SHEED AND WARD
31 PATERNOSTER ROW
LONDON, E.C.4
NIHIL OBSTAT: GEORGIUS D. SMITH, S.TH.D., PH.D.
CENSOR DEPUTATUS
IMPRIMATUR: JOSEPH BUTT,
VIC. GEN.
WESTMONASTERII, DIE 6ᴬ JULII 1935
FIRST PUBLISHED NOVEMBER 1935

FOREWORD

THE facts of Rev. Fr. Pierre Rousselot's life are briefly told. He was born in Nantes on December 29th, 1878. At the age of sixteen he entered the Jesuit Novitiate, then at Canterbury in England. He was ordained priest in 1908. In 1909 he became Professor of Theology at the *Institut Catholique* in Paris.

In July, 1914, the Great War broke out. By September Rousselot was a soldier of the French Army. On April 25th, 1915, Sergeant Rousselot met his death; it was at the Battle of the Eparges. To those who picked him up wounded his last words were : "My friends, I am going to die : it is useless to go any further. . . . I will give you my blessing."

Nothing more is known of his death. He was probably abandoned there and then to lie obscurely amongst the obscurest of his comrades. With his death was extinguished a power of vision that is rare among men, and the present book, *The Intellectualism of St. Thomas*, was the first expression of an intellect that was full of promise.

It would be invidious to indicate certain positions taken by the author that he would have modified had he lived. In his lifetime certain elucidations were called forth in answer to his critics, particularly regarding his doctrine of intelligence as "capax Dei" [1] ; and it seems certain, from indications given by his Editor, the late P. Léonce de Grandmaison, that his doctrine of conceptual knowledge progressed towards a greater degree of realism than is admitted in the text.[2] It is doubtful if Rousselot had solved for himself the problem of the analogy of Being which was so important to his own thesis of the analogy of Intelligence in its different levels. However that may be, the importance

---

[1] See "Métaphysique thomiste et critique de la connaissance," *Revue néo-scholastique* (1910), p. 504.

[2] *Cf. L'intellectualisme de saint Thomas*, 2ième ed., pp. 106, 107, note 2.

of a metaphysic of Intelligence, such as is found in the writings of Aquinas, is beyond question at the present moment. Anti-intellectualism which made its appearance as a reaction against philosophies which failed to grasp the significance of intelligence as the " faculty of being " and against that exaltation of the scientific concept which characterised early nineteenth-century scientific thought has almost run its course. The influence of M. Bergson still remains, but the growth of interest in theories of intelligence, which is the outstanding thing in recent Psychology, must ultimately whet the appetite of our contemporaries for a metaphysical theory of it. As an introduction to a systematic conception of Intelligence the present book will prove invaluable : the Thomistic theory of Intelligence is as actual as his metaphysical account of Being.

If the *Intellectualism of St. Thomas* has not been translated before this, the reason is not to be sought in any low estimate of the value of the book, but rather in the despair of translators. Rousselot is difficult to render into English. The subject-matter is metaphysical, and he seems to have made rather free use of his own language to suit his purposes. " L'autre en tant qu'autre," for instance, is likely to worry any translator, and translation is not the present writer's *métier*.

FR. JAMES, O.M.Cap.

St. Bonaventure's
University Hostel,
Cork.

September 14th, 1935.

CONTENTS

PART I

THE PROCESS OF INTELLECTUAL KNOWLEDGE

PART II

HUMAN SPECULATION

PART III

INTELLIGENCE AND HUMAN ACTION

INTRODUCTION

In the pages which follow I understand by *intellectualism* the doctrine which places the supreme value and intensity of life in an act of intellect, that sees in this act the radical and essential good, and regards all things else as good only in so far as they participate in it. Ordinarily when the term is employed all that it signifies is a rather naïve confidence in intelligence and, in particular, in deductive reasoning. A more precise meaning is to be found in a prevailing acceptation of the term, and this characterises intellectualism by the primacy it is supposed to give to the static clear-cut concept and to the deductive form of inference. The essentially metaphysical doctrine which I have in mind here, however, is something very different from these interpretations. It is a doctrine which goes beyond the theory that all being is capable of being explained, and it is just the reverse of a system which would conceive the life of mind on the pattern of human reasoning. Accordingly, as the common acceptation of the term is developed and pushed to its ultimate consequences, the meaning here adopted would cease to coincide with it, and would tend ultimately to be in diametrical opposition to it.

Words must be taken, remarks Aristotle, in that sense in which everybody employs them. Perhaps it would be opportune, for once, to ignore this precept, and, by enlarging and deepening the significance of a word, seek to unify the various elements contained therein so as to find a meaning which would be the hidden, though for the most part unconscious, reason of what everybody says. That would make for clarity rather than evince a desire to reform common usage.

It happens, in effect, that ordinary language, deceived

by superficial resemblances, gathers under a single word certain elements that are incompatible, and finishes by introducing a contradiction into the meaning for which the word stands. Now, the more sublime and subtle and complex the doctrine of a thinker is, and the richer it is in consequences that do not harmonise save in the midst of apparent contradictions, the more readily will he be permitted to select for this purpose one of these conveniently simple and changeable terms. Strange confusions may ensue for discussion. But the cause itself of the evil contains the remedy. In such a case there is every chance that, by a persistent attempt to give precision to this vague notion, what is purest, most intimate, most original and most delicate in the thought of the master will be discovered, in as much as the idea, the supreme value of which has been obscurely felt without being exactly determined, may stand revealed.

We hear constant references to the intellectualism of St. Thomas. I hesitate to transform into definite reproaches what is more often a vague expression of deep instinctive antipathies. I believe, however, that what is generally looked upon as the outstanding characteristic—and radical defect—of his philosophy is twofold : a certain idolatry of abstraction on the one hand, and an excessive dogmatism on the other. Sometimes, however, reference is made to his theory of the primacy of *contemplation*, without attaching any importance to it.

It seems to us that this last-mentioned principle is the really deep and central thing in his system. It is by setting out from it that one may hope to reach the very heart of the Thomistic metaphysic most easily, for no one can study this principle without seeing it expand and grow and finally develop into an affirmation of the absolute value of the act of intelligence. Arrived at that point, one is in possession of the master-idea which introduces unity everywhere and which links up philosophy and theology in an indissoluble synthesis. If we seek a formula for it, it would be this : *Intelligence, for St. Thomas, is the faculty of the real, but it is the faculty of the real only because it is the faculty of the divine.* Here, in a few words, you have the conception of the doctrine of St. Thomas which it will be our endeavour to expound.

*

* *

The idea that intellect essentially deforms and mutilates reality, that it is the faculty of the unreal, is to-day so widespread that it has found its way into current literature and conversation. " Every word that a child utters," a novelist has said, " is a hecatomb of concrete things. When he plucks a narcissus near by and gives it the name of flower, a name common to a thousand other flowers and narcissi, he classifies it, he expresses its nature, he reduces it to a state of shadow and abstraction, and the flower he names is not the one he has gathered ; it has lost its colour and its perfume."

If we seek among the systems of philosophy the simple child who strips reality in the process of naming it and disowns the flower he plucks, we turn unhesitatingly to Scholasticism. Scholasticism, we are told, is the philosophy of abstractions. And if one particular doctor of the thirteenth century rose up against the common delusion and voiced the rights of living concrete reality,[1] the most celebrated Scholastic, at least, is representative of the state of mind which then held sway. Far from wishing to palliate or excuse his views, St. Thomas is said to have raised to the rank of theory the very error which is his weakness. Above all, he exalts mind ; and it is the universal which, according to him, is mind's proper object. Constantly he repeats, as a definition of intellect, that its function is to divide up what exists as unity. *Intellectus natus est dividere ea quae secundum rem coniuncta sunt.*

It is objected against Scholastic intellectualism that it diminishes and abstracts : it is also reproached with " solidi-

[1] Roger Bacon, *Opus Tertium*, II., 7, 8, 10. *Unum individuum excellit omnia universalia de mundo . . . Singulare est nobilius, quam suum universale. Et nos scimus hoc per experientiam rerum . . . Patet per rationes theologicas, quod universale non habet comparationem ad singularia : non enim Deus fecit hunc mundum propter universalem hominem, sed propter personas singulares . . . Homines imperiti adorant universalia . . . Intellectus est debilis : propter eam debilitatem magis conformatur rei debili quae est universale, quam rei quae habet multum de esse, ut singulare.*

fying." This further grievance, which, at first sight, seems to accord but ill with the first, is, on the contrary, merely the more adequate expression of it. To abstract is to ignore the passing and to postulate the permanent. It is tantamount to crystallising what is expansive, to concentrating what tends to be diffusive, and to freezing the flowing stream ; in a word, to abstract is to " solidify." Human abstraction is a process of solidification implying as it does a breaking up of the real into small fragments and the creation of a certain number of artificial unities which, to satisfy the exigencies of mind, are substituted for the ineffable unity of the data of experience. Not to take account of what as a whole is simultaneously one and multiple is to ignore becoming and to be out of touch with reality.

This advance in the critique of intellectualism helps us, by revealing the connection that subsists between what are supposed to be the two radical defects of Scholasticism, to obtain a deeper insight into the philosophy that it condemns. It is one and the same thing to neglect the multiple of time and space, vital movement, and the complexity of the real. The same fundamental error is also supposed to render Scholasticism refractory to the pure impression of the data, and alienates it from the true spirit of historical method : the world of mind fashioned by Scholastics in the likeness of their own intellects is seen at once to be devoid of reality and stability, *une Néphélococcygie, et un empire de roides entités figées*, a kind of intellectual china-shop.

Following in the wake of systematic abstraction comes presumption in affirmation. If the absolute value of the concept is accepted, then the absolute value of judgment and of reasoning, which are natural consequences, must also be admitted. Since by definition distinct notions represent merely " portions " of reality, they ought to be capable, if they are to represent the real in any adequate manner, of being united into a definite system of stable relations. If indeed reality has anything corresponding to these " portions," it is in the judgment, even more than in the concept, that we must look for the expression of the real. " Complete truth," the Scholastics were wont to say, " is to be found, not in the simple idea, but in the proposition," or, as they called it, " the *enuntiabile.*" Reality, by hypothesis, is capable of explanation, and it follows that we must look for integral truth in science, that is, in a complete picture of the universe, a picture eminently intelligible seeing that it is composed of adequately true ideas and that it expresses merely their interrelations. Such a knowledge would be the ideal goal of intellectualism, just as its possibility is the postulate upon which intellectualism is based.

The claim to equate mind with reality is here palpable and obvious to everybody. No new arguments are needed by philosophers who have no sympathies for intellectualism, for if their criticism of the concept is true, then all knowledge is a mere chimera ; here, at least, they can join in a common jest with popular ideas and with the philosophy of common sense. Both the man in the street and his more educated *confrère* are agreed to see in this pretended equation of reason with reality the delusion of a mind which achieves coherence at the cost of complexity. If the artificial unity that intel-lectualism of this kind finds in reality satisfies it, this can only be the result of narrow vision and of ridiculously sub-jective prejudices.[2] What can such a mind understand of history, of psychology, of metaphysics ? In its knowledge the changing reality of experience is practically denied, since it is petrified in the rigidity of rational categories, and the reality of spirit is completely ousted since it is conceived after the pattern of things in a spatial world.

Add to that the claim to embody in his science not only the reality of experience and of spirit, but also of the divine, and you have intellectualism carried to the limits of absurdity and excess. And that is the form of intellectualism that we find in Scholasticism. Scholasticism is above all a

[2]   *Zu fragmentarisch ist Welt und Leben,—*
Ich will mich zum deutschen Professor begeben.
Der weiss das Leben zusammen zu setzen,
Und er macht ein verständlich System daraus ;
Mit sienen Nachtmützen und Schlafrockfetzen
Stopft er die Lücken des Weltenbaus.
" Too fragmentary are world and life—I will get me to a German professor who knows how to put life together and fashion it into a comprehensible system, by stopping up the gaps in the construction of the universe with nightcaps and the tattered rags of his pyjamas. (Heine, *Buch der Lieder.*)

rationalisation of the divine. It claims to express the divine in formulæ to which it attributes the stability of a truth at once definitive and unchangeable : these formulæ are known as dogmas. New adversaries appear here. These protest no longer in the name of common sense or of a philosophy, but in the name of religion. They are incited not only by the needs of " life " as it appears to the popular mind, nor yet by that " life-experience " which intoxicates such intellectuals as have discovered the emptiness of abstractions, but are inspired by the deep and intense " life " of religious feeling. They are horrified to see the fullness of such a " life " imprisoned by the precision of a formula. They accord, perhaps, a certain relative validity to dogma because of man's felt need to seek expression for the deep realities of his experience in logical propositions. But they are disturbed by exclusive and absolute affirmations, that is, by dogmas in the traditional and Scholastic sense of the word. They scoff at the strange form which religious life assumes under the influence of this ancient conception of the Faith. " Here, then," they say, " you have religion obtained by a process of deduction from phenomena either natural or miraculous. The approach to God is no longer by way of an intimate experience but by a process of reasoning. The divinity of a profession of faith can be demonstrated in such a way as to force man's reason, and, since these dogmatic definitions are identified with religion itself, we discover no vital development in religious history ; certain holy books, belonging to a definite period and fashioned like every other human document, pass for works dictated by God, and enjoy decisive authority in matters of science and history."

They go further. If the affirmations of the partisans of dogma are exaggerated, the reason must be sought in the falsity of their fundamental ideas. St. Thomas, a typical intellectualist, is admittedly a Christian thinker. And yet, what, in his hands, is the fate of those grand ideas that are the strength and the joy of the religious mind—ideas such as liberty, faith, revelation, a Mediator ? What becomes of the very idea of God ? Why, all these realities have fallen to the low estate of pale and abstract notions, their life has vanished, and nothing remains of them but deformed skeletons. The idea of a personal and spiritual will, it is said, is literally lacking in the system of St. Thomas. Revelation whole and entire is for him something bestowed upon human weakness, the merest adjunct to philosophic speculation. It is no longer faith, but thought, which is the organ of approach to the Most High. The Lord whose presence vivified the soul has fallen to the rank of a Logos which illumines the mind, and the living God has become a mere receptacle for exemplary ideas. Intellectually and morally St. Thomas has fallen back into the Greek mentality, and with that the Christian spirit has entirely disappeared, for Christianity stands for a spiritual Personality at the summit of things and not merely for an Idea.[3]

*
* *

This last objection marks the precise point at which the intellectualism of St. Thomas escapes from the clutches of its adversaries, for the objection as it is stated implies a complete misconception. Just when it is thought that the finishing stroke has been given, we find that St. Thomas has gone untouched.

" It is a spiritual Personality which is at the head of

[3] These criticisms are put forward by M. Seeberg. *Cf. Theologie des Johannes Duns Scotus*, pp. 629, 627, 581, 586, 632, 580. I cite him in preference to others, because, in addition to a knowledge of Scholastic problems, he possesses, what is more rarely to be met with, an appreciation, sometimes very accurate, of their significance. I have not here to defend the religious value of Scholastic thought as a whole. There is a tendency at present to acknowledge it : only a pronounced mental rigidity and the lack of psychological imagination would prevent one from seeing the possibility of a subjective co-existence, and even compenetration, of rational Aristotelianism and a mysticism such as that of the Victors or of a St. Bernard. Speculative thought was not, and could not have been, isolated from the religious life which was so intense in the Middle Ages ; the *Itinerarium mentis ad Deum* and the *Incendium Amoris* are not fully appreciated independently of the *Breviloquium*. The recent *Esquisse* of M. Picavet has done much to dissipate the contrary prejudice in France ; as regards Protestant Germany *cf*. M. Seeberg's article, *Scholastik* in *Realencyklopädie für protestantische Theologie*. In this work I take it that this point is beyond doubt, but I contest another opinion, which is rather widespread, that a " voluntarist " Scholasticism, such as we have in St. Anselm, R. Grosseteste, Duns Scotus and others, is better fitted than the intellectualist system of St. Thomas to satisfy the deep needs of the religious soul.

things and not a mere Idea." This assertion implies an
opposition between *Idea* and *spiritual Personality* that St.
Thomas does not admit. It is, in fact, the fundamental
principle of his metaphysical intellectualism that every
spiritual Person is an Idea, and that there is perfect identity
between Idea and spiritual Reality.[4] The "intellect in
act " and the "intelligible in act " are for him convertible
terms. Pure spirits, "subsisting Intelligibles " are the true
Ideas or "noumena," as we should say to-day. Intelligibility is something that belongs essentially to living and
substantial beings. To know is primarily and principally to
seize within the self a non-self which in its turn is capable
of seizing and embracing the self : it is to live with the life
of another.[5] Intelligence is the faculty of the divine because
in this way it is capable of embracing God ; and if we are
to have a correct idea of it we must grasp the fact that the
function of intelligence is not to fabricate concepts or adjust
its propositions but to enrich itself with realities.

Of the ideas put forward in this book the last mentioned
is by far the most important and the one which I shall be at
most pains to clarify and develop ; all the rest will follow
from that.

The coincidence of spiritual Reality and of Idea indicates
that the acquisition of the supreme Reality formally takes
place by means of intellect, and that the destiny of the
universe is linked up with the noblest act of mind, the vision
of God. Now, all religion centres around the beatific vision.
Accordingly, it is clear that those who delude themselves
into believing that in the intellectualist system religious
philosophy is something superadded as an afterthought
simply miss the point.

If it is the intellect which comes to know God as He is in
Himself, then because God is not only Holiness but supreme

[4] This doctrine is not affected by the dogma of the Trinity because each of
the Three Persons is identical with the divine Essence.

[5] For that it is not necessary that knowledge should be immediate in this
sense that the Reality known by me should be identically the idea I have of it.
On the contrary, such immediacy would correspond to the highest ideal of
intellectual knowledge ; it is to be found, according to St. Thomas, in two
cases only, in actual intuitions of itself by the ego on the one hand, and in the
beatific vision on the other.

Reality and essential Source of all being, it follows that it is the intellect that grasps being as it is in itself. Intelligence, we have said, is the faculty of the real because it is the faculty of the divine. This at once explains and justifies the attitude of St. Thomas towards intelligence when he came to consider it as he found it in man and subject to human conditions.

He is disparaging in its regard, as we shall see ; yet he is forced by his principles to ascribe to its operations here below an indisputable value in so far as they exemplify the nature of intelligence as such. Human abstraction and affirmation are justified since they represent on a lower plane the functioning of a being which, despite everything, is mind, and because they are the efforts on the part of an intelligence bound up with sense to find a substitute for pure ideas in its effort to feign a direct intuition of reality.

The abstract concept, then, does not represent an immediate grasp of an intelligible essence, but is rather an unconscious imitation of the intuitive mode of knowledge. It is an artifice on the part of man to impart to material things, by a purification of sensible data, the appearance of spiritual Realities. We must see in judgments that are certain not so much an experience of like-realities as man's way of affirming intrepidly the absolute value of intelligence, and of asserting its aptitude to know these supreme Realities. Dogma, in fine, does not exhaust the divine fact which it translates in human terms ; yet to see in dogma merely a useful symbol for conduct would be to run counter to the nature of intelligence. Intelligence, being the faculty of the real, refuses to acknowledge a " moral order " that would have no affinities with the order of being ; on last analysis, it must refuse to differentiate between judgments of value and judgments of reality.

*
* *

Metaphysical intellectualism, therefore, guarantees the value of those abstractions and affirmations which are the ideals of ordinary " intellectualism." It does not bend the knee to them : it at once disdains and protects them, and

hopes for better. How could St. Thomas, with his ideas of
the intellectual process in its ideal state, exalt human reason
as the highest and best that could be found in the universe ?
" Man," he says, " is not endowed with intellectual nature
as his own proper good and essence ; relatively to what the
angels enjoy, man has merely a spark of it and a comparatively small participation in it." [6] The intellectual
process as we experience it is never pure or perfect because
it can never function, as he likes to repeat, save amidst the
" shadows of space and time." And our right of affirmation, encumbered as it is by our mode of conception, is
necessarily limited to a rather modest number of propositions with a claim to certainty.

Far from pretending to force the whole of reality into that
rigid mould imposed by extended substance (the proper
object of intellect on earth) on our human mode of knowledge, the metaphysic of St. Thomas, on the contrary, stands
out amongst all the Scholastic systems for its affirmation of
realities that lie outside this mould. He affirms the existence
of pure forms where the multiplication of essence and individuality, because they are above and beyond space, go
hand in hand. He also affirms " pure potency" which
" is " and yet is not its act, and it is for him the first step
in metaphysics to admit the possibility of that $\mu\dot{\eta}\ \ddot{o}\nu$ which
nevertheless is $\ddot{o}\nu\ \pi\omega s$. He vigorously protests against those
who, by giving accidents the semblance of material masses,
distort the idea of quality.[7] But he teaches that the terrestrial condition of our understanding, such as it is reflected
in our language, imposes these sensible distortions, and if
on reflection we may condemn them, yet in this life our
concepts can never rid themselves of them. To " solidify,"
then, is for him the essential blemish of our mind, but it
is at the same time the indispensable condition of its
functioning.

Likewise, if he boldly affirms what he believes he sees
with certitude, he is aware of a number of problems that

[6] 2 d. 3, q. 1, a. 2 and 2 d. 39, q. 3, a. 1.
[7] *Cf.* V. 1, Ch. XI ; in 5 *Met.*, l. 7, in 7 *Met.*, l. 1. *Cf.* also Part II, Ch. II.
Compare his theory of the reciprocal priority of the causes, *Ver.* 28, 7, etc.

are insoluble, and he knows that to be carried away by a love of synthesis is to run the risk of chasing after shadows. At the same time, he does not forgo the right of applying his syllogism to all matters ; he detects a subterfuge, and we shall have to study these systems of probable reasonings whose points of contact with reality are, as he says, " outside the nature of being," the outlines of which are furnished by the ordering activity of mind, and which the mediæval philosopher did not hesitate to employ in his effort to fill up what was wanting to his certain knowledge.[8] The syllogistic apparatus served as a kind of general scheme for two kinds of reasoning, certain and probable ; and there is a danger of serious confusion when St. Thomas does not explicitly qualify his statements, if all that he affirms is placed on the same level of importance. In one place he writes that the thought of an angel is not identical with the angel's essence—a metaphysical assertion of the first importance—but on the next page he declares that the angels were created " in the empyrean sky " and he scarcely gives more rational justification for that proposition than would a modern writer who relates that the seraphim soar aloft " in the azure blue." Possibly this procedure is at first surprising and bewildering ; but one thing at least is certain : if in this respect we must reproach St. Thomas we do so less for having affirmed without being certain than for having systematised just for the pleasure of it, while at the same time he was perfectly aware of his inability to affirm.

Thus, neither the paleness of abstractions nor excessive dogmatism is characteristic of this philosopher ; and it was precisely his high ideal of the intellectual process that made him disdainful in regard to concepts and also reserved in his judgments.

Does that mean to say that *in practice* he never succumbed to the delusions which in theory he condemned ? Not to admit this would be to close our eyes to the obvious. Here and there he has attached too much importance to formulæ ; in his explanations of texts he has too frequently substituted a conscious finality for the historical mechanism of psy-

[8] See in 4 *Met.*, 1, l. 1, and Part II, Ch. V.

chology ; he betrayed a tendency to conceive perfection,
even in this world of corruptible things, in terms of constancy and repose.[9] All that, no doubt, has its origin in
an unconscious fascination for the conceptual mode of
thinking. Studied from this point of view one would have
no difficulty in showing the influence of the quantitative
prejudices that he himself criticised upon what I might call
the matter of his own doctrine. Such a work in the hands of
a careful investigator would perhaps prove instructive, and,
conducted with humorous insight, might not fail to prove
amusing. But it seems to us that its historical significance
would be slight because St. Thomas was prevented from
excess in this direction by having his own doctrine already
firmly fixed in his mind, and because in this respect he
cannot be said to have been particularly representative.

*
* *

By taking up the principle of the supreme value of the
act of intelligence, on the other hand, we are conscious of
giving pride of place to what was of prime importance in
the eyes of St. Thomas. Which is the nobler faculty, the
will or intellect ? By what faculty does created being come
into possession of the Infinite, by will or intellect ? These
were problems that the Scholastics set themselves explicitly,
and while the replies they gave to those questions classified
them as voluntarists or intellectualists, it must be said that
these replies were characteristic of their systems as a whole
in as far as they determined their attitude towards the nature
of God on whom all depends.[10]

[9] We shall have occasion to return to these two points later, when we shall
see that St. Thomas, unconsciously restraining the wide application of his
principles, sometimes seems—in his theory of human speculation—to reduce
the whole speculative activity of reason to *rational* forms. As regards a too
hasty identification of an idea with a defined formula, an example may be
found in his discussion, *de Forma Absolutionis* in *Opusc.* 18.

[10] As against St. Thomas, Scotus is of opinion that the possession of God
takes place formally by an act of will (*cf.* p. 49, n. 1 of text). He is therefore
perfectly consistent in denying the coincidence of the intelligible and the real
order ; that is the meaning of his celebrated formal distinction *ex natura rei.*
He is inclined to model all knowledge on the concept-mode of thinking because
the Thomistic ideas of intellectual possession and intellectual immanence were
lacking to him ; this explains his view that being is " univocal " as well as his

For Scholasticism there is one primordial question—one might almost say one unique problem—and that has to do with the conquest of being. It is by approaching the thinkers of the Middle Ages from this angle that one may hope to know them as they really were.[11]

It is, then, the doctrine of St. Thomas on the value of intelligence for the conquest of reality which is the proper object of this study. I have no intention of attenuating the doctrine of St. Thomas in order to make it acceptable to contemporary thought. My aim is to expound it precisely as the author himself understood it, and I shall undertake a critique of it in the light of his own principles. For the same reason I shall follow a method of exposition analogous to that employed by the Scholastics, that is to say, my method of procedure will be *a priori* and in inverse order to that of discovery. A First Part will explain the idea of the intellectual process as such, and will attempt to show that for St. Thomas intelligence is essentially acquisitive of reality and not merely a process of forging propositions. Following this rule, a Second Part will appraise the value of human speculation, that is, the value of those many operations by which our minds, in virtue of Aristotle's principle, *Quod non potest fieri per unum, aliqualiter saltem fiat per plura*, almost entirely deprived of intuition though aided by the senses, strive here below to simulate and supplement that perfection which is lacking to it. The natural substitutes for the intellectual process in its purity are the concept, the apprehension of the particular, science, system, and symbol.[12] The life of contemplation procured for us by the employment of these functions would correspond to

theories of the human knowledge of divine attributes. Were we to define intellectualism on the basis of equating all knowledge with human knowledge, then we should have to say that Scotus is more intellectualist than St. Thomas.

[11] Medieval " voluntarists " attribute to will that acquisition of reality by a process of transformation into itself which St. Thomas regarded as the exclusive privilege of intellect. See besides the texts of Scotus, cited later, Henry of Ghent, *Quodlibeta*, 1, 14 (Venice, 1613), and Matthew of Aquasparta, *Quaestiones disputatae de cognitione*, q. 9, ad 9 (Quarrachi, 1903, pp. 407–408).

[12] There is no need to devote a special chapter to the Judgment, because that which is proper to it, namely the simple affirmation of an existence, possesses no value from the view-point of pure speculation.

what is best on earth, were it not that God, in an excess of love, had promised man a vision more sublime than that which he could have ever hoped for. As a result we have to reckon with a certain transitory reversal of values, because while we wait for heaven we must live by faith, and this faith, which prepares us for the most exquisite knowledge, subjects our reason to the difficult yoke of authority. On earth human values, as a consequence, are not directly of the intellectual but of the moral order. That is why in a Third Part, " Intelligence and Human Action," we shall have to examine briefly, and by way of supplement, the value of the intellectual element in the dynamism of moral action which carries on man to his final end of pure specula-tion. In that context the rôle of intelligence is of a provi-sional and subordinate character. Morals, by definition, leave room for a " something more," a " what next ? " that will complete them, whereas ideas are of their nature absolute. There neither is nor can be anything beyond. It is just here that, in the system of St. Thomas, philosophy and theology are united in a unity not unlike that of matter and form. Seeing that religion claims to have an ultimate value and properly speaking to furnish an ultimate motive for action, it follows that it must find its consummation in some form of contemplation. That amounts to saying that just as created being is simply a participation in the divine, so also supernatural life can only mean a more plenary acquisition of reality. It cannot, then, be said that St. Thomas is religious in spite of his intellectualism ; on the contrary, he believes himself to be an intellectualist *because* he is religious. To seek the supreme good in the practical reason, he avers,[13] it would be necessary for man to be an absolute being.

[13] 1a, 2ae, q. 3, a. 5, ad 3.

PART I

THE PROCESS OF INTELLECTUAL KNOWLEDGE

THE INTELLECTUALISM OF SAINT THOMAS

THE INTELLECTUAL PROCESS AS SUCH

I

" INTELLIGENCE is a form of life, and of living things it is the most perfect." [1] " Being is two-fold : material and immaterial. By material being, which is limited, a thing is merely what it is ; this stone is just a stone and nothing more. But by immaterial being which is vast and, as it were, infinite, since it is not limited by matter, a thing is not only what it is, but in some fashion it is other things as well." [2] These formulæ are a rather good epitome of the fundamental idea underlying the intellectualism of St. Thomas.

They also mark off the only initial conception possible of all that the intellectual process in general meant for St. Thomas. This process of intellectual knowledge is not something " univocal," but is subject to intrinsic variation according to the different modes that it assumes in different intellectual beings. No causal relation of a determinate character, which would express the universal relation that holds between the intelligible object and the intellectual faculty, can be discovered ; now it is the mind which actively posits its object, now it is the object which acts on mind, and sometimes the harmony of mind and object must, without any direct influence of one on the other, be arranged by the action of some higher cause. [3] No necessary modification regulates the external action of object on mind

[1] In 12 *Met.*, l. 5.
[2] In 2 *An.*, l. 5.
[3] *Ver.* 2, 14.

or the receptivity of mind so far as the intellectual process as such is concerned : sometimes the mind, as in the case of angels and of those who enjoy intuition, possesses a collection of images of the universe which belongs to it essentially so to speak ; at other times, as happens in the case of man, mind fabricates a more or less perfect resemblance of things after a series of laborious preparatory actions. In a word, that which concerns the genesis of ideas, and even the relation of idea and object, falls outside the intellectual process as such, and is accidental to it. This process can be made known only when we have looked at the living unity that subsists between the idea and the mind to which that idea is already present.[4]

To mark off this union of the intelligible object with the intellect St. Thomas, like Aristotle, sometimes employs the term " to be " (sometimes " to become "), or " to have," which is a term traceable to an expression of St. Augustine's.[5] This union, he also says, can be compared to the interpenetration of matter and form.[6] But because such metaphors are also applicable to sense-knowledge, it must be added that mind, once it makes contact with reality (which is foreign to it), also grasps itself necessarily and at all times. That these two aspects of knowledge are fused into one is characteristic of the intellectual process and is proper to it. " Aristotle says that by its very nature the intellect knows itself in as far as it bears within it, or conceives, an intelligible object." [7] The difference between intellect and sense is thus sufficiently indicated by the deeper immanence of mind whereby it is capable of reflecting upon itself, or, as will be clear from what follows, the intel-

[4] *Ver.* 8, 6. *Dico ex eis effici unum quid, in quantum intellectum conjungitur intelligenti sive per essentiam suam, sive per similitudinem, unde intelligens non se habet ut agens vel ut patiens, nisi per accidens* . . . , etc.

[5] Aristotle : τὸ αὐτό ἐστι τὸ νοοῦν χαὶ τὸ νοούμενον (*De An.*, III, 4). Ἐστὶ δ'ὁ μὲν τοιοῦτος νοῦς τῷ πάντα γίνεσθαι (*Ib.*, 5).

St. Augustine's idea is best seen in St. Thomas' commentary on St. Paul : *In his quae sunt supra animam, idem est videre et habere, ut dicit Aug.* (In *Hebr.* xi. 1, 1, ed. of *Reginaldus.* *Cf.* Aug., *De diversis quaestionibus*, LXXXIII, c. 35.)

[6] 1 q. 55, a. 1, ad 2. *Intellectus in actu dicitur intellectum in actu, non quod substantia intellectus sit ipsa similitudo per quam intelligit, sed quia illa similitudo est forma ejus.* *Cf. Ver.* 8, 6.

[7] In 12 *Met.*, l. 5. *Cf.* Ar., *Metaph.*, A 7, Berlin ed., 1072, b. 20 . . .

lectual process can also be defined in accordance with a certain gradation which depends on those conditions indicated by the opening formulæ conditions that are correlative to one another. It is an act of variable intensity in which its enrichment by assimilation of what is from without grows in proportion as its immanent life increases.[8] "Its greater extension is not a dispersion over many things, because the intellect, while apprehending many objects, remains more concentrated within itself than do the senses when they apprehend only a few." [9]

If we are asked to characterise with greater precision this union, this possession *sui generis*, obviously we can do nothing better than advise each one to consult the personal experience of his own thinking. It is a presence which resembles the transparent identity of the self with itself without, however, being precisely that, remembering the text *fieri quodammodo aliud*. A survey of the most fundamental theses of Thomistic metaphysic gives the following result : the process of intellectual knowledge ought to be put forward at the outset as an original fact which, before all elucidation, has the power of distinguishing it from what is not it. The question raised by later Scholastics as to whether there could be immaterial beings that were not intelligent could really have had no meaning for St. Thomas. If the presence of sensible qualities excludes the possibility of being purely intellectual, it is the absence of what for want of a better word we must call " intellectuality " that defines matter.[10] Thus the division is complete ; it distinguishes two contradictory things. There are two kinds of beings, those which matter contracts and narrows down to being merely themselves and which are incapable of possessing other forms besides their own, and, on the other hand, there are those beings that are exempt from this limitation and are in a

---

[8] 1 q. 27, a. 1, ad 2. *Quanto aliquid magis intelligitur, tanto conceptio intellectualis est magis intima intelligenti, et magis unum. Nam intellectus, secundum hoc quod actu intelligit, secundum hoc fit unum cum intellectu.*

[9] *Opusc.*, 28, Ch. I. *Anima humana quodammodo est omnia . . . remanet in ea quaedam infinitas . . . nec propter hanc majorem ejus extensionem (Intellectus) spargitur ad multa, sed magis unite remanet in acceptione plurium intelligibilium, quam sensus in paucis sensibilibus.*

[10] *Cf.* 1 q. 14, a. 1.

position to become, after a certain manner, other things as well. The apriorism which renders this dichotomy an absolute one does not solve the further question whether that matter which is exclusive of mind coincides with, or goes beyond, that rather imperfectly knowable reality which affects our senses in an original manner. Intelligence, at any rate, is classed apart and distinguished from other things by a characteristic derived from its own activity.

Here, then, the general idea which must form the starting point of our research has been indicated. What follows will bring light to the fundamental differences that render the different kinds of intellectual process irreducible to one another. These processes will range themselves in different classes according to the diverging development of the essential elements which a first rough sketch has revealed.

II

Contrary to the popular idea of to-day, which regards the intellectual process as an " epiphenomenon " on the surface of true " life," St. Thomas looks upon it as the life-process *par excellence*, and sees in it the deepest and most intense activity of intellectual beings. In opposition to those who see in intellect something necessarily egocentric, he makes of it the faculty which emancipates men from mere subjectivity ; [11] it may aptly be called " the faculty of otherness " if we may employ the term. In a wider sense it is for him, as has been well said,[12] the " faculty of being," the faculty which most truly grasps, and attains, and holds being. It unites in the highest degree subjective intensity and objective extension, because if it grasps reality it does so by *becoming* reality in a certain manner : and in that precisely consists its nature.

Of these two characteristics, immanence and exteriorisation, it is immanence which, on last analysis, imparts to

[11] The word " subjectivity " here is to be identified with the Thomist meaning of " individuality " which implies limitation and contraction as well as incommunicable unity. For St. Thomas God is not an " individual " (*Pot.* 7, 3).

[12] *Revue Thomiste*, 1900, p. 399.

the intellectual act its perfection. The real reason of its superiority over will is that " speaking simply and absolutely it is better to be in possession of the nobility of another being than to have a relation to a noble being which remains beyond it." [13] If, then, intelligence is perfect and supreme life, it is because it can reflect upon itself and because at one and the same time it can know reality and know itself. *Est igitur supremus et perfectus gradus vitae qui est secundum intellectum, nam intellectus in seipsum reflectitur et seipsum intelligere potest.* These words, taken from the last book of the *Summa Contra Gentes*,[14] form the conclusion of a long exposition of the idea of " emanation " as it is realised in the different orders of Nature.

" We find different modes of emanation," it is said, " and further, we observe that from the higher natures things proceed in a more intimate way. Now, of all things the inanimate obtain the lowest place, and from them no emanation is possible except by the action of one on another : thus, fire is engendered from fire when an extraneous body is transformed by fire, and receives the quality and form of fire. The next place to inanimate bodies belongs to plants, whence emanation proceeds from within, in as much as the plants' intrinsic humour is converted into seed, which being committed to the soil grows into a plant. Accordingly, here we find the first traces of life : since living things are those which move themselves to act, whereas those which can only move extraneous things are wholly lifeless. It is a sign of life in plants that something within them is the cause of a form. Yet the plants' life is imperfect because, although in it emanation proceeds from within, that which emanates comes forth little by little, and in the end becomes altogether extraneous : thus the humour of a tree gradually comes forth from the tree and eventually becomes a blossom, and then takes the form of fruit distinct from

[13] *Ver.*, 22, 11. *Cf. Ibid.*, 15, 2. *In verum . . . intelligibile fertur intellectus ut in formam, . . . in bonum autem fertur ut in finem, cum forma sit intus, et finis extra.*
[14] 4 *Contra Gentes*, 11.

the branch, though united thereto ; and when the fruit is perfect it is altogether severed from the tree, and falling to the ground, produces by its seminal force another plant. Indeed, if we consider the matter carefully we shall see that the first principle of this emanation is something extraneous : since the intrinsic humour of the tree is drawn through the roots from the soil whence the plant derives its nourishment. There is yet above that of the plants a higher form of life, which is that of the sensitive soul, the proper emanation whereof, though beginning from without, terminates within. Also the further the emanation proceeds, the more does it penetrate within : for the sensible object impresses a form on the external senses, whence it proceeds to the imagination and further still, to the storehouse of the memory. Yet, in every process of this kind or emanation, the beginning and end are in different subjects ; for no sensitive power reflects on itself. Wherefore this degree of life transcends that of plants in so much as it is more intimate ; and yet it is not a perfect life, since the emanation is always from one thing to another. Wherefore the highest degree of life is that which is according to intellect : for the intellect reflects on itself and can understand itself."

A hundred other passages might be cited to the effect that perfection of life and reality must be gauged by the measure of immanence to be accorded to a being's activity ; the text I have chosen has this in particular, that it excludes from immanent activity not only its consummation in an external object but also the reception of elements from without. This aspect, apparently so incompatible with the extension of mind to the knowledge of the non-self which we have regarded as the second chief attribute of intellectual activity, sends us back to the primal fact which dominates the entire intellectualism of St. Thomas, that is, to the living and personal existence of Absolute Mind. In the chapter cited, once the author has classified the natural powers of operation he goes on to arrange the different degrees of intellectual activity ; in so doing he always assigns the lowest place to those forms of it that are most dependent on what comes from without. Radically complete immanence, he writes down as his conclusion, is to be found in Him Whose being is identical with intelligence and idea, that Mind, namely, which is the Measure of the truth of things.

> "The human intellect can know itself, but because it knows nothing without a sensible image the principle of its knowledge comes to it from without. The intellectual life of the angels is more perfect because their intelligence knows itself without having to make use of anything outside it. Yet, their life does not reach the highest point of perfection since their idea, which is within, is not identical with their essence, and their being and knowledge are distinct. The last perfection of life then belongs to God for Whom to know and to be are equivalent, and in Whom the idea, understanding by idea what the intellect conceives in itself of the object known, is identically the divine essence itself." [15]

Thus perfect consciousness, which is the creative source of all truth, is at the same time exhaustive knowledge and perfect unity, and God is no less one for the fact of knowing ; the thinker and his thought *do not add*, said St. Thomas. In the angelic world, that region which lies between God and man, degrees of reality and life are determined by comparative depth of immanence ; that is the essential thing which remains while the unity of intelligible object is recognised as accidental and transitory. "In God the whole plenitude of intellectual knowledge is contained in one thing, that is to say, in the divine essence, by which God knows all things. This plenitude of knowledge is found in created intellects in a lower degree, and less simply." [16]

---

[15] St. Thomas does not here wish to say that the angelic intellect does not "become" the intelligible object *intentionaliter*, but that in the angel there is something which is not immediately identical with knowledge. This he would prove either by reference to succession in its thoughts or to the presence in its consciousness of acts which are not identically acts of knowledge. See I q. 54, a. 1, etc.

[16] I q. 55, a. 3.

No created mind could pretend to be the universal exemplar of all reality, since such a perfect similitude is necessarily infinite ; the created intellect must therefore depend on a multiplicity of ideas for its knowledge. But " the higher a separate substance is, the more is its nature similar to the divine ; and consequently it is less limited, as approaching nearer to the perfection and goodness of universal being . . . consequently, the intelligible species that are in the higher substances are less numerous and more universal," [17] not indeed in virtue of generalisation, as we shall see, but by a process of condensation. By a multitude of thoughts the energy of a being is scattered and the less dependent it is on many thoughts the more intense does its life become.

III

Now the more intense is the life of an intellectual being, the less limited is it to the narrow circle of itself. Taking up the series of *finite* beings just mentioned, we realise that the second of the recognised perfections, that which has to do with the knowledge of the non-self, is also dependent upon the measure of immanent activity which a being possesses rather than being opposed to it ; it increases and diminishes in direct proportion to depth of immanence.[18]

A little reflection suffices to get beyond the popular opposition that is made between *thought* and *action ;* but it is another thing to see that thought is the most intense and powerful form of action. The latter way of looking at things was, however, natural to St. Thomas. He regarded activity not so much as movement or as passage from potency to act, but as perfection already possessed in that arising out of movement, which implies change and potentiality, it fixed its subject in the extra-temporal consistency of *act*. Given that, he quickly concluded that the possession of the non-self was brought about more fully by means of ideas than by any material form of contact, and that immanence was an implied condition of this intellectual possession of " otherness."

[17] 2 *Contra Gentes*, 98.
[18] *Ver.*, 2, 2.

Undoubtedly, " to have," " to possess," " to grasp," " to hold " are terms borrowed from the exercise of our corporeal powers. At first sight it would seem that to apply such terms to intellectual activity would be to empty them of their real meaning and to content ourselves with describing the shadow activity of intellectual possession working on a shadow of reality. Yet if action implies the passage of influence from one being to another, then it follows that such action will be all the more perfect according as it reaches the other being more fully, that is, in the being's reality and intimacy and unity, and the more imperfect according as it leaves the more of that being untouched by its influence (*Ens et unum convertuntur*). Nothing, however, is more *abstractive* than a material action, and, as a result, nothing is more impotent and restricted. A stone-breaker smashes up his stones, a dog upsets a basket or entangles a reel of thread, the cow crushes the flowers beneath it, but such actions have merely the effect of altering reality ; they reach it in one way only, abstractively if we may so speak they do not invade it, penetrate it, and conquer it whole and entire. By his activity man seeks to subordinate reality to himself, to enrich himself with it, and to saturate it with himself, but by material activity he merely succeeds in transforming some of the qualities of the object ; he does not touch it in its real depths. There is in the permanency of matter a quiet opposition to the most furious animal, to the greatest machine ; and, in addition, the time-duration which conditions their actions introduce an element of instability as an inevitable possibility, if not as a necessary eventuality. Condense it, extenuate it, rarify it as you will, matter still subsists ; overcome and beaten down for a time, the repugnance of the non-self to place itself indefinitely at the disposal of material self is never entirely vanquished. Generation is an almost creative modification, yet it produces merely the same type, and gives birth to a new being external to the first. Material capacity and nutritive assimilation really bring the non-self into subjection to the individual, yet for all that they do not bring about that coincident fusion which is the ideal of action, for the simple

reason that the mere juxtaposition of parts and the agglo-
meration of matter which is impenetrable is opposed to such
fusion.   By definition, knowledge alone permits the ego
while remaining itself to become the non-ego ; and we
cannot speak of real possession except where there is intimate penetration of two unifying principles and where a
thing becomes the other in some sense.   It was that precisely St. Thomas had in mind when he wrote : " The
noblest way of possessing or having a thing is to possess it
in a non-material manner, yet formally, which is the definition of knowledge." [19]

In presence of this immanence of knowledge it is essential
to notice that activity grows immeasurably in extent and,
particularly, in intensity.   The cow may crush one or two
daisies simultaneously, but it sees and lives all the daisies
of the field together.   But this conquest of reality by the
knower varies with the degree of immanent activity it
enjoys.   As there is increase of immanence there is a diminu-
tion of abstraction.   St. Thomas places the oyster and such
animals as are immersed in matter and possessed only of
the sense of touch at the lowest stage of sensitive knowledge.
With these, the most " dispersed of souls," there is no knowledge save of what is actually present to them ; being devoid
of phantasy they are without memory.   Their psychic
content is characterised as " imagination and confused
desire " ; it keeps before them, as in a kind of perpetual
twilight of knowledge, what is good or harmful ; wanting
in " particular judgments," they are neither " prudent "
nor teachable ; of them it may well be said : *In nullo
participant de contemplatione.*   Now that which is particularly
characteristic of them and which explains why they are
lowest in the scale of knowers is precisely the extreme
abstractiveness of their knowledge, or, which comes to the
same thing, its extreme subjectivity.   Out of all the stimuli
that pass from objects to sense-faculties the oyster and the
starfish do not grasp or store or transform save those which
have to do with the sense of touch. [20]   This sense is the

[19] In *Caus.*, l. 18.
[20] In *Met.*, l. 1 ; in 3 *An.*, l. 16 ; in *Sens. et Sens.*, l. 2.

foundation of all the others, and can alone subsist without them. It has this peculiarity about it, that it cannot be entirely denuded of its proper object, and that, in its case, the " real transformation " is more intimately connected with the " knowing transformation " than in others, much in the same way, for instance, that the hand which registers cold and heat is itself necessarily warm or cold already.[21] The oyster, then, has knowledge in so far as a vague unity of consciousness may be said to bring about a certain co-ordination of the *milieu* around it. In its world-system it is *quodammodo alia* if not *quodammodo omnia*. But the extreme abstraction noticeable in this extract of the universe is due to the defective immanence of a shallow consciousness that cannot unite in memory the successive stages of its unity. The higher animals, being endowed with five senses and with more differentiated organisms, furnish a more complete and complex perception of the world. In this respect those animals which possess the sense of sight enjoy a more objective perception than those endowed merely with the sense of touch because the eye is entirely stripped of " the nature of its object " being neither white nor black nor red, devoid, in fact, of colour, and susceptible merely to that of the coloured object. In this case perception is less abstractive : the addition of the other senses to that of touch, and the mutual co-operation which follows, results in a greater grasp of reality, or at least in a view of it from a greater number of angles. The cow of the field not only has eyes to see the colours of the marguerites ; its organs of touch, its snout and tongue tell of their height and resistance, while its sense of smell makes known their perfume. These different perceptions, or memories, are gathered together, according to St. Thomas, in a concrete synthesis by the *sensus communis* and the *sensus estimativus*, which is the organic power of perceiving particulars.[22] In this way the more

[21] For all this development on sense-knowledge see 1 q. 78, a. 3.

[22] *Opusc.* 25, ch. II. To prove the existence of this synthetic faculty Scholatics refer to the facts of experience : the dog will bite the hand of the person who kicks it ; he must therefore have some kind of perception of individual unity. (Domet de Vorges, *La perception et la psychologie thomiste*. Paris, 1892, p. 84.)

complicated organisms of the higher animals allow of a certain advance in the perception of " otherness."

As yet, however, we have not sufficiently emerged out of that subjectivism and abstractiveness of which we have been speaking.[23] The faculty of " otherness," that is, of things distinct from the knower, is to be had in its full sense only in such beings as can apprehend " otherness " as " otherness " with as much facility as they perceive things distinct from them to be such and such. To be able consciously to discriminate between self and non-self one must be capable of judging one's own perception and also of self-reflection. *Omnis intelligens est rediens ad essentiam suam reditione completa.* By definition it is necessary to know oneself in order to know truth as such.[24] It follows that the capacity for reflection on one's act is a condition of intellectual knowledge, and further that the only activity which is perfectly acquisitive of things distinct from the knowing subject is confined to the intellectual process which is the type of immanent action.

It is already clear to what principle we must refer for the proof of the contention that in intelligent beings immanence and knowledge of the non-self go hand in hand. For such beings to possess the non-self is to be in possession of the self. " The better a thing is understood the more intimate is its knowledge to the knowing subject and the nearer is it to being one with him." This notion of unity, so constantly on the lips of St. Thomas and which has just been intro-

---

[23] *Res autem spirituales intellectivae intimius nobis coniunguntur quam res corporales apprehensae per sensum ; sensus enim per apprehensionem coniungitur rebus quasi superficialiter tantum ; sed intellectus pertingit usque ad intimam rel quidditatem. . . . Per similitudines spirituales nobis coniunctas magis pertingimus ad intima quam per ipsam coniunctionem realem quae nobis secundum sensum exhibetur.* (4 d. 49, q. 3, a. 5, sol. 1 and ad 2. *Cf.* 1a, 2ae, q. 31, a. 5.)

[24] See the very clear and adequate developments of this in *Ver.* 1, 9 and 10, 9. A faculty which is capable of reflecting upon itself is necessarily devoid of *all* matter, and so its object is not limited like that of the senses ; it is really capable of " becoming " all being (*Opusc.* 15, ch. II). Sense which is aware of its act (*cognoscit se sentire*) without knowing the nature of its act cannot be styled " faculty of being " ; the mind, on the contrary, knows its essence and therefore truth, that is, being as such. Far from destroying the bridges between mind and reality and obstructing the passage from one to the other, immanence is the very condition of this passage : it is by " becoming " things distinct from us that we know them.

duced here, throws full light upon that correlation which exists between immanence on the one hand and the enriching extensiveness of intellectual activity on the other.

If the intellectual faculty, as a matter of fact, is essentially given to the harmonising of contraries,[25] if it is its nature to be able to become all things, then its ideal will be to gather together whatever is apprehended into the unity of a common idea. If such an idea does not represent for a particular individual the non-self in its totality, the very exigencies of its nature require that it does not feel tied down once for all to merely one representation of reality, but that it is always at liberty to discover in its intrinsic indetermination something with which to form either new complimentary unities or more embracing unities that will combine the present one with those even that are opposed to it.[26] This representative unity (corresponding to the degree of immanence the perfection of which we have seen to be found in the identity of essence and idea) is indeed an essential condition of the idea ; the latter being a second self, that is the self as thought, ought to possess unity like the thinking self with which for the moment it is identical.[27] It follows that the strength of an intellect is to be estimated by the extent of the self as thought, of its idea, and it will be all the more powerful according as it can concentrate within the self a greater portion of the non-self without being impaired in its own living unity. Those intellects are lowest in the

[25] This is also true of the senses, but not in a simultaneous way ; thus the eye sees black and white, but not *secundum idem*. The intellect, on the other hand, knows two contraries at the same time, one by the other, in *Sens. et Sens*, l. 19 ; in 9 *Met.*, l. 2 ; 3 *Contra Gentes*, 82, 3. In this we can recognise an idea of Aristotle.

[26] It is because man desires to know *all things* and cannot do so except by having recourse to a succession of acts that he finds pleasure in the movements of thought (1a, 2ae, q. 32, a. 2). In the thought of God, on the contrary, *immutabilitas consequitur quandam totalitatem . . . quia omnia simul in uno considerat* (*Mal.*, 16, 2, 6).

[27] *Quodl.* 7, a. 2. *Quod intellectus simul intelligat plura intelligibilia primo et principaliter, est impossibile. Cuius ratio est, quia intellectus secundum actum est omnino, id est perfecte, res intellecta, ut dicitur in 30 de Anima. Quod quidem, intelligendum est, non quod essentia intellectus fiat res intellecta vel species eius ; sed quia complete informatur per speciem rei intellectae, dum eam actu intelligit. Unde intellectus simul plura actu intelligere primo, idem est ac si res una simul esset plura.* And *ibid.*, 2 : *Cognoscibilia quae simul cognoscuntur oportet quod accipiantur ut cognoscibile unum numero.* Cp. *Ver.*, 8, 14 and 1 q. 85, a. 4.

scale which depend on material objects for their knowledge since these objects are limited to themselves and cannot therefore give rise to an idea which is representative of many. On the other hand, intellects that are endowed with greater immanence and whose ideas are consubstantial with their essence are free to gather together into a single mental content a vast category of objects. We have already said the degrees of natural perfection to be found in pure intuitive intellects must be fixed according to the decreasing number of their ideas. We find the same thing exemplified, adds St. Thomas, in the case of men, because he that is endowed with greater intellectual acumen is able, by means of a small number of principles, to reach many conclusions at which the less gifted arrive only by means of many reasonings and examples and by reference to particular topics more immediately suggestive of the conclusions.[28]

What is essential to notice here, however, is extent of knowledge and understanding, instead of being in inverse ratio to one another, really go hand in hand, where intuitive intellects are concerned. The universality of the ideal forms by which the higher angels obtain their knowledge makes rather for a deeper penetration of the unique and ineffable character of things than for indistinctness and vagueness. It would correspond rather to a process of condensation than of generalisation ; and the reason of this is to be sought in the nature of intelligence which is the faculty of unity because it is the faculty of being, or, if it is preferred, of being unified in mind, as it is in reality. *Ens et unum convertuntur ;* and particular or transcendental unity, carefully distinguished by St. Thomas from that unity which is the principle of number, must not be separated, either in the real or in the " intentional " order, from reality with which it is identical. It is therefore because the unity of every creature, like its reality, is imperfect that it is better known rather in conjunction with others than by means of others, and also that the process of isolation which cuts it off from the rest of things in the universe deprives it of some degree of reality. *Omnia se invicem perambulant.* For St. Thomas, intelligence,

[28] *Ver.*, 8, 10.

as one of his followers has said, is "the natural order in potency"; *per se*, therefore, and under normal conditions of exercise the more reality it incorporates within itself, and the wider its range of interest, the more true is it to its own nature. To have full and exhaustive knowledge on any detail it would be necessary to have grasped the entire and absolute unity of things. "A thing is known more perfectly," says St. Thomas, "in the Word than itself, even as regards its own particular shape and form." [29]

Once again, then, he has been led by his examination of the intellectual process to affirm Absolute Mind : this Mind alone can reconcile by its absolute unity the twofold perfection we have discovered in the idea. The Cause of all being is the true mirror of reality such as it is in itself ; creative Source of things that exist by participation, "spreading about It all being and degrees thereof," Absolute Mind is at one and the same time perfect Immanence and perfect Extensiveness penetrating to the depths of things. He alone is at home everywhere by intelligence Who knows all things by His own Essence, the unique Source at once of reality and of truth. The human soul is intelligent because it has a "passive capacity" for all being ; God is intelligent because He is the active Source of all being. "God's knowledge is the cause of 'things.'"

Those who are familiar with the writings of St. Thomas well know that we are here at the very heart of his whole doctrine. And it is not difficult to collect from every page of his writings certain formulæ which epitomise his general notion of the process of intellectual knowledge. "The greatest among the perfections of things is that a thing is intellectual because thereby it is, after a fashion, all things, having within itself the perfection of all." "Intellectual apprehension is not limited to particular beings but extends to all." "By the fact that a substance is endowed with intelligence it is capable of possessing within itself all being." [30] We may conclude, then, by saying that, far

[29] (*Una quaeque res*) *perfectius cognoscitur per Verbum quam per se ipsam, etiam in quantum est talis. Ver.*, 8, 16, 11. *Cf. Ver.*, 4, 6.

[30] 1 *Contra Gentes*, 44, 5 ; 2 *Contra Gentes*, 47, 4 ; 2 *Contra Gentes*, 98. *Cf.* 3 d. 27, q. 1, a. 4 ; 1 q. 26, a. 2, etc.

from characterising intelligence as the faculty of abstraction, we must, on the contrary, designate it the faculty of complete " intussusception."

IV

From the foregoing principles it follows that the typical intellectual operation must be sought neither in the judgment (*enuntiabile*), which is the result of a triple abstraction, nor in the concept, which on the Scholastic conception presupposes a certain working up of reality owing to the soul's presence in a body,[31] but in a real grasp of reality, given, however, in the form of ideas and principles.[32] As far as we can judge from an inductive examination of our own defective intellectual capacities, this spiritual possession of reality possesses two characteristics : a living intimacy with reality such as we experience in the concrete perception by the self of its own acts, and an illuminative clarity which we associate with the perception of axioms. Did we apprehend the essence of the non-self as immediately as we do the act of thought, the *cogito*, and as clearly as the principle of contradiction, then we would enjoy a share in typically intellectual activity.

To express the matter in another way. Intelligence must not be defined as the faculty of discrimination or of linking up, of ordering or of deduction, of assigning the " causes " or " reasons " of things. Its work does not consist in isolating things from their surroundings, but directly of grasping what is proper to them, of assimilating to itself that which is most intimate to things and which naturally is supposed to be diaphanous and limpid for mind.

And if *truth* is " reality brought into relation to mind," then perfect truth does not consist in the stable union of two concepts ; its deep and ultimate meaning is less an *adequatio*

---

[31] See Part 11, Chs. 1 and 2.

[32] There is here question of a *being* in the full sense of the word, that is, of a *substance*. St. Thomas frequently says that the proper object of intellect is not the accidents but the essence or quiddity and therefore the *substance* (in 12 *Met.*, l. 5, 208 a ; 3 *Contra Gentes*, 56, 4 ; 3 q. 75, a. 5 ad 2). Accidents considered apart as " quiddities " are no more the natural object of the intellect than they are beings apart from their subject of inherence.

rei et intellectus than an assimilation and union of mind with things. It is due to the infirmity of our minds that truth cannot be attained without recourse to the manipulation of many terms and to the process *componendi et dividendi*. The truth to be ascribed to any particular object of intellectual knowledge is not something unique and static. Just as the union of the thinking subject and the object thought allows of an infinite number of degrees of immanence according to the indefinitely various capacities of the spiritual faculties in question, so we must allow for a proportionate increase of truth according to these different degrees of " limpidity," " clarity " and penetration. So little is true knowledge indivisible that it varies necessarily with the nature of the thinking subject. The whole of a simple object might be known without for all that being known wholly or exhaustively, and fully to grasp the intelligibility of the created world, while at the same time positing it, one would need to be God, that is, subsisting Truth. For if a being is progressive, then, according to St. Thomas, there cannot be an idea corresponding to it which would be arresting and completely definitive ; if a being is finite, there can be nothing exhaustive about its corresponding concept. The indivisible *equality* of true ideas among themselves and in their relations with things is as foreign to him as the idea of the primacy of discursive reasoning.[33]

---

[33] On the inferiority of knowledge by the process *componendi et dividendi*, that is, by judgment, see passages wherein it is denied of God and of the angels, *e.g.*, 1 *Contra Gentes*, 58, 1 q. 58, a. 4, etc. For the infinite varieties of penetration and of " limpidity " which distinguish the different true knowledges (even intuitive knowledges) of one and same object see those passages concerning the degrees of beatific vision (*multis modis contigit . . . intelligere Deum, vel clarius vel minus clare*, 1 q. 62, a. 9 ; 1 q. 12, a. 6, etc.) and also those that have to do with the human knowledge of Christ. As regards his idea of truth, it will be seen that, though he defines it as an *adequatio* in the classical text (*Ver.*, l. 1), yet he explains it in terms of *correspondentia, assimilatio, conformitas* (*cf. Ver.*, 21 : *Conceptio enim nostri intellectus secundum hoc vera est, prout repraesentat per quandam assimilationem rem intellectam . . . sed . . . non potest forma per intellectum concepta repraesentare divinam essentiam complete, sed habet aliquam modicam imitationem ejus. . . .*). If in the case of man truth is more perfect in the judgment because there alone he knows the non-self as " other " existing outside him (*Ver.*, l. 3), yet it is never absolutely pure except in God's intuitive vision (1 *Contra Gentes*, 60, 61 and 1ª q. 16, a. 5), and even then the best description that can be given of it is to say : *Veritas invenitur in intellectu, secundum quod apprehendit rem ut est* (1 q. 16, a. 5). Sometimes, however, it must be admitted, St. Thomas seems to look upon truth as the simple exclusion of error, and

To what extent the view-point adopted by St. Thomas in his intellectualism goes beyond the theory of universal explanation is evident by this time. To say that all things are susceptible of explanation is to be satisfied with a certain equation of thought and reality. That is tantamount to maintaining the duality of the two terms intellect and the object of intellect, and it does not solve the further question whether reality which is intelligible for mind is radically finalised in regard to mind. It is equivalent to arresting the movement of thought at the judgment and concept stage and to allowing or postulating something more ultimate than knowledge in the form of action or such like. To affirm, on the other hand, that the highest form of activity consists in the intellectual acquisition of reality, which in its turn must be distinguished from judgments of fact regarding such and such qualities, is to suppose, if finality be admitted, that everything which possesses reality is also *eo ipso intelligible*,[34] and further that nothing has a title to reality except in function of intelligibility and as object of, or preparation for, intellectual knowledge according to the varying capacities of intelligent beings. Mind comes first, and all being is for mind.

If there is not actual knowledge corresponding to this universal intelligibility, and if the given contains what is relatively opaque for thought side by side with what is perfectly transparent, yet it is clearly insinuated that the material world occupies a position of dependence in regard to mind : in relation to the world of intelligences it is looked upon as a kind of appendix. The true finality of Nature is mind and intelligibility ; the realities " willed for their own sakes " are the subsisting intelligibles.

There are real incorporeal substances intelligible for mind alone, *res incorporeas solo intellectu comprehensibiles*.[35] There are beings at once subsistent and intelligible for whom vision and possession are identical, *quae videre est habere*. This

then truth remains indivisible by definition while the *true idea* remains susceptible of infinite variation (see 1 d. 14, q. 1, a. 2, sol. 1, where the term *adaequare* is applied to the idea as perfectly *comprehensive*).

[34] *Quicquid esse potest, intelligi potest.* 2 *Contra Gentes*, 98.
[35] *Spir.*, 8 ; 2 *Contra Gentes*, 93 ; 1 q. 50, a. 4.

assertion epitomises and rounds off the deduction that we have been making hitherto. Those beings which are also called " separate substances " and which are identified by St. Thomas with the angels of theology play a large part in his philosophy as they did also in the philosophy of the Arabians. To understand them as he did we need to unite the Catholic idea of personal angels capable of knowing and willing with that of the separate ideas attributed to Plato. For St. Thomas there could be no such thing as lion-as-such or man-as-such because every lion and every man implies, besides its principle of life and unity (soul and form), a material element subject to spatial conditions and thereby restricting the possibilities of the essence ; it is just the union of two such elements which constitutes man and lion. On the other hand, once an angelic nature exists it is in possession of all that perfection of which naturally it is capable since it does not imply any material or receptive element which would limit it ; being the expression of its own idea fully, being in fact identical with it, there is no room for another like unto it side by side with it. Of the same species there could no more be two angels than there could be two lions-as-such or two kinds of identical whiteness. In the order of concepts the individuals Peter and Martin can be distinguished from their humanity and both from humanity as such, but from every point of view there could be only one Gabriel because there is no room for a distinction between Gabriel and his own nature. Each separate substance out of that collectivity of them which constitutes the spirit-world represents an original fact in the order of intellectual value and of the idea, and at the same time an intellectual capacity is implied in accordance with the degree that belongs to each one.

These beings, considered both as subsisting as intelligible objects and as subjects endowed with purely intuitive intelligences, are constantly before the mind of Aquinas. With truth it might be said that there is no understanding his theory of the universals unless his doctrine of the angels has been properly grasped. If it was characteristic of Plato at his best to have transcended the view-point of a philosophy of concepts, and to have affirmed the existence of intelligible objects to the contemplation of which the human mind looks for happiness, then it must certainly be admitted that no philosopher has more intimately or vitally incorporated Platonism into his synthesis than St. Thomas. As a result, whoever would study the value of intelligence in a system which is the least " geo-centric " and the most " noocentric " that ever was, can never neglect, no more than did St. Thomas, those perpetual terms of reference, those models of the intellectual process in its ideal state. Not only do they prevent us from identifying intellectual knowledge as such with discursive reasoning, but they help to suppress the opposition that is made between reality and idea. They make us realise that by its nature intelligence is something analogous not only in the eyes of corporeal beings but, if it could be said, for the very organs of apprehension, hands and feet and tentacles : *facultas apprehensiva.*

If, then, after a long period of " notional " spiritualism we are anxious to resuscitate the idea of this ever-youthful spiritualism, let us cease to represent the " intelligible world " as a system of laws and axioms and principles. Beings come before laws : and it is intellectualism that says so. Let us try, following St. Thomas and his contemporaries, to have an adequate idea of " spiritual substance," be it angel or soul, in its exquisite grandeur and its subtle purity. It is less in the world than is the world in it : *continens magis quam contenta.* It is something more real because it possesses a greater degree of being ; that is why it is called " substance." Laws and principles, we must remember, are essentially to man as a rational animal as they are the products of our inferior mode of knowledge.[36] These are

---

[36] That is true even as regards the first principles of reason. Citing a familiar Augustinian comment which likens human truths to so many *defective and broken* images of Unique Subsisting Truth, St. Thomas adds : *Et haec veritas in intellectu nostro resultans primo et principaliter consistit in principiis per se notis* (d. 49, q. 2, q. 7 ad 9). In view of this theory of judgments it is easy to understand that it is not necessary to place a determined number of logical principles at the basis of science. All that reason requires is the unity of the ontological principle, the infinite Intelligence. On earth some of our most precious items of knowledge are not reduced to first principles (*cf.* p. 10). In heaven when we shall enjoy intellectual intuition in its purity the intelligible divine *facts* will appear with much more clarity than no matter what judgments :

enuntiabilia, and the very word *enuntiabilia* with its reference to our vocal organ of expression suggests a time and a space-element in our intellectual knowledge. *The idolatry of the* enuntiabile *is no fitting climax for a philosophy of intellectualism, but implies rather a very suicide of intellectualism.*

All this gives us some idea of the disfavour with which St. Thomas regarded the present life as an initiation into the intellectual life ; according to him this present life is but ill-adapted to intellectual knowledge. Auguste Comte would have it that " feeling experiences the same need of concentration as mind does of generalisation." The philosophy of St. Thomas runs directly counter to this dualism of Comte, this divergence that he places between the different modes of our two chief activities ; though it accepts, indeed, the truth of Comte's aphorism as far as the present life is concerned,[37] and in that spirit evolves a whole critique of human speculation which we hope to unfold in the pages which follow. The fundamental idea has been given which links up the different theses that we shall study, and if there are here and there certain inconsistencies, that must be attributed to no other cause than forgetfulness of this dominating principle. It was necessary, therefore, to speak of it at the very outset. It is now possible for us to go ahead, and in the light of this principle see what St. Thomas thought of the meaning and finality of the universe.

V

If intelligence is that which is the more perfect, it must be said that, on peripatetic principles, Pure Act or the First Being must be identically Intelligence, and further that, if there is intellectual knowledge in the created world, the whole universe will be ordered towards that as to its end.

Pure Act is final end, to put it simply, the final end of all things. Now a twofold relation may be conceived to exist

In patria, ubi essentiam ejus videbimus, multo amplius erit nobis per se notum Deum esse, quam nunc sit per se notum quod affirmatio et negatio non sunt simul verae (*Ver.*, 10, 12). *Articuli erunt ita per se noti et visi, sicut modo principia demonstrationis* (3 d. 24, q. 1, a. 2, sol. 1 ad 2).

[37] See the very similar phrases in 1 d. 47, q. 1, a. 1, and frequently repeated elsewhere.

between the final end and the agents that are referred to it. Either the end depends for its reality and is realised by the activity of the agents (just as victory is in this sense the aim and object of soldiers and health that of doctors), or the end, already in existence, is the object of their tendencies and actions in this sense that if they act, or exert themselves, or pass from a state of potency to that of act, it is in order to acquire and obtain for themselves this end. When it is God Who is the Final Cause? the first alternative is obviously out of the question, since Pure Act and Subsistent Truth are necessarily anterior to progressive natures. " God, there-fore, cannot be the end of things, as though He were some-thing effected, but only as something already existing to be acquired by things," *sed hoc solo modo quia ipse rebus acquiritur*, and again : " things are not directed to God as to an end for which there is question of gaining something, but rather that things themselves may gain something of God for themselves." [38]

This conception of the " acquisition by things of God " suggests in the first instance the idea of an intellectual possession of Him. This is quite natural for the reason that God being pre-eminently incorporeal of Him more than of aught else besides it can be said : He can be grasped only by mind. It would seem, then, that already we have pro-claimed the knowledge of God by creatures to be the only possible final end of all creation.

This way of looking at the Thomistic theory of the finality of the universe is not false ; it must, in fact, be regarded as the principal one.[39]   As we advance, however, in the systematic exposition of this theory given in the Third Book

[38] The reference is evidently to a phrase of Aristotle apropos of the *Summum Bonum* : (εἰ) χω καθ' αὐτό, δῆλον ὡς οὐκ ἄν εἴη πρακτὸν οὐδὲ κτητὸν (*Eth. Nic.*, A, VI, 1096 b). In this passage taken by itself we have an epitome of all the differences that separate St. Thomas from Aristotle in metaphysics and in morals.

[39] It is not necessary to take account particularly of the finality of creation conceived as a " diffusion of divine goodness." This expression is frequently employed by St. Thomas and is taken from Denis the Aeropagite. But good-ness is not merely magnanimity, a quality " of the heart "; it is rather a meta-physical conception which regards being and goodness as identical, goodness being the perfection of being. Taking it in this way it is easily reducible to the idea St. Thomas had of " representative finality." *Ver.*, 23, 4 ; *Comp. Theol.*, 101, 102, 124, 2 ; 1 *Contra Gentes*, 91, 3 ; 96, 2.

of the *Summa Contra Gentes* we notice that a new concept is inserted in the development, even before anything has been said of the divine vision accorded to creatures. This new concept has to do with the assimilation of all things to God, or of the " representation " of God by all things, and it is conceived in the light of a general formula which covers the said " acquisition by things of God." [40] A certain extension of the idea of finality is the result, for on this way of viewing things it is no longer merely angel or man that may be said to " acquire " God but indeed every substance in creation which has being, each in its own way, the birds by flying, the plants by growing and fructifying, and crude matter by its simple resignation to exist. And then it would no longer be some particular mind, but creation entire, which would need to be considered in order to have an adequate idea of this representative finality which requires that multiplicity of parts we find in the universe. For " creatures being unable to attain to the resemblance of that divine perfection in all its simplicity as exists in God, it was necessary that what is one and simple should be represented by diversity and differences in its effects " [41] " just as when a man who finds that he cannot adequately express his idea by one word employs several in order to make his meaning clear."[42]

If representative assimilation be regarded as the most ultimate of created ends—God, in any case, remains the sole final end simply speaking [43]—it is not to an intellectual knowledge outside of that of God that the universe is ordained, but rather to an *intelligible* unity because resemblance and representation can be understood only in reference to mind. Were it true, then, that the universe was devoid of rational beings and consisted merely of the earth and stars and

[40] The doctrine of *assimilatio ad Deum* in its precise form is found in the *Contra Gentes*. It is, however, in the *Summa Theologica* also. 1 q. 65, a. 2 ; 1 q. 103, a. 2 ad 2.
[41] *Comp. Theol.*, 72. *Cf. ibid.*, 102 ; 1 q. 47, a. 1 ; *Pot.*, 3, 16.
[42] Evil itself is embraced by this varied representation of God. 3 *Contra Gentes*, 71 (2 and 6) ; 1 q. 23, a. 5 ad 3 ; In 2 *Tim.*, 2, 3.
[43] *Communicatio divinae bonitatis non est ultimus finis, sed ipsa divina bonitas.* The reason of this is that God acts *non appetitu finis, sed ex amore finis Pot.*, 3, 15, 14, *cf.* in 12 *Met.*, l. 9. Likewise, 1q. 103, a. 2 ad 3.

plants and animals, nevertheless in the theory of St. Thomas the value of the universe would still be of the intellectual and artistic order ; its end would be " the beauty of universal order." [44] If, on the contrary, the most ultimate of created ends were found not in the defective representation that is given by the universe by the mere fact of its existence but rather in the idea formed by intellectual creatures of the world, or yet in the idea which these creatures form of God by contact with His universe, then the final created end would formally consist in an act of intellectual knowledge.

These two final ends, assimilation and vision, ultimate intelligibility and formal intellectual knowledge, do not seem to have been formally subordinated one to the other by St. Thomas [45] ; in certain passages he seems to content himself with merely placing them side by side. Sometimes, as when he says that corporeal creatures were made for mind, he seems to regard assimilation as simply a means in relation to vision.[46] At other times, however, it is the vision of God that is in his mind when he speaks of assimilation, and then this vision seems to be a form of assimilation to God, indeed the most perfect form of it.[47]

In all this there is no contradiction. The problem, in fact, is identical with another one which St. Thomas broaches elsewhere, and this further question asks whether the universe entire is more perfect than the intellectual part of it taken in itself. The same solution will hold for both, and this solution can be effected either by having recourse to many distinctions or by simply ruling out the question altogether : *Vel dicendum quod pars non dividitur contra totum.*[48] The three points of view are all legitimate and comple-

---

[44] *Pot.*, 3, 16 ; *cf.* 4 *Contra Gentes*, 42, 3. God is, as it were, the artist and creatures are simply an expression and a representation of what is contained in the conception of the divine Word. Thus reality finds its ultimate justifica-tion in knowledge which is its source and final end.

[45] *Ver.*, 20, 4 ; 1 q. 65, a. 2.

[46] 3 *Contra Gentes*, 99 end ; *cf.* 112, 6.

[47] *Comp. Theol.*, 103 and 106.

[48] 1 q. 93, a. 2 ad 3. At first St. Thomas had proposed the distinction which may be expressed by saying that, on the one hand, the universal order of the world extends and radiates better the resemblance to God, while intellect gathers it together and intensifies more (*extensive et diffusive . . . intensive et collective. . . .*).

mentary ways of viewing the matter, but the last mentioned
is the most comprehensive because it seems to express God's
idea and intention in the most satisfactory manner : God
wills the means for the end and places simultaneously before
us the work of His hands composed of parts which in their
reality are composite and which have mutual interdependence in the harmony of the whole. It must not be
forgotten that intellectual unity is incommensurate with
individual unity and that it is of another and a higher order
altogether. If, then, spirits as such form part of the universe
and help to make it what it is, it follows that because each
one of them relatively to the whole creation is a spiritual
power of integration, the assimilation of which St. Thomas
speaks will be increased with the number of visions that such
beings enjoy. " Intellectual natures," remarks St. Thomas,
" have a greater affinity with the whole of things than has
any other nature. Each one of them having a capacity to
embrace all reality in its intelligence is in a position to
become all things after a certain manner. . . . Rightly
therefore does God subordinate all things to them." [49]
They are monads that multiply the world by their manner
of reflecting it actively and in a more noble way than that
of its own manner of being.

Moreover, the separate substances " in which principally
consists the perfection of the universe " [50] exceed in number
not only the types or species of earthly beings but even the
whole multitude of material things" [51] to the same extent
that the infinitely great sidereal world surpasses the insignificant sublunary world (ut haec quasi non habeant notabilem
quantitatem in comparatione ad illa). Given that, let us look
at the universe as a whole. We see that its intelligible
perfection is equivalent to its natural perfection and exceeds
it, in fact, both extensively, so to speak, and qualitatively

[49] Naturae autem intellectuales majorem habent affinitatem ad totum quam aliae
naturae ; nam unaquaeque intellectualis substantia est quodamodo omnia, in quantum
totius entis comprehensiva est suo intellectu. . . . Convenienter igitur alia propter
substantias intellectuales providentur a Deo. 3 Contra Gentes, 112, 5. Knowledge,
in the world, is a remedy " for what is lacking to things " (Ver., 2, 2).
[50] 2 Contra Gentes, 93, 4.
[51] 2 Contra Gentes, 92 (4 and 3). Cf. Pot., 6, 7 : sicut punctum ad sphaeram.

also.[52] The world of material objects not only does not dwarf the world of intellects or minimise it in any way, but it is in reality rather the lower fringe of, or a kind of addition to, the spirit-world. " Much more than sun or moon is each separate substance to be considered a principal part of the universe," [53] and their presence in the world is like of the soul in the body, *contines magis quam contenta.* The assimilation of the world to God on the part of minerals, plants and animals cannot, therefore, come into opposition to that finality which is realised in the vision that spirits enjoy.

In fine, even the appearance of contradiction goes if we suppose, in accordance with the principles of theology, that intellectual unity in the case of spirits will be brought about by an immediate vision of God as He is in Himself. In this way alone is all possible intelligibility gathered together into one and the capacities of mind fully realised.[54] Thus every reality and force and natural quality will be seen in their rightful position in the scheme of things entire when the intelligible union of the human soul with the divine essence will be realised, and when the soul will behold in that essence the world which depends on it exclusively for its reality. The divine life that will thus accrue to finite intelligences is as such the highest form of assimilation with God. It is, therefore, the really final end, and it is when we keep it before our eyes particularly that we begin to see in the world a vast *ensemble* of means subordinated to the act of intellectual knowledge.

[52] *Cf. De Anim.*, a. 18 ; 3 *Contra Gentes*, 59, 3. It would be quite in accordance with the spirit of Thomastic " dialectics " to extend what is here said of representative ideas to subsistent ideas : *cf.* final argument of 2 *Contra Gentes*, 92.

[53] 2 *Contra Gentes*, 98.

[54] St. Thomas states expressly that mind, like all other natural forms of energy, tends to realise itself to the fullest extent possible, and, moreover, since " all its capacities can be simultaneously reduced to act," the beatitude of a being endowed with intelligence could not consist in that fragmentary knowledge of God obtainable by demonstration, but must be found in a saturating intuition which conveys in some way a knowledge of all at one and the same time (3 *Contra Gentes*, 39 end ; *cf.* 3 *Contra Gentes*, 59). Already we begin to see that the final end of the universe as an intelligible unity is in perfect harmony only with the theological doctrine of beatitude as consisting in the beatific vision. I have not here insisted on this point as the question of the relation of this vision to the natural capacities of intellect will be taken up later (Part II, ch. 6, 2).

VI

By a profoundly logical coincidence the beatific vision, which is the final end of the world and the ultimate perfection of the created mind, is also, according to St. Thomas, the only example of created knowledge other than that contained in intuitions of the self which directly, not only without recourse to abstraction but without any medium whatever, grasps and possesses being as such. It is the perfect example of intellectual knowledge both as regards its object and the manner of its accomplishment. On this account it must be studied here ; otherwise it would be impossible to have a correct idea of the intellectual process as such. " It must be admitted that the substance of God can be seen by intelligence. . . . As regards the manner of this vision . . . the divine essence cannot be seen in any created species ; it is necessary, therefore, in order that the divine essence be seen by any intellect, that this essence play the rôle of medium by which it is seen and that it must be at one and the same time the object seen and the medium by which it is seen." [55] The intelligence that enjoys the beatific vision has no other idea of God than God Himself ; He takes the place both of the *species impressa* and of the *verbum mentale*. It could not even be otherwise, adds St. Thomas, for if it were necessary to employ any created representation, then it would no longer be God Himself Who is seen. To fulfil its rôle a representation should participate in some way in the nature of its object. The appearance of a circle or of a house which is depicted on paper or reproduced in memory may differ from the circle and the house as regards their reality, but essentially and from point of view of their nature this appearance is similar to them and can therefore be employed to represent them. But in God nature and being are one and the same, and it follows that every representation of God or idea of God which is not identical with Him cannot make known the divine essence as it really is ; they are circumscribed,

[55] 3 *Contra Gentes*, 51.

limited and belonging to a *genus*, while the object to be represented is both incommunicable and infinite.

But how can God Who is absolutely Pure Act and therefore essentially opposed to all forms of combination with things, how can He be the intelligible species that will actuate and inform the created intellect ? " To understand this truth we must remember that every substance is as such either form only or composed of matter and form."

A material object, such as a stone or a dog, cannot immediately inform intellect by its material reality ; the stone precisely as matter does not actuate mind as mind. Likewise, finite intelligible objects which are at the same time thinking subjects, but not identical with intelligibility as such, and whose thought is distinct from their reality, cannot so come into contact with another spirit that this spirit should remain itself in its depths while receiving the first and " becoming it after a certain manner." That a finite spirit should by its very substance actuate another is a contradiction, for either the second by receiving it becomes identical with it and then they will be no longer two, or the first must be such that it enjoys personal consciousness and total intelligibility (that is to say, endowed with the pre-eminent value of universal consciousness), and this latter supposition is true of God alone. But let us try to refine our idea of spiritual substance so as to empty it of all phenomenal determination and restricting limitation, of all subjectivity that would bar the way to adequate apprehension of reality, even of all dependence in regard to external things (nothing less is demanded by the idea of perfect consciousness) : then we are in the presence of thought as *pure form* which, by definition, is identical with intelligibility as such and truth itself, the subsistent and universal Mind. This thought, moreover, is conscious of itself, that is to say personal, since thought by definition is conscious. Undoubtedly, this absolute could not be the form of something distinct from it in that being's material reality so as to form with it a substance of nature : such a composite would be unthinkable because it would mean the lowering of that which is infinite to the rank of a genus.

Such a contradiction is absent, however, when there is question only of intentional or intelligible union which is compatible with a substantial distinction. Hence " that which is pure form in the order of intelligible objects, Truth itself, that is God," can alone, and to the exclusion of all other intelligible objects which are true but not Truth, determine in an intellectual manner created intelligence and become the idea of angel and of man.

The same demonstration may be presented from another angle if we employ the notions of *being* and of essence. " Everything is intelligible in so far as it is in act," and " the actuality of a thing is, as it were, its own light." In order, therefore, that a thing directly of itself be the idea of an intelligence it would be necessary that there would be nothing in it which would not be in act. In the finite consciousness of a pure created spirit, however, everything is not in act. The angel has many ideas and several acts which succeed one another in his consciousness ; there is room for differentiating between substance and phenomena where he is concerned. The phenomenal surface of his being corresponding to his acts of knowledge is intelligible by hypothesis, but these acts do not express the thinking subject in its entirety and they are therefore inadequate expressions of the angelic essence as such. Suppose that this phenomenal surface were detached, so to speak, and were to inform intelligibly another being, it would be incapable of giving a full knowledge of its owner : it does not exhaust the many virtualities that belong to the essence and beyond it there are other capacities that might be actualised otherwise. The next instant, once the idea or perception had changed, the realisation of the same nature would be different. The natural life of finite beings with their imperfect unity is either a perpetual flux, or else a succession of discontinous actuations the collection of which does not exhaust the capacities of the essence. In God there is nothing of that, *and because in Him there can be no distinction of reality and phenomenon* it is possible for Him to *appear* entirely, as it were. Where the nature is itself act there is no room for light and shade. " The divine essence

is intelligible light," perfectly and entirely luminous.[56]
Intellectual union with a distinct being, this possession of a
living mind without any mediation, can be conceived of
no other object than of Him Who is Thought or Pure Form,
Who is Being and not merely a subject endowed with being,
Truth itself. And this conclusion, for St. Thomas, followed
from a philosophic analysis of the intelligibility of act and
of the immanence of intellectual knowledge.[57]

Brought into line with the Arabian theories of beatitude
these discussions presented a very lively interest in the eyes
of contemporaries. The particular point of interest, however, which concerns us here was this : the mussulman
philosophers, in order not to tamper with the inaccessibility
of God, placed human beatitude in a union with the angels,
and the Jew, Ibn-Gabirol, denied all " proportion " between
God and even the " separate " intelligences and went so
far as to declare the Absolute unknowable, but the Catholic
Doctor, not fearing to compromise the transcendence of
God, affirmed that the lowest intellect was *capax Dei*.[58]
In this we must recognise a triumph for intellectualism and
at the same time we cannot fail to see how different and
other this form of intellectualism is from everything that might
come under the title *rationalism*. True, to express such a
possession of God with the term " intellectual knowledge "
may seem pale and of the earth ; the term " vision," which
is metaphorical, has generally met with greater favour.
But the word is without importance. No matter what term
is selected, be it " union," " intimate possession," " conscious coincidence " or the like, the point of capital import
is that, for St. Thomas, the faculty which renders us capable
of this transcendental action is the self-same faculty which,
under another form, is responsible for our concepts and

[56] See *Quod.*, l. 7a, 1 and 4 d. 49, q. 2, a. 1.

[57] 3 *Contra Gentes*, 51, and also 2 *Contra Gentes*, 98. If intellectual knowledge
is understood as an immanent transformation in the sense of Aristotle, then
the angel is known directly in itself by its own personal consciousness. If such
knowledge is understood as a kind of spiritual " contact " *secundum positionem
Platonis*, then it might be held that there is a mutually immediate knowledge
of one another among the angels.

[58] *Capax Dei* (3, q. 6, a. 2, and elsewhere. The phrase is that of St. Augustine,
De Trinitate, XIV, 11). Ch. 57 at Book III of the *Contra Gentes* is entitled
Quod Omnis Intellectus Cuiuscumque Gradus Particeps Esse Potest Divinae Visionis.

rational deductions here below. " The divine substance is not so completely beyond the power of the created intellect as to be radically alien to it, as for instance sound is to the sense of sight or immaterial substance is to sense in general." " In so far as man by creation participates in intelligence, he is made, as it were, in the ' specific image of God.' " [59] In these words, which are employed by St. Thomas not merely *en passant* but as conveying the very soul of his thought, opposition is declared not only to the theories of the Arabian philosophers. The Saint is also seen to reject the vague and metaphorical anti-rationalism of a Plotinus for whom this union with God and the simplification that it brings is not properly due to an act of intellect since it implies the denial of all movement. Opposition is not less marked to the inconsistent doctrines of so many heterodox mystics whose zeal ran ahead of their knowledge. Finally, he is opposed to certain illogical Scholastics of his own day who had inherited the psychology of the twelfth century : these thinkers, the most typical of them being, I think, William of Auvergne, having distinguished, as was the custom, between *knowledge* and *wisdom*, failed to reduce these two cognate knowledges to a common principle and, like the voluntarists of all ages, attributed to the " heart " all that was simple, direct and profound in the activities of intellect.[60] As against these " Augustinians " St. Thomas, in this nearer to St. Augustine than they, maintained with the whole Greek tradition that in intellect as such all that

[59] 3 *Contra Gentes*, 54. *Divina enim substantia non sic est extra facultatem intellectus creati quasi aliquid omnino extraneum ab ipso, sicut est sonus a visu vel substantia immaterialis a sensu . . . sed est extra facultatem intellectus creati sicut excedens virtutem ejus, sicut excellentia sensibilium sunt extra facultates sensuum.* 3 d. 10, q. 2, a. 2, sol. 1 : *Homo autem in quantum per creationem producitur in participationem intellectus, producitur quasi in similitudinem speciei ipsius Dei : quia ultimum eorum secundum quae natura creata participat similitudinem naturae increatae, est intellectualitas.* The Scholastics find no little difficulty in reconciling this " likeness to God " imposed by the Bible and accepted by their metaphysic with the infinite dissimilarity implied by God's transcendence and which renders God more distant from the most luminous angel than the angel is from the smallest eel. In one of his latest works St. Thomas suggests that intelligibility might be represented rather as a negative attribute than a purely positive one (in *Trin.*, l. 2, 4).

[60] *Cf.* William of Auvergne, *De retributionibus sanctorum* (Paris ed., 1674, Vol. I, p. 319) and *De virtutibus*, ch. XI (*ibid.*, pp. 146–147).

is of highest value is to be found and that it is the noblest faculty *simpliciter*.

Wisdom, though a celestial gift, is more intellectual in its nature than is science because it brings with it a greater unification and marks a greater triumph over multiplicity. Deductive reasoning, upon which science is built up, is so little characteristic of intellectual beings that in us it is the result of our composite nature. If by intuition we possess something of the life of angels, our dependence on discursive reasoning lowers us towards the successive, multiple and relative knowledge of animals. Taking the beatific vision itself into account we see that, instead of representing a violent stretching of intelligence beyond its reach, a development of the principles of St. Thomas leads to the view that it is the capacity we enjoy for this vision, being the only common basis for differentiating the different aptitudes of intelligence, which defines intelligence itself. Intellect is the faculty of *being in general* because it is the faculty of the *Infinite Being*. If reason is capable of forming judgments that possess an absolute value and of perceiving laws from which not even God can derogate, if the indivisible certitude of its clear assertions puts all intellectual subjects, as it were, on the same level, the reason of this is to be found in that potential participation which makes intellect to be what it is and in that capacity for the divine which God will fill up in the beatific vision.[61] How could that act, which renders all forms of intellectual knowledge possible, not be itself a form of intellectual process as such ?

It must be added that the intellectual possession of God which is given by the beatific vision must not be likened to such acts as those which are said to " bring us near " Him, or which help us to reach Him in some figurative and inexact

---

[61] Because, in effect, the unity of the specifying object of intelligence must be secured and this cannot be done by having recourse to being in general or " predicamental " being which will not give the mind's capacity for the beatific vision, we must reverse the argument and say that it is the capacity for seeing God which accounts for the unity of mind's object and for its capacity for being as such. In the terminology of Scholastics it would be said that we have not the *potentia obedientialis* to be elevated in the vision of God because of our natural capacity to know the " quiddity " of things, but rather *vice versa. Cf.* also p. 71.

manner. The love of God, for instance, and the desire of
God are mere expressions which have to do with the appetitive side of our nature and are dependent on the abstractive
perception of our intelligence. The intellectual possession
of God, on the contrary, is something which gives us God
as He is in Himself and makes Him known to us in the naked
intimacy of His own nature, as He can be possessed and
known, as He knows Himself, in fact, *illo modo quo ipse videt
se ipsum*. This vision marks the true participation in His
life and a real communion with His consciousness : being
a common life in one and the same idea between two
intellectual beings, it is the most perfect example of friend-
ship.[62] Once this union has been brought about everything
that is God's belongs also to the soul. Beyond what He
has, and what He is intellectually, He has nothing and He
is nothing. How this strong assertion which is postulated
by his doctrine of intelligence and intelligibility is compatible,
for St. Thomas, with innumerable differences of perfection
in the vision of the divine essence, how it leaves intact the
incommunicability of that vision as enjoyed by God Himself, " comprehensive " to such an extent that glorified
souls regarding the whole of God yet do not see Him
" wholly," is explained by him without recourse to any
new theory because he admits, as we have said, infinite
degrees of limpidity in all intuitive knowledge. Besides,
it is easy to see that this last assertion merely confirms our
general theory of intelligence. Intellectual knowledge is
simply a linking up in the development of the same act of
an objective extension with a new intensity of subjective life.
The intellectual being ought, therefore, to remain himself
throughout. Did we, however, fully comprehend Him Who
is identical with intelligibility as such, did we perceive the
infinite in an infinite manner, then because our capacity
would be equivalent to that of God, our own limited and
restrained individuality of nature would have disappeared.[63]

[62] *Cf.* Aristotle, *Eth. Nic.*, IX, 9 and 12.
[63] 3 *Contra Gentes*, 55 : *Cum omnis intellectus creatus sub certa specie terminetur.
Impossibile est igitur quod visio alicuius intellectus creati adaequet in videndo divinam
substantiam. Cf.* 1 q. 12, a. 7, and particularly 1 q. 12, a. 4, where he reasons
from the concept of intellectual knowledge to a certain natural proportion

If, therefore, the finite intellect is to remain itself and not be lost in an impossible expansion, it must be that God, while actuating it, does not cease to transcend its powers. On this condition only will God continue to retain His ineffable character of " otherness " where finite intellects are concerned, and bearing this in mind we can still employ what is perhaps the best formula drawn as it is from experience near at hand, to express the union of the finite with the Infinite in the beatific vision : *fieri quodammodo Ipse*. In heaven I shall possess Being, and God will still be " other," much in the same way as here below I am conscious of the *ego :* in this will consist eternal life.

VII

To bring precision to the metaphysic of the intellectual process as such it will now be necessary to examine briefly the ontological value of will as compared with intellect. To this effect we shall examine two Thomistic theories which are of equal importance though of unequal difficulty : the first, which explains the subordinate character of volition, completes those two doctrines already outlined and is continuous with them ; the second, at first sight apparently opposed to what has been already said, proclaims in certain circumstances the pre-eminence of love.

The subordinate rôle of will is very clearly expounded by St. Thomas when he discusses the question we have just been studying, that of the beatific vision. His solution of this question, as is well known, depends on the union of a dogma with a philosophical explanation. If, according to the Catholic Church, the beatitude of the just consists in the possession of God, this possession may be explained by Scholastics with more or less precision according to the philosophical principles governing their views of being and of the soul and the limits fixed for philosophical speculation by other dogmas. It would have been heresy to assert that in heaven the essence of the creature becomes identical with

between knowing and being : *Cognitum autem est in cognoscente secundum modum cognoscentis. . . . Si igitur modus essendi alicuius rei cognitae excedat modum naturae cognoscentis, oportet quod cognitio illius rei sit supra naturam illius cognoscentis.*

that of the Creator, or that each particular humanity was united to God therein hypostatically as in the case of Christ. But it was possible to remain a Catholic whether this possession was explained formally as due to an act of will or an act of intellect. St. Thomas elected for intellect ; Scotus for will.

In the theory of St. Thomas the decisive factor was his concept of intellect as " possessive " of reality as opposed to will which rather *tends* beyond itself to things. Not indeed that St. Thomas saw only in will this centrifugal tendency ; he also recognised in it the seat of pleasure (*subjectum delectationis*). Before the acquisition of its object there was for him desire or better urge on the part of will ; with acquisition came pleasure in the object's possession, and these were the two forms of volition and of its characteristic act, love. His doctrine, then, stands in opposition first of all to a certain form of theological hedonism which would place beatitude for man in soul-pleasure as such, but historically this system may be put aside : the real struggle was between the partisans of knowledge and the advocates, not of pleasure, but of " fruition " or " unitive love " as the final end.[64]

The latter view, according to St. Thomas, is even less tenable than that of hedonism ; both, in fact, he refutes at one and the same time. " I say, then, that as to the very essence of happiness, it is impossible for it to consist in an act of will. For it is evident from what has been said that happiness is the attainment of the last end. But the attainment of the end does not consist in the very act of the will. For the will is directed to an end, both absent, when it

---

[64] In the *Opus Oxoniense* Scotus expresses himself thus : *Delectatio sequitur finis assecutionem, nedum primitate generationis, sed etiam perfectionis ; sequitur enim actum diligendi finem visum, qui est vere actus elicitus voluntatis. Porro omnino falsum est voluntatem circa obiectum amabile sibi praesens non elicere actum aliquem, sed solum recipere delectationem et passionem* (4 d. 49, q. 4, n. 6). This act of the will is not desire but love ; it is preceded in time by a certain acquisition on the part of intellect, but it alone " simply " reaches the perfect good : in this act, therefore, consists essentially and formally man's beatitude (*ibid.*, n. 4). And in q. 3 the will-act is spoken of as *adductiva formaliter possessionis summi boni.* It is to be noted that St. Thomas does not exclude all activity on the part of appetitive faculties once they have obtained their object : *Assentit rei delectabili, et in ea quiescit, quodammodo se praebens ei ad eam interius capiendam. . . . Quasi se tradens ad continendum interius rem delectantem.* 1a, 2ae, q. 33, a. 1. But in so far as this same activity is a form of movement it could not be the end.

desires it, and present, when it is delighted by resting therein.
Now, it is evident that the desire itself of the end is not the
attainment of the end, but is a movement towards the end ;
while delight comes to the will from the end being present ;
and not conversely is a thing made present by the fact that
the will delights in it.   Therefore that the end be present
to him who desires it must be due to something else than
an act of the will.   This is evidently the case in regard to
sensible ends.   For if the acquisition of money were through
an act of the will, the covetous man would have it from the
very moment that he wished for it.   But at that moment it
is far from him ; and he attains it by grasping it in his
hand, or in some like manner ; and then he delights in the
money got.   And so it is with an intelligible end.   For at
first we desire to attain it ; we attain it through its being
made present to us by an act of the intellect ; and then the
delighted will rests in the end when attained.   It follows
that the essence of happiness consists in an act of intellect [65] :
" Neither physical generation . . . nor much less movement
could be the end. . . . Thus, the final end of the intellectual creature is to see God, not to find pleasure in this vision ;
as for desire and love, much less can they be the final end,
seeing that they exist before the end is attained." [66]

It is unnecessary to elaborate what seems obvious ; the
pivotal point on which the doctrine turns is that there is
no possession of a thing for will except it be by desire or
pleasure.[67]   If it be supposed that pleasure ought to constitute the very substance of beatitude, St. Thomas is ready
to admit in technical terms that pleasure is its formal complement.[68]   Following up the discussion he very justly points
out the real union which obtains between these two terms,
which by analysis we separate : what is desired, he says,
is both act and pleasure as a whole, both forming a single

[65] 1a, 2ae, q. 3, a. 4.
[66] Comp. Theol., c. 107 end.
[67] This comprehensio of which there is question is not something distinct from
vision. 1a, 2ae, q. 4, a. 3 ad 3.
[68] Quod., l. 8, 19 ; 3 d. 34, q. 1, a. 5 ; 4 d. 49, q. 1, a. 1, sol. 2. St. Thomas
recalls that Aristotle has not solved the question whether the act is sought for
the pleasure, or the pleasure for the act. He himself pronounces in favour of
the act (4 d. 49, q. 3, a. 4, sol. 3 ; in 10 Eth., l. 6 end).

good : *Nec illa duo sunt consideranda quasi duo bona, sed quasi unum bonum.*[69] The two are really inseparable, but of the two intellect is the more essential.

Taking the argument of St. Thomas in relation to the rest of his system, we may recognise how harmoniously it fits in with the theses examined up to this by simply stating the fundamental presupposition upon which it is built up. This presupposition is simply the axiom that movement or tendency as such cannot be an end : *Motus non habet rationem termini.* If there is movement, it must be towards something. There is no such thing as tending to tend. An absolute and radical dynamism is impossible, and that is the basis of all his arguments.[70]

When he undertakes an examination of this principle the intrinsic reason he puts forward in its support is drawn from that determinate unity of finality which rapid induction reveals in nature.[71] Movement could not be the end because it stands for duality, multiplicity, dissimilitude (*difformitas*), in other words because it is essentially a combination of potency and act as opposed to perfection which eliminates potentiality to bring about the full realisation of act.

The voluntarists are mistaken, according to St. Thomas, because they confuse movement and action, and they do this because they have not grasped the significance of perfect act which is static as opposed to the potentiality implied in movement as such. Of them it might be said, as of those described in the Seventh Book of the *Ethics*, that they have erred " concerning operation by confounding it with becoming when in reality they are not identical, since operation or activity arises out of, or succeeds, becom-

---

[69] 4 d. 49, q. 3, a. 4, sol. 3. Also 1ae, 2ae, q. 2, a. 6 ad 1 : *Ejusdem rationis est quod appetatur bonum et quod appetatur delectatio.* It is remarkable that Scotus, though he denies the real distinction of faculties among themselves, nevertheless speaks of them when he comes to treat of them psychologically as more or less separable : *Plus appetit voluntas perfectionem sui in fine ultimo, quam perfectionem intellectus* (*Opus Oxeniense*, 4 d. 49, q. 4). *Quamvis potentiae intellectivae felicitas summa sit penes propriam operationem* (*ibid.*, q. 3).

[70] This is seen specially in 1a, 2ae, q. 1, a. 1 ad 2, *Comp. Theol.*, c. 107, etc., where St. Thomas declares that the act of will itself could not be the first thing willed.

[71] *Pot.*, q. 5, a. 5   3 *Contra Gentes*, 23, 5.

ing. Every becoming has for term a nature, but activity is the nature or form in use." [72]   A Scholastic axiom has it that the agent as such is not changed except when there is a passage from potency to act ; and what is here said of act may be also said of pleasure, which is the complement of act : " Pleasure that is present without movement is more intense than pleasure which is mixed up with movement because the latter is in the order of becoming while the former belongs to the order of perfect being." [73]

Besides, where shall we find act that is static as opposed to movement and pleasure that does not entail change if not in intellectual activity ? If we examine the characteristic dynamism of man, that is, the history of those activities to be found in beings whose minds are imprisoned in matter, what do we discover ? Do we not see the quantitative multiplicity of human activities converging towards the singular unity of one end and aim which is reconquest of the qualitative similarity of things by means of ideas ? Where matter is, there also we find a certain impenetrability of things among themselves : one thing remains itself distinct from *other* things.[74]   But mind is such that while it remains itself, it can also " become " other things. This comprehensive unity of mind with reality is possessed by intuitive beings from the outset, each according to its own nature.   But it must be sought after by men by means of a multiplicity of laborious acts : their natural end is to evolve the full capacities of their minds, to arrive at the maximum of consciousness, to become nomads which have the power of reflecting all things (*ut in ea describatur totus ordo universi*). It is the unity of this end which is responsible for bringing intelligible unity to the complex series of their different activities.   Everything in them which may be described as desire or tendency has for aim the emergence of man out of

[72] In 7 *Eth.*, 1, 12.
[73] In 7 *Eth.*, l. 14.
[74] On Scholastic principles matter may be described as that which is apt to become " Other," but successively, *in sensu diviso*, that is, by ceasing to be itself.   It can neither penetrate, nor be penetrated by, its like, and of itself as such it is also impenetrable for mind (there is no idea corresponding to it, *Ver.*, 3, 5), and has no title to reality or intelligibility except by its conjunction with a form which raises it to the rank of essence.

the *regio dissimilitudinis* into the luminous home of mind. As long as there are two minds, or groups of minds, which have not communicated with one another, which have not enriched themselves upon one another, by such communication there still remains a potentiality which calls for progress. But when the last term of progress has been realised and all potentiality actualised, then movement is no longer conceivable, and the only thing left for the act of will is contentment or pleasure. Every other state implies the possibility of movement or progress ; this alone is one both of activity and repose.[75]

The static concept of perfection then, which contains the refutation of the voluntarists, is perfectly logical for St. Thomas, and is seen to be demanded by the fundamental parts of his system which we have been considering up to this.

" The operation of the apprehensive power is completed in the very fact that the thing apprehended is in the one that apprehends : while the operation of the appetitive power is completed in the fact that he who desires is borne towards the thing desirable. Therefore the operation of the apprehensive power is likened to rest : whereas the operation of the appetitive power is rather likened to move-ment." [76] Elsewhere the Saint says : " Contemplation is not a form of becoming but rather a form of perfect activity." [77] Voluntary activity, accordingly,[78] is some-

---

[75] *Assimilatur quieti.* F. C. S. Schiller, in a very suggestive article on ἐνέργεια ἀκινησίας (*Bibliothèque du Congrès international de Philosophie*, Paris, 1902, Vol. 4), remarks very justly that in this context ἠρεμία might be translated more accurately as *constancy* rather than as *repose*.

[76] 1 q. 81, a. 1.

[77] 1a, 2ae, q. 35, a. 5. *(Contemplatio) non est generatio . . . sed operatio quaedam perfecta.* For the superiority of intelligence over movement see 2 *Contra Gentes*, 55, 11.

[78] It follows that from the Thomist point of view a philosophy founded on the analysis of appetite or volition is legitimate, though of an inferior kind : it does not directly envisage the perfection of activity but either its preparation or its result. It is deeper philosophy to argue in favour of the beatific vision or in proof of the existence of God from the nature of intelligence than from an analysis of the " aspirations " of the will. Ultimately, to satiate will is simply to satisfy intellect. This subordinate character of volition explains why all forms of voluntarist philosophy are so easily made to fit into an intellectualist metaphysic. See the curious passage taken from the Sentences : *Ille quippe beate vivit qui vivit ut vult, nec male aliquid vult. Haec sententia Augustini concordat*

thing essentially relative and imperfect, whereas intellectual
activity is the example of perfect action and hence an end
in chief.

VIII

The arguments put forward thus far prove metaphysically,
that is, rigorously, and in regard to all possible hypotheses,
the supremacy of intellectual activity as such, or they serve
no purpose at all. It may happen then, once this intransi-
geant attitude of St. Thomas has been grasped, that, finding
elsewhere certain affirmations of the supremacy of love, we
are inclined to see in this a veritable contradiction. Viewing
things in the abstract, St. Thomas says more than once it
is true that knowledge is superior to love. But in the concrete it is necessary to make a distinction : if the object of
the act in question is one which is superior to the human
soul, then we must admit that love is superior to knowledge.[79]

Must we see in this an unconscious concession to the
dogmatic piety of the mystics and of the Fathers,[80] or is it
a concession to a vague instinct of the human heart which
is awed by the nakedness of pure speculation and which is
tempted to find a greater sense of reality and of value in this
tendency towards union which we call love ? As a matter
of fact, a reconciliation is not far to seek. St. Thomas has
assimilated this principle of the Doctors on the supremacy
of love into his philosophical synthesis ; for him it is no
longer something merely superadded from without. To this

cum sententia Philosophi 2 de Anim., ut per vivere operatio vitae intelligatur ; per hoc
autem quod dicitur ut vult, ostenditur operatio non impedita ; per hoc autem quod dicitur
nec aliquid male vult, ostenditur esse connaturalis, quia mala sunt contra naturam
(4 d. 4, Exp. t. 3). Likewise, when there is question of a general classification of
beings St. Thomas refuses to base his division on the different kinds of appetite :
Appetititivum non constituit aliquem specialem gradum viventium (in 2 An., l. 7).
For him appetite is really in function of something else ; in this philosophy it is
reduced, so to speak, to the position of something " mediate " and is explicable
in terms of something other than itself.

[79] Ver., 22, 11 ; 1 q. 82, a. 3.   In these passages St. Thomas has not forgotten the principles that we have already expounded. On the contrary, the
superiority of intellect in the abstract is proved in the first passage by a reference
to that immanent possession of reality which characterises it, and in the second
by the natural priority of the intellectual act over the act of will as well as by
its more simple relation to being.

[80] The phrase so dear to Scotus which he cites as that of St. Anselm is
well known : Perversus ordo esset, velle amare ut intelligeres.

extent the vague instinct of the human heart has been brought into line with his whole system.

It might be said that St. Thomas, by a deep analysis of those concepts which for his Masters and contemporaries had solidified into opaque metaphors and literary formulæ, came to look upon love as something destructive, as it were, of individualities. (In intellectual knowledge, on the other hand, he saw a means of multiplying reality.) In the love of mere desire I subordinate the object loved entirely to myself, I destroy its own individual finality, and make of it an instrument in regard to self : such an object no longer exists on its account, it has become part of me, and as a whole subordinated to my interest. It is in this way that we love the rose we pluck, or the water we drink. In the love of good will, on the contrary, it is I who assume the rôle of instrument, and become part of the object loved, no longer seeking my own happiness but rather that of the object loved. Love, then, as it arises in me is a principle of activity which has for end and object something outside of me, something that forms part of a whole which surrounds me, goes beyond the self, and subjects me to its empire. To take an example from St. Thomas, we see that the hand, in order to safeguard the body from sudden danger, goes out spontaneously and of itself, and is ready to sacrifice its own well-being to the good of the whole to which it belongs.

This whole can be, as in the love of passion, something co-equal with the lover, but it happens that the person loved can come to be considered arbitrarily (and under the influence of sensitive subjectivity) as something superior to the lover and so induces by disorder and immorality a subordination of self on the part of the lover. When it is a question of social sentiments, it is the greater *ensemble* to which we belong, as for instance the Fatherland or especially Humanity, that we prefer naturally to ourselves, seeing that it embodies more fully the nature that is ours. Thus all lions, if Plato spoke truly, would prefer the separate Lion to that participation in lionhood which they enjoy.

Let us now consider the scheme of things entire in the light of its common participation in the attribute being.

Everything, according to St. Thomas, prefers that Being which is transcendent, absolute and subsistent to the limited and participated form of being that finite things enjoy. The angel, man, even the things of nature, naturally love God, each in its own particular way, more than they love their own essence.[81]   Now this important and very explicitly stated doctrine serves to remove an apparent contradiction which, in the peripatetic doctrine, seems to vitiate the very concept of " pure love " ; and in the same way it will help to reconcile the rigorously intellectualist conception of perfection that we find in St. Thomas with the supremacy of love affirmed by the Fathers. All that is necessary is to bear in mind the distinction that holds between man viewed in his isolated individuality and man as he forms part of the universe, or, better, as an analogical participation of God.

For the first case, all the arguments of Aristotle hold good : in the human microcosm the highest faculty, reason, subordinates the rest to itself, and man's end is contemplation. In the second, contemplation is not excluded : it is still the perfection of the part, and indeed may also become the good of the whole if the well-being of the whole so demands. Yet the more certain and more immediate perfection of the part is to realise its end as a part to subordinate itself as far as possible to the good of the whole, and where this end is as yet unknown to keep itself in expectant readiness. Could not God require from me the sacrifice of my happiness—*ad decorem universi ?* The distinction between these two cases permits us to distinguish between perfection and beatitude. Saints have acted on that distinction in their " impossible suppositions." They argued with themselves thus : " Did God place my partial perfection (as a lover) elsewhere than in my beatitude (perfection of the individual), which would I choose, happiness or love ? " And they elected in favour of love.

In the thought of St. Thomas, however, such a distinction

[81] 1 q. 60, a. 5, 1a, 2ae, q. 109, a. 3. I have tried to elucidate some points that arise out of this doctrine in my thesis, *Pour l'histoire du problème de l'amour au moyen-âge*

belongs merely to the order of ideas, and these suppositions are impossible. Not only has God as the intelligent Cause of all things created things with definite natures destined to find their perfection in particular forms of activity, but He upholds and watches over intellectual creatures with such immediate care that it were impossible so to escape the laws of nature as to bring perfection to the universe by the definitive sacrifice of self or by destruction.[82] As we shall see later, the perfection of the intellectual creature, at least when it is not conditioned by being subject to successive duration, corresponds to the good *simpliciter* without restriction or possible hindrance. Hence the perfection desired by God for man is identically man's beatitude. There would be a contradiction in the very heart of God's creative and all-powerful idea to which human nature corresponds were it possible for the human will to be in a perpetual state of tension with no final end beyond itself.

The logical disjunction implied by these " impossible suppositions " is really due to lack of intuition regarding the divine designs in our regard. Up to a certain point it may be natural for a mind which views everything through the prism of the quantitative to regard the hierarchy of duties as something in the form of a bifurcation. But in reality and precisely because we are participations of God, the duality must disappear for him who sees things at their source in the First Truth. In heaven, logical artifices will have to go : there it will be seen that what God wishes for us covers that which unites us to Him, and is in reality formally to be identified with it. The basis of the distinction will remain, it is true, and for that reason it will still be possible to say that the love of God transcends the knowledge of God in excellency. At the same time it will have to be admitted, prescinding even from the reactions of knowledge on love which will be intensified and expanded by the beatific vision,[83] that obedience, which is the peculiar work of love, can have no other object than to tend towards

---

[82] *Cf.* 3 *Contra Gentes*, c. 112 and 113.
[83] *Ver.*, 29, 3, 5. *Caritas enim viatoris non potest adaequari caritati comprehensoris : aliter enim aliquis afficitur ad praesentia, et aliter ad absentia.*

knowledge. Thus, from every point of view, the act of union with God will be one of *knowledge.*[84]

[84] Because it is intellect which shall attain to God as He is in Himself there can be no real divergency between tending *ad rem ut est in se* and *ad rem ut est in intellectu.* In the same way, the pleasure of love *ex parte objecti* and the subjective pleasure of the act of contemplation which we can distinguish here below will then coincide necessarily. For those in possession of God to " gain one's soul " is to " gain God," and that is so because of the very nature of the intellectual process. It is just the perfection of intellectual activity that on earth prevents it from directly possessing its object and which forces it to be satisfied with faith which is ultimately destined to disappear. *Aenigma est essentiale fidei, accidentale caritati* (3 d. 31, q. 2 ad 3). The act of will, on the other hand, attains to God as immediate on earth as it is possible for it, precisely because it does not imply true contact or immanence of what is " other " in the self; for the will to attain its object in its own way it suffices that intellect has perceived this object in an imperfect manner (3 d. 27, q. 3, a. 1 ; d. 23, q. 1, a. 5 ad 6, etc. And it is for that same reason that there is not an exact proportion between love and knowledge (1a, 2ae, q. 27, a. 2 ad 2 : *Car.*, 4, 4).

PART II

HUMAN SPECULATION

CHAPTER I

THE INSTRUMENTS EMPLOYED IN HUMAN SPECULATION

I

THE nobility and strength of the intellect lies in the fact that it is an *acquisitive* faculty. The intellectual process by which the reality of things is grasped by mind is the highest form of activity, and consequently it ranks as the measure, *raison d'être*, and end of appetite in all its forms. When we regard this intellectual activity, however, under the ordinary conditions of its terrestrial exercise we find that it is possessed of very different attributes. This undeniable observation brings home to us the unreal character of intellectualism in the form in which we know it. But this cannot alter those absolute exigencies of intellectualism in the abstract and for a metaphysician who accepts finality it will have the effect of convincing him of the existence of a supreme reign of intelligence in a better world than the one in which we live.

In the hierarchy of intellects man comes lowest and last : before the splendours which Nature unfolds he is blind like the bat in the presence of the noonday sun. The whole poetic system of Aquinas is simply a development of this fundamental idea and his intellectualism as applied to man is conditioned by it. It will be necessary, therefore, not to lose sight of this idea as we proceed. To overlook for a moment this capital restriction upon which St. Thomas insists, and to read him upon the implicit assumption of the identity of human intellect with intelligence as such (*ut sic*), would be to render his whole system at once puerile and contradictory. When Averroes identified intelligibility as such with what man is capable of comprehending St. Thomas could not refrain from saying that in that Averroes put forward a " most absurd " proposition.[1]

---

[1] In 2 *Met.*, l. 1. *Cf.* 3 *Contra Gentes*, 45.

The inferior form of the intellectual process that is found in man is characterised by a multiplicity of acts and of different forms of knowledge. This is in keeping with a general law of nature which harmonises with man's position in the hierarchy of things,[2] characterised as he is by plasticity, progressiveness, and potentiality. There is a twofold kind of multiplicity to be found in human knowledge.[3] On the one hand there is a special and simultaneous form of it which is due to the collaboration of many faculties ; and, on the other, there is a successive form of it which appears in human reasoning that is made up of several acts.

Nature is good : hence it is the body which is for the soul. The soul is made for knowledge : the body therefore is intended to be an aid to knowledge. The nearer knowledge approaches reality, and the more intimate its grasp, the better it is. It follows that if in the pursuit of knowledge recourse must be had to other helps and factors that are not of a purely intellectual order, the deep reason must be that such knowledge as is possible for the particular intellect in question is too vague to delineate reality in its fullness, and because without these infra-intellectual helps this knowledge would remain in a cloud of general conceptions far removed from the clear-cut precision of existing realities and the concrete individuality which belongs to them. Did human souls come into possession of their knowledge without having had recourse to sensible images, said St. Thomas, " such knowledge would be imperfect, of a general nature, and confused. It is therefore with a view to having perfect and proper knowledge of things that their constitution requires a union of body and soul. These sensible objects impart by their impression a proper knowledge of themselves, and in their regard human souls are like the uneducated who have need of concrete examples for their instruction. The greater good of the soul, then, demands its union with the body, and it is for that reason that it cannot grasp things without

---

[2] *Multis et diversis operationibus et virtutibus indiget anima humana . . . anima humana abundat diversitate potentiarum, videlicet quia est in confinio spiritualium et corporalium creaturarum ; et ideo concurrunt in ipsa virtutes utrarumque creaturarum,* 1 q. 77, a. 2.

[3] 2a, 2ae, q. 180, a. 6 ad 2 ; in *Div. Nom.,* 7, 2.

having recourse to sensible images." [4] In virtue of the same reasoning we see why a whole organism of subordinate faculties is joined to intellect. Besides the external senses there are in man certain internal senses such as the *sensus communis*, sense-memory, and the *sensus cogitativus*. Even his intellect is affected by an inherent duality in so far as it is distinguishable into active and passive intellect. All this corresponds to that simultaneous multiplicity which implies passivity and receptivity in regard to external objects. It is this which distinguishes the intellect of man from that of God. In God there is identity of essence and intelligence, the distinction of subject and object is ruled out whether we view God in relation to His own essence or in relation to any other objects of intellectual knowledge, and the knowledge that God possesses is both the creative source and measure of all things. This characteristic multiplicity in human knowledge also serves to distinguish men and angels. The angel receives his ideas directly from God, and these ideas are in the first instance perfect and are less numerous according as the recipient is endowed with a greater degree of activity and less subject to the limitations of potentiality.[5] But man, instead of acquiring his knowledge by a kind of *a priori* condensation, is dependent on his sense-faculties which are in search of knowledge for the impressions of different essences. These sense-faculties are continuous, so to speak, with the external world, and hence it is that in man his potential receptivity in regard to knowledge is linked up with a spatial multiplicity.

The multiplicity that is inherent in reasoning is not less characteristic of human knowledge. The antithesis that holds between the intellectual process in its purity and human reasoning is marked by the opposition which St.

[4] *Ille modus intelligendi, prout erat possibile animae, erat imperfectior . . . in quadam communitate et confusione . . . ad hoc ergo quod perfectam et propiam cognitionem de rebus habere possent, sic naturaliter sunt institutae, et corporibus uniantur, et sic ab ipsis rebus sensibilibus propriam de eis cognitionem accipiant, sicut homines rudes ad scientiam induci non possunt nisi per sensibilia exempla. Sic ergo patet quod propter melius animae est ut corpori uniatur, et intelligat per conversionem ad phantasmata . . .* 1 q. 89, a. 1, likewise 3 *Contra Gentes*, 81 ; *De Anim.*, a. 15 and 20 ; 1 q. 55, a. 2. *Competit eis ut a corporibus et per corpora suam perfectionem intelligibilem consequantur ; alioquin frustra corporibus unirentur.*
[5] 1 q. 89, 1 c.

Thomas introduces between *intellectus* and *ratio*. The importance, in fact, of this distinction in Thomistic philosophy could scarcely be over-emphasised. According to the Neoplatonic law of continuity the lower orders reach up in the highest forms of their activity to a certain participation in the nature of the higher orders of beings above them. The human intellect in this way really functions as *intellect* in some of its activities, but what has to be borne in mind is that the typically human exercise of intellect is that of reasoning, and reasoning serves to disintegrate the perfection of intelligibility as such.

"Intellect and reason [6] are not two different faculties, but are distinguished as are perfect and imperfect," [7] "intellect meaning intimate penetration of truth, and *reason* the research for truth." [8] "Reason differs from intellect as does the multiple from unity ; according to Boethius its relation to intellect is that of the circumference of a circle to the centre, or of time to eternity. It is characteristic of reason that it traverses the ground around a number of objects in its effort to obtain a simple knowledge of them. Intellect, on the contrary, commences with one simple truth which it grasps and from this it obtains a knowledge of many things, much in the same way as God Who by regarding His own essence knows all things. Thus it will be seen that the reasoning process converges towards that of intellect and terminates therein and also that intellectual process is the underlying principle of reasoning which serves to collect and prepare the necessary elements." [9] "*Ratiocination is an attribute of the genus, animal* ; it cannot be predicated either of God or Angel." [10] "The lower

---

[6] In the German there are different renderings of *intellectus* and *ratio* (M. Schneider, *Psychologie Alberts des Grossens*, Münster, 1903, pp. 185, 253) : *Vernunft* (*intellectus*) and *Verstand* (*ratio*) ; others, such as Stöckl (*Gesch. der Phil. des Mittelalters*, Mayence, 1865, vol. 11, p. 488), read them inversely.

[7] 2a, 2ae, q. 83, a. 10 ad 2.

[8] 2a, 2ae, q. 49, a. 5 ad 3.

[9] In *Trin.* 6, l. 3 (Vol. XXVIII, p. 543). The twofold function we have here assigned to *intellect* is that which is the most clearly marked and emphasised by St. Thomas (see especially *Ver.* 15, 1 ; *cf.* Aristotle, *Eth. Nic.*, VI, 12). It would be superfluous for our present study to go into all the details of this usage here.

[10] 1 d. 25, q. 1, a. 1 ad 4. *Rationale est differentia animalis, et Deo non convenit nec angelis.*

intellects, namely the human, obtain their perfection in the knowledge of truth by a kind of motion and discursive intellectual working ; that is to say, as they advance from one thing to another. But, if from the knowledge of a recognised principle they were straightway to perceive all its consequent conclusions, then there would be no discursive process at all. Such is the condition of the angels, because in the truths which they know naturally they at once behold all things what-so-ever can be known by them. Therefore they are called intellectual beings : because even with ourselves the things which are instantly grasped by the mind are said to be understood (*intelligi*) ; hence the intellect is defined as the habit of first principles. But human souls which acquire knowledge of truth by the discursive method are called rational. And this comes of the feebleness of their light." [11] " Knowledge by the method of reasoning is due to the imperfection of the intellectual nature, because that which is known by means of another thing is less known than if it were grasped directly by itself and because this is due to the fact that the knowing subject is dependent on intermediaries for its knowledge. Now knowledge which is the result of the discursive method does employ middle terms, whereas that which is known intellectually is grasped directly in itself and the nature of the knowing subject suffices for this without having recourse to anything external to it." It follows that recourse to reasoning marks a certain defect on the part of the intellect in question (*quod defectus quidam intellectus est ratiocinatio*).[12] Again, "the certitude of reason comes from the intellect. Yet the need of reason is from a defect in the intellect, since these things, if the intellectual power is in full vigour, have no need of reason."[13]

[11] 1 q. 58, a. 3.
[12] 1 *Contra Gentes*, 57, 8.
[13] a, 2ae, q. 49, a. 5 ad 2. From all these texts it is clear that the distinction of *intellectus* and *ratio* is based on the mode of apprehension. It is a distinction which is not less characteristic of St. Thomas than is that other distinction of *ratio superior* and *ratio inferior* based on the value of objects in regard to a soul which is free in the psychological mysticism of St. Augustine. St. Thomas is aware of the Augustinian distinction (1 q. 79, a. 9), but he does not incorporate it into his own synthesis and sometimes in his hands it is reduced to a purely verbal distinction (2 d. 24, q. 3, a. 4 ad 1). It would be a serious error to identify the distinction here mentioned with that of St. Augustine. Nor

The foregoing accumulation of texts I have considered
necessary. The composite imperfection of human knowledge
as well as the sensible origin of ideas is readily admitted as a
constituent part of the Thomistic theory of knowledge. But
what is less frequently emphasised is that imperfection of
human knowledge which is due to the discursive method.
The exclusive exaltation of simple knowledge might indeed
appear more appropriate to a certain type of mysticism such
as that of the Visitors than to the peripatetic system of
Aquinas, and yet it is in intuitive knowledge that St. Thomas
seeks the ideal and measure of all intellectual activity. And
it is this very distinction which we have been emphasising
which allows him to " Platonise " when he takes the whole
universe into consideration while remaining very much
Aristotelian in his explanation of the sublunary world. We
must, beware, therefore, in what follows where we are
striving to obtain an idea of the coherence of his system in
the appraisal of those values we are about to examine, of
considering the judgment or any number of judgments as
more perfect in themselves than the simple idea, always
bearing in mind the doctrine condensed in the formula :
necessitas rationis est ex defectu intellectus.

We have yet to see whether St. Thomas has subordinated
our two multiplicities, sensitive and discursive, to one
another, or whether he has simply left them as two facts on
the same plane. Certain isolated expressions would seem to
imply an explicit subordination of one to the other.[14] It is
certain that we should not be doing violence to his thought
in linking up the two together. For the general idea, or
concept, is to be found only in minds that are united or

---

must we allow ourselves to be deceived by an isolated text where the *ratio*
designates the cogitative faculty. In *Caus.*, l. 6, 531 b. ; *cf.* in 6 *Eth.*, l. 1.
Elsewhere (in 6 *Eth.*, l. 9, 511 b.) St. Thomas distinguishes for the cogitative
faculty itself a function analogous to *intellectus* and another to that of *ratio*.

[14] *Ratiocinatur homo discurrendo et inquirendo lumine rationali per continuum et
tempus adumbratic, ex hoc quod cognitionem a sensu et imaginatione accipit*, etc. (2 d.
3 q. 1, a. 2 ; *cf.* 1 b., a. 6).
The two multiplicities are juxtaposed, without being subordinated in In
Trin., q. 6, a. 1 (Fretté, Vol. XXVIII, 541 b. and 2 q, 2 ae, q. 180, a. 6 ad 2).
Sometimes they are classified together under the title *ratio* (in *Trin., loc. cit.*,
2 ad 4, 543a ; and 2a, 2ae, q. 180, a. 3). Naturally the faculty employed in
discursive reasoning is linked up with that of judgment (1 q. 58, a. 4).

bodies ; and judgment, and much more *a fortiori* reasoning, necessarily presupposes the general idea. Or, to express the matter otherwise : time, for St. Thomas, is dependent on space ; hence only beings endowed with sense are to employ discursive reasoning.[15] All intellects that are linked up with sense are naturally discursive. The time-element in their progressive knowledge is the ransom to be paid for the imperfection brought about by their spatial limitations. If then men are to live beyond the moment, either they will be like the oyster whose perception is confined to the *hic et nunc*, or they will be capable of a number of subordinate intellectual activities that takes place during a definite duration of time. In one case, intellect as a unifying faculty and one which is above the conditions of spatial conditions would have no meaning. In the other it is implied that the series of acts which go to fill up the time-duration is with a view to obtaining a more perfect idea which, in its turn, may help to integrate the intelligibility of the object which in its changing reality is presented successively to the intellect.

Now that we have examined human knowledge in general under its time and space condition, we can understand that our study of its speculative value will be determined by the further question : How does the human intellect, by the means of knowing at its disposal, take the place of, or at least imitate, the truly intellectual acquisition of reality ? To meet this we shall have to examine the instruments of human knowledge in their different combinations and from the view-point of their results. We shall take up successively the concept, science, system and symbol, and the apprehension of the particular or singular. These may be said to represent the effort on the part of the human intellect to overcome its own deficiencies according to the principle of Aristotle : *quod non potest effici per unum, fiat aliqualiter per*

---

[15] See 2 *Contra Gentes*, 96 end (*cf.* 3 d. 26, q. 1, a. 5 ad 4). The unstable aspect of knowledge is an imperfection in the eyes of St. Thomas. Sometimes we hear references to-day to the " static dispersion of an argument." For St. Thomas it is precisely because the judgment is simply a thought that is broken up that it is capable of that fuller development given to it by the discursive argument ; in the case of pure spirits intuition is perfectly stable because it is independent of time.

plura [16]. But, before passing on to a detailed study of these substitutes for the idea in its purity, we must stop to consider for a moment the luminous influence of intuition which unifies every one of them to the extent of raising them out of the level of mere crude apprehensions of reality to a participation in intellectual life.

II

In the matter of the apprehension of being as such the competence of the intellect, according to St. Thomas, is at once exclusive and infallible. In the light of modern attitudes this apparently would form the very central point of his intellectualism. For it is here that St. Thomas comes nearest to the rigorously mathematical leanings of Descartes. It is here also that he reveals his views on the logical critique of knowledge, a problem that has been of paramount importance in the philosophy of recent centuries. He opposes the sceptic who denies that man can justify his spiritual relations with things and refutes him. He also rejects the views of voluntarists and philosophers of every shade who make final appeal to feeling or to the *raisons de cœur*. Examining for himself their arguments and methods he finds room for them in a more comprehensive synthesis. As a matter of fact such problems were far from occupying a prominent position before his mind, and to look upon them as primary and essential would be to falsify historical perspective. On the other hand, it would be no less erroneous to imagine that he was completely ignorant of them, or that he did not think it necessary to raise them and to solve them.

To say that in the absolute apprehension of being, intellect alone is competent is to deny, first of all, the possibility of an approach to reality completely inaccessible to intellect and so far transcending it as to render all its activities merely provisional and subject to radical transformation. *No power, not even that of God, could produce the contrary of what reason*

---

[16] See in 2 *Cael*, l. 18.

apprehends under the direct influence of evidence. In this the attitude of St. Thomas is strongly marked as opposed to those theologians who held that God could be the originating source of things contradictory.[17] For St. Thomas to take any other stand would be clearly to go back on his principles regarding the essential nature of intellectual activity. Further, it need scarcely be said that for the same reason this doctrine in no way implies any limitation or restriction of divine power. The dignity of God remains unaffected, since He is subjected to no lesser law outside Himself. It is intelligence rather which is honoured, since its absolute competency in such matters is grounded in the fact that it is the faculty of the divine. This has been already stated. Intelligence has been defined by its capacity for possessing the Absolute (by the beatific vision), and its power to reach contingent things in a manner at once definite and unchangeable has been looked upon as traceable to its divine prerogatives. Mind is $\Theta\epsilon\acute{o}s$ $\pi\hat{\omega}s$ before being $\pi\acute{a}\nu\tau a$ $\pi\hat{\omega}s$. It is because intelligence is a participated perfection of God that "what reason declares impossible" is impossible simply speaking without any reference to the productive capacity of any power.[18] If God cannot realise the impossible, it is because before a thing can be actuated it must first be thought by God. Thus from every point of view God comes first. To be *capax Dei*, however, and open, as it were, for the ultimate acquisition of Him by intellect is to be endowed with strange ambitions that come precisely of man's divine dimensions. St. Thomas recognised this when he referred to the remarkable person, Job, who entered into dispute with God. "This dispute between God and man," he says, "may seem inappropriate because of the great distance that separates man from God. But we must remember that where truth is concerned difference of personality is relatively unimportant. To proclaim the truth is to render a person

[17] See *Pot.*, 1, 3, and questions as are contained in *Quodl.*, 3, 2 ; 4, 5 ; 5, 3 ; 9, 1 ; 12, 2.
    In *Op.* 16 St. Thomas mentions Catholic adversaries outside the followers of Averroes naturally. In this work of his youth his own questions lack that precision that appears later.
[18] *Pot.* 1, 3, 3.

invincible no matter who his adversary may be." [19]   It is
scarcely necessary to repeat that this is in no way derogatory
to God's dignity, since the whole value of intellectual judgments comes from the fact that intelligence is the faculty of
the divine.

In the eyes of St. Thomas, then, it is perfectly meaning-
less to suppose that truths, no matter to what order of
reality they belong, can clash with rational evidence.   How
could faith contradict reason ?   Faith, on the contrary,
presupposes reason and perfects it.[20]   Antinomies can never
be more than apparent :   their hidden defect is always
susceptible to the scrutiny of Logic.   Undoubtedly God has
power to accomplish things that surpass the comprehension
of man, but things that run directly counter to what is
certainly perceived by the human mind God cannot do.
*Otherwise we should have to admit that God could contradict
Himself.*[21]   If therefore it is reasonable to accept a supernatural revelation with greater conviction than even the
evidence of demonstration, that cannot be because it is
anti-intellectual but because it is more intellectual and
endowed with a greater degree of truth.[22]   There was no

[19] *Videbatur autem disputatio hominis ad Deum esse idebita propter excellentiam qua
Deus hominem excellit.   Sed considerandum est, quod veritas ex diversitate personarum
non variatur ;   unde cum aliquis veritatem loquitur, vinci non potest, cum quocumque
disputet.* In *Job* c. 12, 1, 2.
[20] *Sic enim fides praesupponit cognitionem naturalem, sicut gratia naturam et ut
perfectio perfectione.* 1 q. 2, a. 2 adl.
[21] *Cum enim fides infallibili veritati innitatur, impossibile autem sit de vero demon-
strari contrarium, manifestum est probationes, quae contra fidem inducuntur, non esse
demonstrationes, sed solubilia argumenta* (1 q. 1, a. 8).   *Per Apostolos et prophetas
numquam divinitus dicitur aliquid quod sit contrarium his quae naturalis ratio dictat; dicitur
tamen aliquid quod comprehensionem rationis excedit, et pro tanto videtur rationi repug-
nare, quamvis non repugnet ;   sicut et rustico videtur repugnans rationi quod sol sit
maior terra, quod diameter sit asymeter costae ;   quae tamen sapienti rationabilia apparent* (*Ver.*, 14, 10, 7).   *Quae sunt fidei, quamvis sint supra rationem, non tamen sunt
contra rationem :   alias Deus esset sibi contrarius, si alia posuisset in ratione quam rei
veritas habet* (4 d. 10 *Expositio textus*).
   Cf. the counterpart of this in 4 d. 20, q. 1, a. 3 sol. 2 :   One single error in
the Bible or in the dogmatic teaching of the Church would be sufficient to
undermine the whole of religion.
[22] In 8 *Phys.* 1, 3 beginning :   *Omne enim quod ponitur absque ratione vel auc-
toritate divina fictitium esse videtur.   Auctoritas autem divina praevalet etiam rationi
humanae, multo magis quam auctoritas alicuius philosophi praevaleret alicui debili
rationi, quam aliquis puer induceret.   Non ergo assimilatur figmento* (*cf.* text of Aristotle :   ἔοικε πλασμαῖ) *quae per fidem tenentur, licet absque ratione credantur.
Credimus, enim divinae auctoritati miraculis approbatae id est illis operibus quae solus
Deus facere potest.   Absque ratione* here means devoid of intrinsic demonstrative

J. S. Campbell

error against which St. Thomas fought more fiercely than that of the Latin Averroeists. In their theory of a twofold truth he sensed a form which was the most opposed to his own thought as it was to that Catholic dogmatism which he loved so passionately.[23]

III

To accept the exclusive competence of intelligence will mean also the exclusion of the senses and the appetitive faculties. This statement, where the senses are concerned, may not seem devoid of paradox. In Scholastic writings we find a certain opposition, either explicit or implicit, between Thomistic criteriology and that extreme form of "mentalism" which may be styled Platonic or Augustinian. What is proper to the latter theory is the rather simplified division it introduces when it marks off the senses as the source of opinion and the domain of error from pure intellect to which belong light and truth. St. Thomas, with his peripatetic theory of the origin and object of human knowledge, aver his commentators, could not pass a theory of knowledge so disdainful in regard to the data of experience. Study St. Thomas himself and you will see how he dissipates the vaporous Augustinianism of his contemporaries and discovers an Aristotelian interpretation of the "contemplation of eternal ideas." Further, you will see that he demands the collaboration of the senses not only to supply data for judgments but he even assigns to them a certain critical rôle in regard to the judgments themselves of intellect. In the latter case we have what he

evidence. If, in effect, the act of faith is intellectually justified thanks to the motives of credibility (as, for instance, miracles here mentioned), yet the object of faith remains essentially obscure in itself and mysterious. (See Ch. VI, where the theory of the act of faith is discussed.)

[23] *Opusc.* 15. *De Unitate Intellectus contra Averroistas*, c. 7 end. *Adhuc autem gravius est quod postmodum dicit : " Per rationem concludo de necessitate, quod intellectus est unus numero ; firmiter tamen teneo oppositum per fidem." Ergo sentit quod fides sit de aliquibus quorum contraria de necessitate concludi possunt. Cum autem de necessitate concludi non possit nisi verum necessarium, cuius oppositum est falsum et impossibile, sequitur secundum ejus dictum, quod fides sit de falso et impossibili : quod etiam Deus facere non potest. Quod fidelium aures ferre non possunt.* In view of the detailed attention that this problem of the Averroeists has received in recent years it is unnecessary to multiply citations.

calls the *resolutio in sensibilia*, which, though simply referred
to rather than analysed, is worthy of notice, as it presupposes
the need of harmony between the whole complexion of the
being who thinks and the particular acts of his thinking.[24]
In these circumstances is it possible to refer all certitude to
intellect as to its unique source ?

There is no escape from this alternative, however, if we
bear in mind the nature of the senses according to the
really vital needs of the system. The senses, according to
St. Thomas, are endowed with *a nature*, that is, a restricting,
limiting nature which confines them to the world of their
own subjectivity. The whole rhythm and direction of their
movement is not, as in the case of intellect, towards drawing
the whole of reality as such towards them : they are not
faculties of that which is " other " in their regard modified
by the object " in so far as they are things in themselves,"
all that they " indicate," as a matter of fact, and all that as
a matter of right they can indicate, is *identically* (not to say
univocally) a modification of their own subjective state.
That granted, what becomes of the truth of the senses ?
In the first place, seeing that truth arises only for a rational
being, there could be no question of truth for a sense-
consciousness : it could have no meaning for such. *Falsitas
non est quaerenda in sensu, nisi sicuti ibi est veritas.*[25] Since
truth properly consists in the conformity of intelligence and
reality, nothing more than a resemblance to truth or false-
hood could be found in the senses. Secondly, this resemblance will be greater according as a multiplicity of sense-
organs helps such a being to get beyond the circle of its
abstractive subjectivity to increase its contact with reality

[24] The *resolutio in sensibilia* is simply a verification of the normal state of the
thinking subject which is necessary for the validity of the judgment. In this
way the senses as a whole acquire a criteriology value. Sleep is distinguished
from the waking state by the impossibility of this operation, since the sleeping
person is unable to verify at the starting point the connection of his thoughts
with reality. See on this rather neglected point 4 d. 9, q. 1, a. 4, sol. 1 ;
Ver. 12, 3, 2 ; 1 q. 8, 4 a. 8 ; 2a, 2ae, q. 173, a. 3 and q. 154, a. 5 ad 3. For
marvellous visions see 3 d. 3, q. 3, a. 1, sol. 2 ; 3 q. 30, a. 3. "My body is
myself," and even in the beatific vision where God is seen intuitively my
tendency towards Him will be even greater when my body shall have been
given back to me (4 d. 49, q. 1, a. 4, sol. 1 and ad 3). Here we are far removed
from the ideas of the *Phaedrus* and the *Phedo*.

[25] 1 q. 17, a. 2.

distinct from it by some form of contemplation. Thirdly, it is only where the senses are linked up with reason, as in the case of man, that the information they convey can be of any use to pure reason, and even then their information will have to be constantly controlled by mind. In an article devoted to the question of error as it is found in the senses St. Thomas, basing his remarks on the relation of senses to intellect, reduces all possible classes to two chief headings.[26] If the sense is unique and autonomous, " a kind of mind in presence of reality," then not only will it be infallible by definition when it " declares " a subjective modification as such, but the simple impression that it receives from its object will necessarily be what it ought to be, and, as St. Thomas says, will represent the object such as it is, provided the sense-organ is in a normal state. The higher animals are capable of certain individual syntheses owing to the collaboration of their various faculties. To this extent their knowledge approximates to pure knowledge and to a certain resemblance with truth, but to the same degree the possibilities of error on their part will have augmented.[27] In the case of man, however, who is capable of conceiving truth as such and of reflecting on the conformity of his intellectual act with reality, there is a brusque change of nature and of value where his sense-apparatus and its relation to reality are concerned. Instead of being reduced to the humble office of passively reflecting the nature of its objects the senses co-operate in their humble, though necessary, way with the effort of intelligence to reach the essence of things. By them the autonomy of the senses has disappeared. No longer may sense be spoken of as a kind of mind face to

[26] *Ver.* 1, 11.

[27] They are, however, not devoid of what will help to correct their impressions in the interplay of the different senses (*Mal.* 3, 3, 9, etc.). In the light of these principles it is easy to see how in practice an animal arrives at discerning individuals. It is not so easy to see how man, in view of the fact that he has no intellectual intuition of the individual, comes to affirm absolutely the identity of an individual seen on different occasions ; the only thing he has to go upon for the basis of his judgment is the similarity of sensible accidents and these are essentially communicable (see Ch. III, 2). St. Thomas does not fully solve this problem, though he concedes the possibility where the different impressions are subject to control. (See those questions that treat of the manner in which the Apostles could have been certain of the Resurrection. 3 d. 21, q. 2, a. 4, sol. 4 ad 3 ; *Comp. Theol.*, 246 ; 3 q. 55, particularly a. 6 ad 1).

face with reality, but is rather itself an object, a thing in presence of mind : *intellectui comparatus, quasi res quaedam.*[28] From the sphere of relative apprehension of reality we have entered the domain of the absolute. What hitherto could not be classified as error is on the way to becoming error from the moment that intellect begins to apply to things in themselves what the innocent subjectivity of the senses announces to it. A rational control becomes, then, a prime necessity. And this control will have to be all the more vigilant when we remember our tendency to transform our representation of things distinct from us into intellectual knowledge and absolute judgments. " When sense represents that which it receives there is no error in it, as Augustine says, but there is error in the intellect which judges that things are as the senses represent them." [29] It is clearly indicated, then, that in spite of the inconsistencies of the imagination, which it would be foolish to ignore,[30] the sensitive organism, according to St. Thomas, has radical need of

[28] *Ver.* 1, 11.
[29] *Ver.* 2, 6, 15. To the eyes of Adam, even in the state of innocence, the sun seemed " other than it really is," that is to say it seemed smaller than its natural size, and because imagination naturally follows the senses, reason had necessarily to intervene in order to correct these impressions (1 q. 94, a. 4 ad 3). St. Thomas has expressly denied that there is really an error in the senses in presence of the Eucharistic Bread (4 d. 10, a. 4, sol. 11 ad. 3).
[30] I speak of the attribution of a certain reality (*en-soi*) to sensible qualities. In the absence of indications to the contrary it is natural to believe that St. Thomas in this respect shared the opinions of his contemporaries. But there is inconsistency because the opposite conclusion follows from his principles : *Sensibilia . . . nata sunt apprehendi per sensum, sicut intelligibilia per intellectum* (*Contra Gentes*, 96, 1) and *Sensus in actu est sensibile in actu,* just as *Intellectus in actu est intellectum in actu.* It is not to be inferred from this comparison that it is the realist opinion which is implied : it is just the contrary which is true because of that kind of divine subjectivism implied in the formula ; *Scientia Dei causa rerum.* Though devoid of senses, pure spirits are able to reach all there is to be known of concrete material things in their reality. Thus they know sensible things in their proper setting, that is, as registered by the sense-organs of those beings endowed with senses, just as they are capable of knowing judgments in the rational subject, though their knowledge is exempt from reasoning. Intelligence is that pure capacity for seizing Being, that which exists in and by itself. If then God is incapable of sense-knowledge, it follows that things of sense have no title to reality. Were I not afraid of indulging in a rather paradoxical *rapprochement,* I should say that St. Thomas was led by the logic of his system to a position not unlike that of Kant in the *Dissertation* of 1770. Certain formulæ on the correlation of the senses and their objects might appear here and there to declare explicitly the conclusions we have been indicating. But when these formulæ are placed in their context it is seen that the problem still remains.

the presence of intelligence if it is to contribute in some way to the knowledge of being as such and of the reality of things. Further, this collaboration on the part of intellect with the senses must be an active one if this knowledge of reality is to be valid. Where speculative certitude is concerned the whole meaning of the senses is bound up with their relation to intelligence, and intellect, in its turn, must bear all the responsibility.

The question of the cognitive rôle of the appetitive faculties might seem much more simple than that of the senses. Yet, if the senses, which represent the demi-transparent parts of the human mechanism, stand in constant need of the light of intellectual intuition for true illumination of reality, how can tendencies essentially opaque and devoid of light collaborate in the pursuit of knowledge unless they also are brought within the same light cast by intellect? In the thirteenth century there were philosophers to suggest to St. Thomas the necessity of pursuing truth with " one's whole soul." All were ready to admit, on the other hand, the necessity, as subject-matter for judgment, that feelings, desires and tendencies which are so near to consciousness and so expressive of human instincts, were useful and indispensable elements in any philosophy. In an effort to correct the celebrated dictum of Plato they would have all without exception, I feel sure, advanced the same distinction : it is necessary to pursue truth with one's whole soul, that is, one must pursue an object which is true, *concedo ;* one must pursue truth as such, *nego.* But that in the actual process of knowing one should be anything else than a knower ; that is a thing they would not have understood. Prior to their reduction to ideas emotional factors were inexistent as far as the pure order of knowledge was concerned.[31]

---

[31] It is known that St. Thomas denies liberty in presence of self-evident principles and conclusions properly demonstrated. *Sciens cogitur ad assentiendum per efficaciam demonstrationis* (2a, 2ae, q. 2, a. 9 ad 2. *Cf.* explanation given in 2 d. 25, q. 1, a. 2).

A propos of those imperfect demonstrations which go from effect or sign to the cause (see Ch. IV, 1), the value of which is, in his eyes, very small, he admits that in certain cases they can guarantee a fact with certainty and force assent (see 3 q. 43, a. 1, a. 4 ; 2a, 2ae, q. 5, a. 2 ; 3 q. 76, a. 7 ; *Ver.* 14, 9, 4 ; 3 d. 24,

Like the others St. Thomas affirms not infrequently the necessity of a moral preparation for the perception of certain truths.[32] In this he was not guilty of contradicting himself, as is clear from the consideration that not every condition that is necessary for the constitution of the knower enters directly into the act of knowledge. There is another doctrine of his, however, which seems quite opposed to that rigorous intellectualism which characterises the Thomistic theory of knowledge. This opinion is embodied in what is called *cognitio per modum naturae*, a form of knowledge which is looked upon as co-ordinate with rational knowledge rather than as subordinate to it. " There are two ways," he writes, " of possessing rectitude of judgment. This rectitude may arise either from the perfect use of reason or it may be due to a certain connatural harmony between the subject and those matters upon which the subject is called upon to pronounce. In things relating to chastity he who knows moral principles is capable of good judgment in accordance with the rational method : but to judge well as the result of an existing natural harmony between the subject and chastity can only come from habitual virtue." [33] Elsewhere he says : "Just as a man gives his assent to first principles by the natural light of reason, so the habitually virtuous man by reason of his habit of virtue judges correctly as to what virtue demands." [34] Is not this juxtaposition significant ? Does it not almost reach the point of suppressing the very idea of the transparency of intellect ? Would it not be better frankly to acknowledge that here we have an instance that does not fit in well with the general scheme, and see in it rather a concession to the needs of common speech at the expense of reason ?

Strong as all this may seem, however, it seems to me that

q. 1, a. 2, sol. 2 ad 4) ; but at other times it is possible that will could intervene to command unreasonable scepticism and withhold assent : St. Thomas very clearly teaches the possibility of a certitude which is free and employs it to explain the act of faith (1a, 2ae, q. 17, a. 6 ; 3 q. 47, a. 5 corp. and ad 1. Cf. the precise formulæ of *Ver.* 24, 1 : *fides astringit . . . manifesta indicia inducunt . . . evidens ratio cogit*).

[32] 4 d. 33, q. 3, a. 3 ; 2a, 2ae, q. 46, a. 2.
[33] 2a, 2ae, q. 45, a. 2.
[34] 2a, 2ae, q. 2, a. 3 ad 2.

the most probable explanation is really intellectualist in character. This theory of connatural knowledge is frequently cited by modern authors, but it is rarely explained. A rational explanation of it would seem to be along the following lines. The acquisition of virtue implies for St. Thomas that a course of action has become what is called " second nature." When that happens virtuous action is raised to the level of spontaneous action and accordingly it is no longer necessary for reflection to go back on each occasion to first principles. In given circumstances the man of such habits has merely to glance, as it were, at his own inner *tendencies* to *see* how they react. Granted that a certain habit has been consciously formed, then *it would be possible for the subject to judge of the specific object of that virtue by noticing the greater or less facility entailed in the exercise of its corresponding actions.* A Londoner who knows nothing of the classification of instances where *shall* and *will* must be employed will in given circumstances reply accurately and without hesitation. This will hold as long as he allows his organs to function normally and as long as he does not allow himself to become entangled by reflection. The little child who is not as yet quite sure of the use of the words *right* and *left* will help himself out of the difficulty by commencing to make the sign of the cross. Between the action and the judgment an inference is slipped in with the rapidity of a flash and this inference is based on the known relation which exists between the action and its habitual object. In this way both the examples and the formulæ of St. Thomas can be explained without prejudice to the intellectualist character of his system.

The fact that such a perception is not consciously linked up with first principles does not make it less rational or intellectualist in character on the principles of St. Thomas. It is the contrary rather which would hold. Take the classical example of chastity. The moral philosopher sets out from pre-existing moral ideas and then makes a deduction ; the chaste man experiences a feeling of sympathy or revulsion and this guides him to a conclusion. Which of the two may be said to have the better grasp of reality ?

Recall the view of St. Thomas as expressed in the words, *castitas proprie non est, sed est aliquis castus*. The moralist possesses a generalised abstraction while the other is in presence of what is for him an *esse castum*. In modern language we should say that while the one has an idea which is communicable and easily interchanged the other enjoys a "real" intuition. In Thomistic language we should have to say that while the philosopher in this instance has merely an idea abstracted from human sensations, the chaste man is enriched by something approaching the angelic idea. What the *cognitio per modum naturae*, then, is opposed to is knowledge of first principles in the form of conceptual judgments, and for that reason the opposition is rather to logical knowledge than to knowledge of purely intellectual character. It might be said in fact that the *cognitio per modum naturae* is a higher form of knowledge than merely conceptual knowledge because of its more intuitive and personal character : *est enim aliquid scientia melius, scilicet intellectus*. Whether this explanation was put forward in detail by St. Thomas or not, it does seem to be the one that accords bests with his general principles.

IV

In addition to this exclusive competency of intellect in its own sphere there is that other aspect which emphasises the absolute character of its pronouncements, its infallibility. There is no necessity to insist on the classical thesis that when intellect confines itself to the conception of the essence of a thing it cannot err. This form of its infallibility was already recognised by Aristotle. St. Thomas repeats the observations of Aristotle under this heading. For a similar reason, when he goes on to speak of angelic knowledge he excludes from the angelic intellect all error where the purely natural order of things is concerned. True to his principle of continuity, St. Thomas treats the angel as the highest form of created life and the lowest forms of life, such as the oyster and the star-fish, in much the same way : if the angel is a "separate substance" these lowest forms of life are instances, as it were, of "separate touch," since touch is the only sense with which they are endowed. In both cases the simple and primitive forms of their activity are necessarily what they ought to be, with this proviso for the lower forms of life, *si materia est disposita*, since the corporeal organ may be damaged or ill-adapted to its environment from the cognitive point of view. Between the oyster and the angel, between pure sensation and pure spirit, there is a system of increasing differentiation and complexity. For that reason error is possible where man or monkey or eagle is concerned even outside the case of a disordered condition of the sense-organs. The root-cause of all human error lies in the twofold multiplicity that characterises human knowledge : St. Thomas says so expressly. The cause of error is to be sought either in sense-knowledge, or else in that multiplicity which is implied in discursive reasoning.[35]

If all error is ultimately traceable either to sense or to discursive reasoning, truth will have to be sought with reference to intellect. Just as the truth of sense-perfection arises on last analysis from the intellectual principle, so the whole value of reasoning and deduction goes back to a simple intuition. *Necessitas rationis est ex defectu intellectus*, but *certitudo rationis est ex intellectu*. In this sentence the whole theory of knowledge is contained if by *ratio* we mean all our instruments of knowledge that are not purely intuitive in character. It is not to be expected that we shall delay to prove that St. Thomas believed in the value of deduction. If he is exacting in his conditions for a strict demonstration, he is perfectly confident in results once these conditions are fulfilled. " The proper motive which determines intellect is that which is true with infallible truth : every time that intellect allows itself to be determined by some fallible sign

---

[35] 1 q. 94, a. 4 ; *Mal.*, 16, 6 and ad 16 ; *Ver.*, 13, 5, 1. For the infallibility of simple intellectual knowledge see In 3 *An.*, l. 11 end . . . whence the difficulty of explaining error in angelic knowledge. *Ex hoc quod daemon non utitur phantasia nec discursu rationis et per alia huiusmodi, potest haberi quod in his quae ad naturalem cognitionem pertinent non errat ut existimet aliquid falsum esse verum. Mal.*, 16, 2, 5. *Cf. ibid.* ad 7 and 1 q. 58, a. 5. The intrinsic and primitive goodness of the knowing faculties also exclude the possibility of complete and radical error in the case of man : every human opinion has its share of truth (2a, 2ae, q. 172, a. 6 ; In 1 *Eth.*, l. 12 ; In 1 *Tim.* c. 21, 2. *Cf.* 3 *Contra Gentes*, 9 and In 1 *Phys.*, l. 10).

it makes room for disorder whether its movement be perfect or imperfect." [36] Elsewhere he says that " once intellect has reduced things correctly to first principles it cannot be in error." [37] " Nor can there be any error in the intellect which cannot be removed by contrary reasonings." [38] This " reduction to first principles," which is a form of necessary verification for all series of syllogisms, is understood by St. Thomas as the intellectual perception of the interdependence of the different moments of the reasoning-process and of their connection with the starting point in virtue of the formal principle that unites them. The doctrine is contained in an expressive metaphor which says that it must be possible for us to see the principles in the conclusion : *oportet in conclusionibus speculari principia.* [39] A tower is built over a well. If it is in a perpendicular position one can see from its height the beams and the stone-work reflected upside-down in the water at the bottom of the well. This would represent the analysis here in question, which is a counterpart of that other form of analysis (*resolutio in sensibilia*) of which we have spoken above. Thus the intuition of first principles brings unity to the rational dependence of the plurality of propositions and on this will depend the certitude of all science. " All knowledge where true science is in question is possible in virtue of its reduction to first principles immediately present to intellect so that knowledge is rendered perfect by the vision of reality present to mind." [40] A completed system of knowledge, or a science which would be concentrated in the intuition of the principle which unites all its conclusions to one another, would then serve to illustrate the beauty of an intelligible idea. The thought of St. Thomas might be happily expressed in those words of his to be found in his

---

[36] *Ver.*, 18, 6.

[37] *Ver.*, 1, 12.

[38] *Ver.*, 24 ,10. *Quando ratio in aliquo errat, ex quocumque error ille contingat, potest tolli per contrarias ratiocinationes.*

[39] 1a, 2ae, q. 90, a. 2 ad 3. *Nihil constat firmiter secundum rationem speculativam, nisi per resolutionem ad prima principia indemonstrabilia.* The reduction to first principles is generally given as something following on the reasoning process : it is evident that what is required is a formal condition which renders this reduction possible.

[40] *Ver.* 14, 9.

Commentary of the book, *De Causibus: Omnis scientia radicaliter non est nisi intelligentia.*[41] In the light of the ideas developed in previous chapters it will not be difficult to grasp the connection of this proposition with the whole Thomistic system.

A word must now be said as to the infallibility of the first principles themselves. These intellectual intuitions are usually put forward as ultimate and fundamental. But in what must be sought their justification for the thinking subject who posits them? Though the question is an important one we can afford to be brief. St. Thomas was no doubt aware of the problem. It is treated of in his *Commentary on the Metaphysics* with his discussion of ancient scepticism. But these pages are amongst the least original that he has penned : he simply gives a commentary on Aristotle. His thought on the objective evidence of first principles may be expressed tersely in a short formula taken from another of his Commentaries : " That which is characteristic of these principles is not only that they possess necessary truth but that they are seen to be of themselves necessarily true." [42] The intuition of these principles carries with it its own justification : all things are judged in the light of this intuition and it is itself its own light. It is the same theory which is expressed more briefly in that other formula : " First principles are known naturally."

Naturaliter cognoscuntur. The first term of this formula is not to be so emphasised as merely to suggest that there is here question of a subjective necessity that no one disputes. " These principles are known naturally and error in their regard would imply a corruption of nature : there can be no question of passing from a true appreciation of such principles to a false one without undergoing a change of nature." [43] Neither are such expressions as these to be

[41] In *Caus.*, l. 18. And again *ibid.*, *Intelligentia enim est sicut unitas quaedam, ut Proclus dicit, omnis cognitionis.* On this question of the reduction of knowledge to intellect from the view-point of certitude, see In *Hebr.* xi., l. 1.

[42] In *Post.*, l. 19. *Proprium est horum principiorum, quod non solum necesse est ea per se vera esse, sed etiam necesse est videri, quod sint per se vera.*

[43] 4 *Contra Gentes*, 95. The words *naturalia, naturaliter* must not be taken as suggesting innate ideas. The origin of these principles must be sought in the collaboration of the senses and intellect : they arise, as it were spontane-

taken as suggestive of some form of pragmatic philosophy. The author does not argue in favour of these principles by saying, "Nature must be safeguarded. These principles are a constituent part of nature. Hence they must not be questioned." He does not take nature and reason as two distinct terms and place the burden of justifying one on the other. Every nature in its own order is its own justification by the very fact that it is. Likewise intellect which is reduced to act by the perception of such principles ranks as a nature with its own proper sphere which is that of the absolute. If therefore it is in a position to justify all other knowledge, that can only be because of its own particular nature (that is to say because it is the faculty of being and of the absolute). As also such intelligence, being ultimate and present to itself in the limpidity of its own essence, will be justified simply speaking, once it can satisfy itself as to its own inherent justification.

The evident intuition of these principles, then, which is the basis of deductive reasoning permits of the a posteriori construction of the world just as the reality of the universe requires as a necessary pre-condition the reality of the divine knowledge. This will serve to suggest the intimate relation that holds between the Thomistic theory of knowledge and that of St. Augustine. Ultimately the exaggerated "mentalism" of the Theologian of Hippo is seen to coincide with the carefully thought out intellectualism of Aquinas. It is the Aristotelian concept of the immanence of knowledge which forms the link between the two systems. *Veritatem videre est eam habere*, said Augustine ; Scholastic analysis would

ously, from primitive concepts. 2 *Contra Gentes*, 78, 3 and 83 ; *De Anim.*, a. 5 ; 2 *Post.*, l. 20 ; 4 *Met.*, l. 2. Once acquired they carry with them the necessity for affirming them. They can be denied only with the mouth, or in imagination (In 1 *Post.*, l. 26 ; In *Met.*, l. 3, 477 a.). If it appears that they can be denied that is only because they assume the forms of propositions, and then their terms seem to be dissociated by the mind. As judgments they are not above the mind ; they are simply its functions and a means of expressing itself in a fragmentary way. *Et principia sunt regula conclusionum, et intelligens est quodammodo regula principiorum.* 3 d. 33, q. 1, a. 3 sol. 3 ad 1. Conviction as to the objectivity of knowledge must be sought in something deeper than any principle formally announced. It is to be found in the consciousness that mind possesses of itself when it reflects upon its own activity (*Ver.*, 1, 9 ; *cf.* p. n. 2). It is this consciousness which allows us to say : *Veritatem esse, est per se notum* (1 d. 3, q. 1, a. 2).

add, *et quodammodo esse.* The consciousness of that perfect vision which is implied by the identity of intelligence and truth explains the calm and imperturbable bearing of St. Thomas throughout the course of all his reasonings. This is something that grows upon one with practice, and it must not be overlooked amidst all the restrictions which follow. On last analysis it is his robust confidence in human reason which gives the characteristic note in the intellectual temperament of Aquinas.

CHAPTER II

In its higher forms intellectual activity consists in a simple act of knowledge. Amongst the characteristic activities of the human mind, therefore, we must begin with the concept [1] which we now purpose to isolate and consider apart. Ideally, the simple intellectual process is one whereby " one subsisting intelligible object " is brought into contact with another. But the question to be elucidated here is concerned with human knowledge. We must see to what extent it is possible for man, in his present position, to simulate this higher form of intellectual activity, and also in what measure he is capable of knowing supra-sensible realities. That done, we shall pass on from the realm of pure spirits, the *proper* knowledge of which according to St. Thomas is beyond our reach, to examine our ideas of material essences. These latter form the really proper object of human knowledge, and it will be of interest to determine what speculative value is to be ascribed to our knowledge of them.

I

The human intellect is one that is conjoint with a sensitive organism. In these circumstances man's intellect is radically dependent on sensible objects for its knowledge both of being in general and of supra-sensible realities. " Our knowledge can go as far as it can be led by sensible objects." [2] The image, or *phantasm*, which is distinct from the immaterial idea, is necessary not only for the acquisition of ideas but

---

[1] St. Thomas is acquainted with the word *conceptio*. But habitually he designates the simple act of intellect as *simplex apprehensio, indivisibilium intelligentia*, and the product of this process, the idea, as *verbum mentale*.

[2] I q. 12, a. 12. *Tantum se nostra naturalis cognitio extendere potest, in quantum manu duci potest per sensibilia.*

also for the " inspection " of these ideas once acquired.[3] From this it follows, as against certain Arabian philosophers, that it is impossible for us in this life to obtain direct knowledge of separate substances as they are in themselves. Though being in general is the adequate object of intelligence, the proper object of the human intellect is none other than the " essence of sensible things " (*quidditas rei materialis*).

It is only by the aid of the senses that the human mind acquires its knowledge of rational principles. The conditions of material objects and the differences that hold between them suggest in particular the idea of negation. This note of negation in fact is something naturally applied to sensible things. In view of the sensible origin of our knowledge and at the same time bearing in mind the possible extension of rational principles to objects of all thought, it is natural to concede the negative character of our ideas of supra-sensible realities even though we are capable of positive judgments regarding their existence. " Everything that transcends these sensible things known to us is conceived by us only in virtue of a negation. (We say) immaterial, incorporeal and so forth." [4] Out of this arises the defective character of all knowledge which we call *analogical*.

In the formation of analogical judgments St. Thomas distinguishes three distinct moments. To grasp the defective character of the knowledge imparted by such judgments we had better analyse the three stages mentioned by St. Thomas. I have in my mind the idea of a certain perfection, A, which is subject to corporeal conditions. I then go on to deny a certain quality, B, which for me is subjectively but inseparably bound up with my knowledge of A. I then declare a being possible which unites in its complexity the conjunction of A and B. Here we have a judgment intervening between me and my intuition ; the *ratio* is employed to criticise my intuition ; and finally I possess no unitary idea in my mind corresponding to the object of my affirma-

---

[3] In *Trin.*, 6, 2, 5. *Non sicut transiens, sed sicut permanens, ut quoddam fundamentum intellectualis operationis.*

[4] In 3 *An.*, l. 11, 171 b. Our ideas of celestial bodies are also for the most part negative in character. In *Trin.*, 6, 3, 548 a. *Cf.* In *Caus.*, l. 7.

tion. For me, in fact, it is an object of thought only in so far as I have superimposed a reflex idea on the subjective act previously elicited which in itself is not simple : I have succeeded in thinking the possibility of an unknown object the unity of which has been brought about by what must for ever remain divergent and multiple in my idea.[5]

Little difficulty is presented by the first stage of the process. It must be borne in mind that the concept employed for analogical knowledge remains *heterogeneous* in regard to the object that the mind is seeking to know. That which is simply defective is not to be confused with what is vague, and analogy is not to be identified with knowledge that is merely general. To know spirit by means of body, or God by having recourse to creatures, says St. Thomas, is not unlike knowing an ox by the idea of an ass or a stone.[6] He does not say : by the idea of " body " or " animal " for in that case the idea, though generic and approximate, would be correct ; as such it would pass, it would be applicable to reality, it would be completely verified and would need no subsequent correction.

The second stage, wherein this correction is introduced, is rigorously necessary if, like St. Thomas, we desire to exclude positive error from analogical knowledge. The whole difficulty of the process lies in this second stage. The correction does not consist in *substituting* a new intuition for the actually existing one (as, for instance, the substitution of " ass " for the idea of " ox," which by hypothesis is absent), nor yet does it consist in the elimination of notes which would leave behind the generic notion in the form of a residue. It consists rather in rationally rejecting, while the whole representation continues to exist in the mind, a mental attitude which was a necessary condition of the first apprehension. Once this subjective element falls to the ground it disintegrates the concept that it has helped to form, and

---

[5] It would seem in keeping with Scholastic principles to say that objects which are known by means of analogy are " unknowable " though not " unthinkable." See L. de Grandmaison, in *Bulletin de littérature ecclésiastique de Toulouse*, 1905, p. 198. Mercier, *Les origines de la psychologie contemporaine*, Louvain, 1897, pp. 411, 418.

[6] *Comp. Theol.*, 105.

carries with it all that must be denied of the unknown object, which in itself of course cannot be isolated by our minds for examination. An example will help to clarify this. We cannot think, for instance, without a corporeal image of some kind, yet we can think, in the presence of the image, of a being and deny of that being what properly belongs to the image.[7] Or again, by means of a purely logical distinction we can form propositions such as " Socrates is identical with himself." Suppose the existence of a being for whom this distinction, which for us is a purely rational device, were a subjective necessity. In that case such a being might rationally affirm the unity of Socrates ; there would be nothing to prevent it. Now it is in that way that we affirm the existence of pure spirits.

In the same way, to take an example from Thomistic Theodicy, we are unable to conceive things as bearing a relation to God without in the very same act conceiving God as relative to things. Yet by a judgment of reason we can correct this false conception of things.[8]

---

[7] *Non possumus intelligere Deum . . . esse . . . absque corporeitate, nisi imagine-mur corpora.* In *Trin.*, 6, 2, 5, 546 a.

[8] According to the Scholastics there is a real relation between creatures and God just as there is between knowledge and its object. There is not, however, in God a real relation to creatures any more than the object of knowledge is relative to the knowledge of it. We are forced to this conclusion by reasoning, says St. Thomas, and yet " our intellect is unable to conceive one thing as related to another without making such a relation reciprocal " (*Pot.*, 1, 1, 1). Elsewhere he says more explicitly : " This order implied in the mind's conception of relation is not invented by mind ; it follows rather on the mind's exercise by some kind of necessity, and, such relations are attributed by intelligence not to its ideas but to the object " (*Pot.*, 7, 11). This latter point, which is a delicate one, is explained by the context : these subjectively necessary ideas of which there is question here are not reflex ideas but ideas about ideas (*Pot.*, 7, 11, 2 ; *cf. Pot.*, 7, 99). We have here therefore an example of concepts that arise spontaneously which have to do with reality in itself, some of which are true and others false, but at the same time their co-existence in the subject is a necessity. Note that in these pages even where St. Thomas refers to this expedient he denies explicitly that " intelligence is in error " or that it affirms something of things not to be found in them. At first sight it would seem that there is a contradiction here, as he adds a few lines down : *Hujusmodi relationes intellectus . . . habentia secundum se ordinem ordinate intelli-guntur, licet intellectus non intelligat ea habere ordinem, quia sic esset falsus* (*Pot.*, 7, 11. *Cf.* 2 *Contra Gentes*, 13, 3). The only way of explaining this doctrine without such a crude misunderstanding is to recognise that intellect can announce this order of things without judging that it is immanent in the order of reality and that by reasoning (*ratio*) the intellectual intuition (*intellectus*) is corrected.

This method of purifying our concepts, by rejecting on reflection a necessary mode of mental activity on our part, borders on positive falsification. It is quite different from that segregating process of which St. Thomas frequently speaks when he distinguishes, as against Plato, the twofold manner of being which characterises a thing as it is in its own nature and as it is for the mind in knowledge.[9] St. Thomas argues against the " Platonic " theory of the universals that it is a naïve form of realism which consists in predicating of things themselves the abstract and simple nature of the ideas corresponding to them. He criticises the human conception of supra-sensible reality as a spatial and composite representation which in its concrete form is far removed from the simplicity of the original. There are too many elements in our human and quasi-animal intuition to allow us to see spirit as it really is in itself.

What indeed is this subjective condition of our mental activity which we reject in analogical knowledge ? It is always reducible to some form of multiplicity, though this will vary according as there is question of man's knowledge of self, or created spirits, or of God. Take, for example, man's knowledge of the angels. If it be held that man has a proper knowledge of his own soul, then it would also have to be conceded that he would know the angels just as he knows an ox by the idea of animal or of body. His purely analogical knowledge of them would extend not only to the

[9] 2 *Contra Gentes*, 7, 5. *Quamvis enim ad veritatem cognitionis necesse sit ut cognitio rei respondeat, non tamen oportet quod idem sit modus cognitionis, et rei : quae enim conjuncta sunt in re, interdum divisim cognoscuntur . . . licet natura generis et speciei nunquam sit nisi in his individuis, intelligit tamen intellectus naturam speciei et generis, non intelligendo principia individuantia, et hoc est intelligere universalia.* Here there is segregation and intellectual abstraction which may be compared to sense-abstraction in virtue of which given a certain object which is both white and sweet the sense of sight perceives only the colour and that of taste its sweetness (*ibid.*). But the underlying principle of the difference between the *modus cognitionis* and the *modus rei* implies not only a certain extenuation of material beings but also on the part of mind a certain " concretion." I q. 50, a. 2. *Intellectus non apprehendit res secundum modum rerum, sed secundum modum suum. Unde res materiales quae sunt infra intellectum nostrum, simpliciori modo sunt in intellectu nostro quam sint in se ipsis. Unde intellectus noster non potest attingere ad apprehendum eas, secundum quod sunt in se ipsis, sed per modum suum, secundum quod apprehendit res compositas : et sic etiam apprehendit Deum.* From an epistemological point of view it will be seen that the difference between the two incapacities of our mind is fundamental.

individual essence of each one but also to that particular
quality by which as pure spirits they are distinct from man.[10]
As a matter of fact St. Thomas is of opinion that the thinking
mind knows itself only in its acts of knowledge. These acts
of knowledge are prompted by species received from material
things. The soul knows itself accordingly in the process of
knowing other things, as, for example, in knowing colour and
in " becoming " intelligibly white or blue.[11] But what is
characteristic of all knowledge of material things is that it
takes a special concrete form which is implied in the
" subject " and " attribute " relation. Not only is there in
the human mind an innate desire to judge and to define,
but in its highest flights of so-called intellectual perceptions
there is an incurable duality. We say : *a* horse, *a* tulip, *this*
rose, and without a certain amount of practice it is impossible for us to identify an " abstract " quality with a " real
being " and find an intelligible meaning for such expressions
as " God is *His* Truth, *His* Goodness." If, then, the human
soul has anything corresponding to a proper idea of spirit,
it can only be of spirit as affected by the sensible duality
that is implied in its own cognitive activity. And that
precisely is what must be excluded when we attempt to
represent to ourselves the reality of pure spirits. These
pure spirits correspond to " separate " ideas, they are above
and beyond space, they fall outside that category which
St. Thomas designates as " unity, the principle of number."
" Our intellect, since its knowledge originates from the
senses, does not surpass the mode which we find in sensible
objects, wherein the form is distinct from the subject of the
form, on account of the composition of matter and form.
In these things the form is found to be simple indeed, but

[10] *Contra Gentes*, 46 end. *Cf.* preceding chapters and parallel passages
against the Arabians. *Cf.* also In *Trin.*, 6, 3, 547 b.
[11] The doctrine of the soul's knowledge of itself is epitomised in these words :
*Ex objecto . . . cognoscit suam operationem, per quam devenit ad cognitionem sui
ipsius* (*De Anim.*, 3, 4. *Cf. Opusc.*, 25, Ch. I). As this object is something material
then *Cognitio Dei quae ex mente humana accipi potest, non excedit illud genus cognitionis quod ex sensibilibus sumitur, cum et ipsa de se ipsa cognoscat quid est, per hoc
quod naturas sensibilium intelligit, ut dictum est* (3 *Contra Gentes*, 47 end. See also
Ver., 10, 8 ; 3 *Contra Gentes*, 46, where St. Thomas tries to force his own meaning
into the texts of Augustine). This conception is far removed from all forms of
Cartesian Theodicies.

imperfect, since it is non-subsistent, whereas the subject of
the form is found to be subsistent, but not simple, nay more,
with concretion. Wherefore, whatever our intellect signifies
as subsistent, it signifies it with concretion, and whatever it
signifies as simple, it signifies it not as subsisting but as a
determination or particular form of being. Accordingly in
every term employed by us there is a certain imperfection
of expression." [12] Thus there is imperfection of expression
whether we speak of God as *good* or as *goodness*, since " goodness evokes the idea of non-subsisting being and *good* the
idea of a subsisting thing with concretion." In the same way
all our efforts to speak of angels testify to the incapacities of
our minds and reveal their subjection to the conditions of
space and number. We are inclined to think that there
could be many " Gabriels " just as there could be a number
of men, and we distinguish the quality of being Gabriel
(" Gabrielite ") from Gabriel. To avoid this dualism of our
thought a judgment and a number of subtle reflections are
necessary which are beyond the capacity of the majority of
people. Thus in all our intellectual excursions we are
weighed down by what St. Thomas calls " the corporeal
conditions of human expression," which in their turn are
simply the corporeal conditions of human intuition that
debar us from a vision of separate substances. Human
intuition cannot avoid confounding mental abstraction,
which implies generalisation with real abstraction which is
synonymous with immateriality. The knowledge of purely
spiritual conditions is radically excluded for man because of
the quantitative and spatial aspects of his knowledge. [13]

[12] 1 *Contra Gentes*, 30. *Cf.* 1 d. 33, q. 1, a. 2 ; 1 q. 13, a. 1 ad 2. What
has been said of God here is also repeated in connection with the angels who
are also " pure forms " (1 q. 13, a. 12 ad 2).

[13] *Conditiones corporales . . . quantum ad modum significandi* (1 q. 13, a. 3 ad 3).
It is certain that though St. Thomas ordinarily speaks of *language* he is really
judging human *intuition* (see 1 *Contra Gentes*, 30 ; *Pot.*, 7, 5, 2, etc.). As for the
impossibility of multiplication of individuals outside the species to which he
refers in the text he usually accompanies the general principle with a comparison, *sicut albedo, si separata existeret, non posset esse nisi una numero* (see *Spirit.*, 8,
etc.). But the supposition implied in this image (which is the Platonic paradox), as well as the violent contradictions with which the theory has always
met, clearly shows to what extent human intuition is the slave of " unity,
the principle of number." To complete the critique of the category of number
according to St. Thomas it would be necessary to enter into details concerning

Our idea of God is in an even greater plight. There are qualities to be found in the angels which are not identical with their essence ; an angel, for example, may be good or bad. Since they are composed of potency and act their existence is not something that belongs to them by virtue of their essence. There is, then, something here which appeals to our intellects so prone to multiply, and since the angels belong to a genus a duality of terms is still possible even if these terms are extremely general. I may say that an angel is a being, or *an* intellectual being, that he is *something*.[14] But of God such predication is impossible. He is pure Act and subsisting Being from Whom all duality is excluded. He is above and beyond *genera* or categories and for that reason He transcends every created concept of Him that we can entertain. " What is the Nature of an idea," it has been well asked, " which can be explained only by reference to other ideas with which it is identical and yet at the same time from which it is distinct ? " [15] To have some idea of the intellectual process as it is found in God, it would be necessary to be capable of conceiving a form of knowledge which formally and identically is an act of love or a justice which at one and the same time is justice and mercy. This is true of all God's attributes since when I predicate something of man " the thing predicated is circumscribed and cannot escape me while a thing affirmed of God is necessarily not fully comprehended ; its meaning outsteps the terms employed to express it." Everything predicated of God must be taken out of the category of quality.[16]

---

the Holy Trinity and the Incarnation and also to study his concept of *aevum* or the duration proper to angels. What has been said here suffices to indicate how spatial conditions restrict intellectual knowledge, especially if we remember that the spatial universe is simply a single point in the intelligible world. A purely philosophical application of the principle will be found in the theory that governs knowledge of the infinite. *Per accidens* and in so far as intelligence receives impressions from the senses it knows *sub ratione quantitatis dimensivae* and for that reason *impeditur a comprehensione lineae vel numeri infiniti* (4 d. 49, q. 2, a. 3).

[14] And this knowledge remains positive, " affirmative." 1 q. 88, a. 2 ad 4. The angel is not outside the categories of substance and accident.

[15] M. Sertillanges, *Revue de philosophie* (February, 1906, p. 153).

[16] 1 q. 13, a. 5. Certain words are applied to God which designate accidental qualities, but the category of accident must first be denied of them (*Pot.*, 7, 4, obj. 3 and 4 ; 7, 7 ad 2 in contr.). The same is to be said of

Take even the term Being, as applied to God. It is the most indeterminate of all possible attributes and for that reason also it is the least imperfect.[17] The specification which is implied in attributes is absent. Yet, for all that, does such a notion convey a proper idea of the divine substance? Not in the least. Whether it be taken as a single word (*Ens, esse*) or as a composite (Being, that which is) the unavoidable duality is still present. We can call to mind the hundred odd perfections that we associate with being, but the fact remains that we are thinking in terms of *a* being, one amongst many, which like them participates in existence but is not identically existence itself. Here then, as elsewhere, there must be a constant understanding that my intellect in the very moment of its exercise condemns what for it is a necessary condition of its activity.

All this goes to show, it seems to me, that the method of negation was something quite distinct in the *eyes* of St. Thomas from a " refinement of method." " In the things of God negations are true, and affirmations are defective." [18] The negative idea " is the *proper* knowledge of God obtained by demonstration." [19] These well-known pronouncements must be taken as rigorously true. It would not indeed be exact to take them as stating that " our concepts of God are purely negative." Strictly speaking such concepts are neither purely positive nor purely negative, for the simple reason that as concepts they lack unity. There is really no idea that is common to God and creature and therefore there is no idea which *as such* is attributed to God. But hidden in every idea there is a positive element which con-

---

"relation" (the πρός τι of Aristotle) in speculative theology—the *ad aliquid* is retained while its accidental inherence is rejected (see *Pot.*, 8, 2 and the explanation for the word *person, Pot.*, 9, 4, 6). The *quid est* of God being precisely the Trinity of persons, the substance itself, *leaving out* the relations, must be only a mode of being : *dici secundum substantiam pertinet ad modum significandi (Pot.*, 8, 2, 5). " Substance " and " Relation " are besides the only categories to be employed when speaking of God, because they are the only ones that do not imply composition and inherence (1 q. 28, a. 2 ; *Quodl.*, 7, 4).

[17] " The more common a name is the more appropriate it is as applied to God . . . because the more specific it is the more it *determines* a mode of being and that applies more to creatures " (1 q. 33, a. 11, *cf.*, 13 a. 11, etc.).

[18] 1. q. 13, a. 12 ad i. It is a quotation from Pseudo-Dionysius.

[19] 3 *Contra Gentes*, 49. *Cf.* in *Trin.*, 2, 2, 2.

stitutes the only proper knowledge that is to be found in what we call an analogical idea, and every idea which is not only limited but concrete or complex [20] demands a negative judgment. The three "ways of causality, negation, and eminence" are reducible to one unique process [21] which is suggested by the names invented for them by Pseudo-Dionysius. When I say *supersapiens* after *sapiens* and *non-sapiens*, the singular term must remind us that every perception must be accompanied by a negation of our method of perception because we can always envisage a greater measure of being. It is also seen why God Who transcends all categories must not be designated as "species or individual," "nor as universal or particular." [22] For these are designations which presuppose a genus.

Words themselves must not be allowed to deceive us. The third stage of the analogical process consists in the effort to unite together its first two moments. But a true grasp of the second stage shows us that an intuition of the whole taken together is never present. Nothing assuredly can prevent us from imagining a *word* that would stand for the object with which these many activities of the mind are concerned, if it is known that such an object exists. But when the word has been found, that does not mean that the ideas have stirred out of position or that they have come together to fuse into one single idea, no more than a group of trunks becomes a single trunk by the fact that a covering has been thrown over them. Human language can cover many things and suggest much, but we can never get out of it more than human knowledge is capable of putting into it. Thus I may desire to speak of a square circle and designate the circle A, but the choice of label has not made the object for which it stands a whit more thinkable. The idea of God, though it contains no contradiction, is complex. To write *Ipsum Esse* in one word will not succeed in unifying the mental process. The only difference between the "analogical name" and the analogical idea is that the same envelope serves successively

[20] See in *Trin.*, 1, 4.
[21] *Pot.*, 7, 3, and in *Trin.*, 3, 3, 1.
[22] I q. 119, a. 1.

to hold two different contents.   Besides the name itself will
reveal its own insufficiency.   Language offers only two kinds
of marks for the phantoms of our ideas.   These take the form
of concrete and abstract terms and we have seen that reality
is always too large for such terms.   Whether we say the
living God, or *Life Itself*, we always speak subject to
correction.

In a word, these two parallel criticisms of language and of
intellectual knowledge bring home to us our inability to
grasp subsisting intelligible objects by means of the pure
idea.   So great is this inaptitude on our part that we fail
to form a concept of their nature which would be subjectively one.   Let us come back, then, to our proper sphere,
that of material essences :   *nos non scimus nisi quaedam infima
entium.*[23]

II

This doctrine of analogy allows for the affirmation of supra-
sensible realities, but it postpones to another life what is
nevertheless the characteristic activity of intelligence, the
perception of such realities.   It has the twofold advantage
of making provision for the most daring of our intellectual
desires and of recognising the vanity of such desires as far
as the present life is concerned.   In this way it lays the
foundation for a critique of intelligence as it is found in man.
It remains to be seen whether these principles have been
consistently developed by St. Thomas.   It may be also
asked whether a corresponding examination of our ideas of
material essences should not have made him extend the
domain of analogical knowledge and thus help to remove
some of the illusions he entertained in their regard.

How do we know those " low forms " of reality, material
substances ?   The perfection of intellectual knowledge is
gauged by the measure in which it seizes the reality of

---

[23] 3 *Contra Gentes*, 49.   It is to be noted that St. Thomas would not have
been under the necessity of pointing out this impossibility on our part of
forming unitary concepts of things supra-sensible had he adopted, instead of
his theory of analogy, the more convenient and simpler view of symbolism.
He did not do so, however, and it would be wrong to give a general interpretation in this direction to the curious passage, *De Anim.*, 9, 18, where St.
Thomas is speaking simply of man's tendency to clothe his ideas of spiritual
realities with some form of imagery.

things as they are in themselves. Now, the real properly speaking, or " first substance," as far as the present world is concerned, is identical with beings that are composed of matter and form, the individual realities of experience. Human nature, for instance, has no existence except as endowed with its individuating principles and as it exists in the concrete. And since reality is the measure of truth it is clear that " true human nature " such as is found " in Peter or Martin definitely connotes a particular soul and a particular body." Without a complete notion of a material being it is impossible to form an absolute judgment concerning such a being.[24] Purely intuitive intelligences have true ideas of such objects because they are capable of gathering together in the unity of their ideas all those determinations that are found together in the real unity of such objects.[25]

The human intellect, however, instead of directly grasping the individual in its particularity, is reduced to forming an idea of the essence of individuals on the occasion of its coming in contact with them. For this contact the human intellect has need of the senses for a certain (*quodammodo*) apprehension of the individual.[26] When we place this last assertion side by side with that which proclaims the exclusive reality of the individual, what must be inferred ? Does it imply a contradiction between ontology and theory of knowledge ? Many have charged Aristotle with it. The same might certainly be urged against any philosopher who maintains the intellectualist equation of reality and idea and yet does not allow for the existence of any intelligence superior to that of man. But this cannot be urged against St. Thomas. The legitimate conclusion which he drew was simply a disproportion which must be recognised as existing between the human intellect and being. The

---

[24] *Cf.* 3 d. 20, a. 5, sol. 2.
[25] *Quodl.*, 7 a. 3 ad 1.
[26] There is this much in common between our perception of the individual and our analogical ideas that the former is neither direct nor single, but is the result of a reflection of the subject on its own acts. *Per quamdam reflexionem, in quantum scilicet ex hoc quod apprehendit suum intelligibile, revertitur ad considerandum suum actum, et speciem intelligibilem quae est principium suae operationis, et ejus speciei originem ; et sic venit in considerationem phantasmatum et singularium, quorum sunt phantasmata* . . . (*De Anim.*, 20 ad 1 in contr. Also 4 d. 50, q. 1, a. 3, etc.).

human concept is too vague and ill-defined to embrace within it the fullness and rich determination of reality. This lack of esteem on the part of St. Thomas for conceptual knowledge is clearly delineated in certain texts. " The nature of a stone and such things which belong to the order of nature cannot be known truly or adequately except in such cases where knowledge grasps it in a particular subject." [27] Again : " In the hierarchy of intelligences that of man comes last. The intelligible species received by him are accordingly the least effective of all. They allow of a knowledge of things which is simply universal, generic or specific. . . . That is why he knows the individual by means of the senses and the universal by his intellect." Further on he says, " The more elevated a knowing faculty is, the more universal it is. That does not mean that it knows only the universal, for then instead of being more perfect it would be less so, since to know things in this universal manner is not a perfection but rather the sign of imperfection, owing to the margin that it leaves between potency and act. If it is said then that the higher form of knowledge is more universal that can only mean that it implies a greater range of power and a more intimate grasp of the reality of things." [28]

The principles of Thomistic ontology allow us to mark off with great precision this disproportion which exists between the human idea and reality. It would not be sufficient to say that it is simply a question of *inadequate* knowledge : according to St. Thomas intuitive knowledge need not be entirely exhaustive of reality as happens in the case of angels.[29] Nor yet would it be entirely accurate to speak in this connection of *partial* knowledge, for in the real essence, leaving aside the accidents and the *esse*, St. Thomas recognises only one form of composition, that of matter and form. For him matter is the individuating principle, and this matter which is intrinsic to the actualised essence cannot be looked upon as adequately distinct from it. But to say that, accord-

[27] 1 q. 84, a. 7.
[28] *Opusc.*, 14, c. 14.
[29] *Spir.*, 1. 11.

ing to him, mind knows only the physical form (as, for instance, *anima*) and does not know the material element (*corpus*) would be totally erroneous.[30] What the mind knows then is a being conceived in the form of an abstraction (as, for instance, *humanitas*, or the " metaphysical form " of the later Scholastics), but this abstraction represents the essence as a totality including matter and physical forms. What is left aside by mind is the particularity of the being which makes it to be *this* matter and *this* form. And yet this particularity thus left aside is not distinct from the being itself, but is a determination that is intrinsically constitutive of the object.[31]

This would be unintelligible if it were a question of knowledge directly produced by the object itself. It is easily grasped, however, once we begin to see in the concept an original creation, so to speak, of the human mind, its autochthonous fruit and a new product of its own activity. A study of the mechanism of knowledge is here seen to be of great utility in determining the value of knowledge. We must recognise that our ideas of material things are for St. Thomas *concepts*, not *percepts*, and due allowance must be made for the activity of the *intellectus agens* which creates the idea : *FACIT intelligibilia esse actu*. These *intelligibilia* do not exist as such outside the soul, but " the thing understood is constituted or formed by the activity of intelligence whether there is question of a simple idea or of a judgment." [32] It is precisely for that reason that the existence

[30] The distinction between " forms " like *anima* and " forms " such as *humanitas* so vague in Aristotle is very clearly marked in the metaphysic of St. Thomas. See in *Met.*, l. 8 (542) ; in 7 *Met.*, l. 9, l. q. 75, a. 4 ; *Pot.*, 9, 1, etc. It is surprising to see the same confusion still made in works so able as those of Seeberg, *Die Theologie des Johannes Duns Scotus*, p. 634 ; and of Ueberweg-Heinze, *Grundriss der Geschichte der Philosophie*, 11[8], p. 271.
The clear consciousness of the distinction enables St. Thomas to see clearly that matter which is something impenetrable to our minds is intrinsic to the object to be known and that forces him to have a low estimate of our knowledge.
[31] *Humanitas . . . dicitur quod est forma totius . . . sed magis est forma quae est totum, scilicet formam complectens et materiam, cum praecisione tamen eorum per quae materia est nata designari* (*Opusc.*, 26, Ch. 3). *Humanitas . . . pro tanto non est omnino idem cum homine, quia* importat *tantum principia essentialia hominis, et exclusionem omnium accidentium . . . humanitas* significat *ut pars* (in 7 *Met.*, l. 5 end). Assertions of this nature occur frequently.
[32] *Spir.*, 9, 6.

of an *intellectus agens* must be admitted even when there is no
question of a *sensus agens*.[33] This comparison in fact brings
out the thought of Aquinas much better than the most
systematic subtleties. The senses possess intuitions whereas
intelligence which is destined for intuitions and desirous of
them must be satisfied for the present with *concepts*. And
the essential mark of these concepts which are formed by
intellect in its reaction to the passive impressions of the
senses is that they are stripped of everything which is
particular in the image : as such they are immediately
prepared for generalisation.

The imperfection of our conceptual knowledge, then,
consists in a certain " indistinctness " if by a distinct idea
we understand that which suffices to distinguish the object
to be known from all other objects. The object to be known,
it may be repeated, is a reality and therefore particular.
But the concept (unless joined with numerous sensitive
apprehensions) cannot be employed to distinguish individuals
of the same species ; it unites them all together in the unity
of the *absolute essence*. The best image we have of the concept,
the official one in fact in the Thomistic system, is that sup-
plied by those troubled visions we possess of a distant object
when its exact shape is indecipherable.[34]

" This particular soul, this body, these bones belong to
the essence of Socrates, and if it were possible to define the
essence of Socrates these should form part of such a definition." But the man whose eyes are fixed on Socrates can
intellectually extract from the object only a notion which is
vague enough to apply equally well to Plato. By insisting
on the necessity of considering individual matter as an
integral part of the essence while at the same time refusing
reality to common matter outside of its concrete realisations
thus identifying *humanitas* and *Socrateitas*, St. Thomas may be
said to have introduced into the depths of things a certain
nominalism. He holds that mind merely knows what is
common to things which in their reality are distinct from
one another, and by his avowal of a certain incapacity and

---

[33] 1 q. 79, a. 3 ad 1. *Cf.* 1 q. 85, a. 1 ad 3.
[34] 1 q. 85, a. 3, and parallel passages.

" unreality " in the part of human concepts he very definitely solved that problem that arose for Aristotle.

III

We have now made the first step in the critique of that mental resemblance to reality which is the result of intellectual abstraction. The concept is admittedly general in character, and even for the most imperfect representation of individual substance the collaboration of many elements is a necessity. But here a further question arises which concerns the concept itself. If the concept is general, how can it be one ? If it is abstract, can it be said to convey an immediate representation of reality ? Take for example the " absolute essence " or nature conceived by mind as undivided, yet devoid of individuality and plurality. As such this nature does not exist. Can we say that mind knows it " as it is in itself " ? If I do not see what is the constitutive essence of an angel do I see what constitutes an ox ? Some of the later Scholastics [35] replied in the negative and invoked the authority of St. Thomas for their views. It is my opinion that their view is in accordance with the principles of St. Thomas though contrary to his usual assertions, if not indeed to his final doctrine. There is here a certain lack of logic in his system which is of no importance, and simply illustrates the power of words over the minds of the greatest and most sincere thinkers.

I propose to indicate rapidly that St. Thomas was of opinion that in concepts of material essences he possessed that living and ineffable unity which is the goal of mind's grasp of reality ; that he looked upon the concept as " the similitude of the essence," of which it could only be said that it was " the thing in its intelligible state " as distinct from its " natural reality." [36] It will not then be difficult, I think, to show that his poetic principles conflict with such

[35] Suarez, for instance. *Disputationes metaphysicae*, XXXV, 3, 5 ; Tolomei, *Philosophia mentis et sensuum, disp.* 12ᵃ *logico-physica*, sect. 2, n. 8 ; sect. 3, n. 1.

[36] *Quodl.*, 8, a. 4. *Species intelligibilis est similitudo ipsius essentiae rei, et est quodammodo ipsa quidditas et natura rei secundum esse intelligibile, non secundum esse naturale, prout est in rebus.*

a position. By a peculiar coincidence the very reason that inclined St. Thomas to believe in the perfection and adequateness of concepts will lead us to the opposite conclusion.

This precious middle term is the equation of definition and the true concept. Actually the vision of a thing as it is in itself goes hand in hand with the possibility of defining it. We do not see God as He is in Himself, nor pure Spirits. God, Gabriel, a Raphael are no more capable of definition than are individual men like Socrates and Plato.[37] Natural substances such as man, ox, olive-tree we can define, and therefore we are capable of conceiving them as they are in themselves. *The two processes, in fact, of conception and definition are identical.*

" He presupposes that the definition of a thing signifies the essence of a thing." What St. Thomas here says of Aristotle may be also affirmed of himself.[38] Not only do we constantly meet with such phrases in his writings as *forma speciei quam significat definitio*, but he goes further and says simply that the " definition of a thing is the same as the thing," [39] and concludes by explicitly identifying definition with the perfect concept. With greater reason, then, he who can define a thing possesses vision. " When a man has an intellectual knowledge of a thing he conceives a certain form which is the similitude of the thing in its full perfection, and it is in this way that intellect arrives at the definition of things." [40] " Once we have succeeded in forming the

[37] The reason of this in the case of the Angel is that we have no proper idea of the angel and that the idea of an angel cannot be broken up (*Opusc.*, 26, c. 6 ; In 7 *Met.*, l. 15, etc.) ; in the case of Socrates it is to be sought in the fact that the individuating matter, unknown to us, forms part of his essence : *Oportet igitur, si singulare definitur, in ejus definitione poni aliqua nomina, quae multis conveniant* (In 7 *Met.*, l. 14, etc. ; *cf.* later p. 115). Ultimate Abstractions are naturally not subjects for definition, since definitions cannot go on indefinitely *ad infinitum* (*In. Post.*, l. 32). *Genera* are definable in so far as like species they can be subjoined under higher classes (In 5 *Met.*, l. 3 ; In 7 *Met.*, l. 11, etc.).

[38] In 2 *Pot.*, l. 8. Aristotle's phrase is : λόγος τοῦ τί ἐστι (2 *Post.*, c. 10). *Cf. Top.*, 7, 5.

[39] *Definitio enim est idem rei.* In 7 *Met.*, l. 9 (p. 3a).

[40] *Ver.*, 2, 1. *Cf.* 1 d. 2, q. 1, a. 3, where St. Thomas explains the dictum of Aristotle cited above. The *Ratio* (λόγος), he says, is *id quod apprehendit intellectus de significatione alicuius nominis : et hoc in his quae habent definitionem est ipsa rei definitio.*

definition of a thing we have a perfect knowledge of it." [41]
" A thing is understood once the definition of it is known,
that is, if the definition is itself understood." [42] Elsewhere
he repeats this assertion and goes on to add significantly :
definitio enim est virtus comprehendens rem.[43] The same is to
be understood of definition not only when it is applied to
concepts but also to words, " the word *man* expresses by its
meaning the essence of man because it signifies the definition
which in its turn makes known the essence." [44] Finally,
" we can know the essence of a stone as it is in itself by knowing what constitutes a stone." [45] Greater precision is brought
to such declarations by the difference he indicates in certain
passages between the vision of the pure essence of a thing
and those notions of it that may be formed by analogy.[46]
They are supremely important in relation to his theory of
science. The essential definition ranks at the summit of
the deductive process and constitutes the major premise of
the scientific syllogism. The specific properties which are
virtually contained in it may be determined by deduction.[47]
It is beyond all doubt, then, that St. Thomas believed that
definition reveals the intelligible reality of things, and that
he saw in it the mental counterpart of the essence of things
which is proportionate to the human mind's capacities and
satisfies it perfectly.

It must be clearly understood, however, that St. Thomas
never loses sight of the principle which declares the sensible
origin of all our ideas. Never does he say or think that

[41] In 5 *Met.*, l. 22, 571 a.
[42] *Ver.*, 8, 2, 4.
[43] *Ver.*, 20, 5.
[44] I q. 13, a. I.
[45] I q. 13, a. 8 ad 2. *Substantiam lapidis ex ejus proprietate possumus cognoscere
secundum seipsam sciendo quid est lapsis* and so the name stone signifies its *quod
quid est,* which is not true of the name God. Elsewhere, apropos of the Blessed
and God's incomprehensibility, he says, *Non videbitur Deus ab eis sicut videtur res
per suam definitionem, cujus essentia comprehenditur* (4 d. 49, q. 2, a. 3 ad 5).
[46] Note particularly 3 d. 35, q. 2, a. 2, sol. 1. This text is very valuable on
account of the comparison it suggests with angelic intuition. It indicates
that the human intellect also arrives (though as a result of reasoning) at a
unified vision which St. Thomas does not consider as merely analogical.
See how differently he speaks regarding spiritual objects (*ibid.* and sol. 2).
Cf. also *Div. Nom.*, c. 7, 1, 2, 3, d. 23, q. 1, a. 2.
[47] In 2 *Phys.*, l. 15, 380 b, etc. ; *Ver.*, 2, 7 : *Intellectus autem cognoscens essentiam speciei, per eam comprehendit omnia per se accidentia illius speciei.*

substance can be known *except by means of* its accidents. But it is one thing to give an exact account of the genesis of definitions and another to make a general pronouncement on their value.[48] If the passages here in question are examined closely it will be found that they may be divided into two distinct classes. On the one hand it is undoubtedly affirmed that we do not go beyond the accidents, and yet, on the other, there are certain texts which clearly assert that we do get beyond them and that in virtue of mind's own activity we succeed in discovering that intimate substantial note (*differentia*) which characterises the " essence " of an oak or a tiger as clearly and as distinctly as the essence of a triangle or a square.

When, for example, we define blackness or whiteness by one of its properties relative to our eyes (*congregativum* and *disgregativum visus*) we are simply employing an accidental difference in the absence of an essential characteristic. In this instance we are not going beyond a certain accidental effect of the colour because the real cause and the true specific difference must be sought, says St. Thomas, in " a certain fullness of light " which is found in white light and which cannot be determined exactly.[49] On the contrary, when we define man as a " rational animal " we have reached beyond accidents and activities to the really constitutive and substantial element which is the specific difference of man as such. This definition of man, it might be said, is put forward by St. Thomas as representing the ideal definition [50] ; he seems to have regarded it as a magic formula which lays bare the hidden depths of reality, the *speculum adaequans essentiam rei*. Between these two extremes furnished by the definition of man and the attempted definition of whiteness there are numerous intermediaries. The passage from one to another is sometimes rather obscure,

[48] In the following discussion I leave aside the difficulties that might be urged against the method followed in order to arrive at definitions. Whether the method is that of division or induction (*cf.* In 1 *Post.*, l. 32, 33 ; In 2 *Phys.*, l. 1, 13–16) the result is always a dual concept, and it is the value of this resultant in which I am at present interested.

[49] In 10 *Met.*, l. 3, 125 a.

[50] See particularly *Spir.*, 11, 3. *Cf.* the reasons given why only one species of rational animals could exist. In 2 *An.*, l. 5, 73 a. *Cf.* 1 q. 85, a. 6.

and it is not a rare occurrence to find that differences of
meaning may conceal themselves behind an identical form
of expression on the part of St. Thomas. The method of
progress from accidents to the knowledge of the essence is
marked out in accordance with the Aristotelian formula,
but it must be admitted that sometimes the progress is not
very great and that one must be satisfied to remain more or
less distant from the goal. Some accidents are more deeply
set than others ; they lie " nearer to the essence " of an object
than those of white and black, as for instance the accident
of " figure " in the animal and vegetable domains.[51]
Others are proper, in fact essentially characteristic, effects
of the cause, and in such instances it might even be possible
to reason from such effects to the specific difference of the
object (as when from the accident *biped* one concludes to
the difference, rational).[52] In other cases the name given
need not be changed provided it is understood not to refer
to an accident but to the essence and to imply " something
qualitative " rather than a simple quality.[53] In these
last-mentioned cases the essence of the object is really
reached and grasped. In a word, when we mark off a
camel by the colour of its skin we are not going beyond an
external accident, and when we describe its outlines, its
appearance, its hump we are suggesting a good basis for
a zoological classification, but a definition will not be
reached until we have discovered that particular temperament to be associated with the camel's characteristic
realisation of the genus animal which is responsible for
its particular form of sensitive reactions.[54] St. Thomas

---

[51] In 2 *Phys.*, l. 5. *Cf.* 2 d. 3, q. 1, a. 6, etc.

[52] *Ver.*, 10, 6 ; 1a, 2ae, q. 49, a. 2 ad 3 ; In *Trin.*, l. 2 ; *Opusc.*, 26, ch. 6.

[53] *Secundum quod quale invenitur in genere substantiae secundum quod differentia
substantialis dicitur praedicari in eo quod quale.* In 5 *Phys.*, l. 4. The qualities
sensitive and *rational* are differences *per se*, one generic and the other specific.
Though taken from the faculties (sight, smell, intelligence) they are applied
to the natures themselves. (*De Anim.*, 12, 8 ; also 4 d. 44, q. 1, a. 1, sol. 2
ad 3 ; *Ver.*, 10, l. 6, etc.)

[54] In 2 *An.*, l. 5, 73 a. *Diversificantur species sensitivorum secundum diversas
complexiones, quibus diversimode se habent ad operationes sensus.* The essence of a
lion is said to be that of an animal (*Quod habet animam sensitivam*) *talem, scilicet
cum abundantia audaciae.* In 7 *Met.*, l. 12. *Cf.* In *Trin.*, 5, 3. St. Thomas is
anxious to express in a word the principle of the internal harmony of a being
which determines all its details. The quest for this original and unique

believes that such a definition can be obtained. It is possible to get beyond the many physical accidents of a thing
to their unique and common source in the nature from which
they spring. Like the essence the ideal metaphysical definition is itself unique : *simpliciter significat unum de una re,
cuius ratio est. . . . Quia essentia cuiuslibet rei est una.*[55]

We shall see later the influence of this idea on Thomistic
epistemology and the degree to which it favoured the extension of the deductive method to all the sciences. For the
present the only important point to be settled is to what
extent this pretended perfect grasp of essences is in harmony
with the poetic principles hitherto expounded. Would
St. Thomas have been more consistent had he not spoken
of the knowledge of material essences " as such " ?   Or
must we not speak of our ideas of material substances as
analogical ideas, meaning by analogy something distinct
from that vital presence of things in the mind by means of
an idea which, because it is the representation of the thing
as it is in itself, at once represents the object and unifies
our consciousness ?

principle which will not go beyond the species in question (*in equis, puta hin-
nibile,* 2 *Post.,* l. 16) conflicts with certain responses inspired by a wise agnosticism which he gives elsewhere (2 *Post.,* l. 13). This agnosticism is to the effect
that the work of definition must be reduced to circumscribing and marking
off the object to be defined as the only one in which a certain number
of common accidents come together. It is precisely because he has this ideal
before his eyes that St. Thomas carefully distinguishes not only external
" notifications " by means of " properties " (In 7 *Met.,* l. 12 ; In 2 *Post.,* l. 8),
but also definitions furnished by partial causes from the perfect form of definition. Frequently he says that many definitions arising out of different causes
are possible in regard to one and the same object, but he always holds that only
one definition is perfect and that it includes all the others (3 d. 23, q. 2, a. 1
ad 8 ; In 1 *Post.,* l. 15 ; In 2 *Phys.,* l. 5 ; 1a, 2ae, q. 55, a. 4, etc.). There are
many definitions because " there are several ' quiddities ' belonging to the
same thing " (in 2 *Post.,* l. 7, 250 b), but these, according to his doctrine, are
so many partial and abstractive aspects of the object. *Cf.* the principle (*Pot.,*
7, 6) : *Unius formae non potest esse nisi una similitudo secundum speciem, quae sit
ejusdem rationis cum ea ; possunt tamen esse diversae similitudines imperfectae.*
[55] In 2 *Post.,* l. 8. This theory of definition is somewhat the same as the
view of explanation which looks to the " chief form of activity " or " pre-
dominant trait " of things (see Taine's *Philosophie de l'art,* T. 1er, for his celebrated description of the lion. Neo-Scholastics have referred to this as illus-
trating their idea of *form* rather well). The pretention of anthropomorphic
intellectualism to impose on reality the unity demanded by intellect is very
palpable. For that reason St. Thomas might be accused here of inconsistency.
Such a conception of the power of human formulæ implies logically the deduction of species and also the reduction of harmonised multiplicity to a rational
unity. This, of course, runs counter to Thomistic principles (p. 113).

It seems to me that the very duality of terms implied in his theory of definition should have suggested the latter alternative to St. Thomas. Duality of terms means duality of ideas, and as long as there is this duality of ideas the thing as it is in itself is not grasped. To what object, in fact, would the " difference " correspond ? Would it not be to something implying the contraction of the " genus " by an intrinsic determination ? The note " animal " is not distinct from the note " lion," except as the result of reflection on our part, and in spite of all metaphors " genus " remains of " second intention." Just as properly speaking matter cannot be conceived without form, and *vice versa*, so " animality " cannot be conceived except as contained in some specific object : man, lion or dog, since by definition knowledge and its object go hand in hand.[56] If, then, the ideas corresponding to " genus " and " difference " are true and proper, there will be complete coincidence of the two and consequent fusion of them. In such a case there would be a perfect grasp of the intelligible object (*ens* and *unum*), but then it would have ceased to be a definition.[57] The " difference " and the " genus " go to form one being just like matter and form, and as it is one and the same nature that results from matter and form, so the difference does not add an extrinsic nature, but " simply determines the nature

---

[56] There is a natural equation of the intelligible and the " definable " in the system of Scotus with its formal distinction *ex natura rei*. But when St. Thomas holds that we conceive or define *by means of addition* and compares this method with syllogistic reasoning (*Quodl.*, 8, a. 4, *cf.* in *Trin.*, 6, 4, etc.), he must necessarily be aware that this latter process is necessarily broken up and far inferior to the ideal of intellect. His doctrine of being forces him to see in all abstraction a sign of incapacity. He is right no doubt in associating the unique " difference " with a unique *form* (In 7 *Met.*, l. 12, 21 b : *Si enim essent plures formae secundum omnia praedicta, non possent omnes una differentia comprehendi, nec ex eis unum constitueretur*), but it would have been much better if he had refused to see in definition (*ce concept doublé*) the ideal perfection of intelligence. (If he sometimes declares that genus corresponds to the matter and the " difference " to the form he is, like Avicenna, speaking simply metaphorically. Matter and form for St. Thomas are only one reality and have only one idea corresponding to them.)

[57] *Ipsa enim definitio, scilicet secundum se, oportet quod sit divisibilis* (In 5 *Met.*, l. 6, 535 a. *Cf.* Ar.). The notes may be more numerous than two, but the ideal is to discover a proximate genus which will contain the higher genera (In 7 *Met.*, l. 12, 18 b, 20 b), the number of words is unimportant. What is of chief importance is the two ideas are present : *In specie hominis intelligimus animal et rationale.* 1 q. 12, a. 10 ad 1, etc.

to be what it is." [58]   It follows because of the broken unity
of the concept that we must admit something other in the
definition than a mere transposition of a thing from the
" real " to the " ideal " state : we must recognise in it a
certain rupture of *ideal unity* and a knowledge that is imperfect and analogical.

It would be also possible to reason along the following
lines. The real essence comprises matter, and the absolute
essence comprises the common matter. But the intellectual
knowledge of matter, according to St. Thomas, is possible
only in two ways. Pure spirits who obtain their ideas from
God can know the material individual in its particularity,
but for man, whose knowledge is obtained from the objects
themselves, every idea of determined matter implies a
certain reflection upon the perfection of sense. With this
necessity for reflection a certain complexity is introduced
into human ideas, not unlike that implied in analogy, which
absolutely excludes the possibility of a unique idea corresponding to a material substance. And that is tantamount
to admitting that such knowledge is not appropriate to its
object. This explanation, which is an echo of the general
principles of St. Thomas's theory of knowledge, would have
the advantage of showing that *all general ideas of substances are
necessarily analogical in character*, and that the true and adequate
idea could not be the result of abstraction but rather the
product of *a priori* condensation. It is in this latter way that
the angels perceive things. They possess innate forms which
are natural to their intelligences and which are types of all
reality (including the determinable and the determining).
The lowest of Angelic ideas are at least equivalent to natural
species.[59] In a similar way the human soul has a true and
adequate idea of " things " (non-substantial) of which it is
itself the measure, namely the *artificiata*. In this way the
theory of St. Thomas is amended and brought into harmony
with his general principle, which says that " when a thing is
known intellectually it is known *per se, and for this knowledge
the intellectual nature is of itself sufficient and needs no external*

medium." [60] Might it be said, however, that St. Thomas has here contradicted himself? The word "contradiction" requires to be understood in a special way when it is employed to express an opposition between an author's profound and certain principles and certain secondary superficial assertions. The very naïveté of some of St. Thomas's expressions cited leads to the belief that he did not go very deeply into the question of the definability of natural substances. The absence of restrictions when he speaks of definition in general and simply gives examples of abstract things like eclipse, thunder, triangle, may be an index of the absence of distinctions in his mind, but they do not warrant the conclusion that he would have explicitly dogmatised to the effect that a camel is just as definable as a triangle. The fact that he was not disconcerted by bad results only goes to show that he did not trouble very much about the consequences of his theory. What shall we say of the ease with which on occasion he abandons the ideal definition itself, that of man, upon which the system seems to rest? Because many of the Fathers had looked upon the celestial bodies as so many

---

[60] I *Contra Gentes*, 57, 8. It will be noted that this idea implied in the "artificiatum" is complex without for that reason being untrue or inappropriate. As a thing is, so it is known. An object whose unity is dependent on human purposes and human use is not perceived in this accidental unity (*unum per accidens*) without a corresponding perception of this dependency. In psychology and in scientific morals definition might still be regarded as proper and perfect precisely because it creates the unity of its object. *Cf.* reflections in 1a, 2ae, q. 18, a. 10 : "*Species moralium actuum constituuntur ex formis prout sunt a ratione conceptae . . . . Sed processus rationis non est determinatus ad aliquid unum ; sed, quolibet dato, potest ulterius procedere. . . .*" Finally, the existence of an appropriate idea corresponding to accidents and sensible phenomena, which are only abstractions and are relative to the human mode of apprehension, might, for a similar reason, be granted (*cf.* p. 33), though such an idea would, of course, remain a complex one, implying the reflection of intelligence on the act of sense-perception. Within these limits the theory of the concept would be in perfect conformity with the principles of St. Thomas : rooted in the direct intuition of the ego and branching out from it will be found those true and proper concepts of realities relative to it. For the most part the definitions envisaged by St. Thomas belong to those kinds referred to here ; it is a question of "house," " eclipse," "magnanimity," etc. Nevertheless (and here we have additional proof that he looks upon definition as a veritable taking possession of reality), St. Thomas affirms theoretically that substance alone is truly capable of being perfectly defined : "*Secundum quod aliqua habent esse, possunt definiri . . . ideo nil perfecte definitur nissi substantia* (2 d. 35, q. i, a. 2 ad 1). The whole discussion in the In 2 *Post.*, 1, 8 also indicates clearly that he places natural substances in the category of things that are subject to definition.

" rational animals " St. Thomas, apparently seeing no contradiction in such a supposition, is quite ready to include under this definition as many species as there are stars in the firmament.[61] It is well to remember these vacillations and concessions. Yet, all the time the dream remained of extracting from the stuff of accidents the real note that would point to their true source in the mysterious unity that lay behind them. Having clearly shown how a thing could be identical with an idea, he failed to recognise the contradiction implied in the effort to make one essence identical with two ideas or with one phrase. The logical consequences of this inconsistency will be developed in the following chapters. The psychological explanation is not far to seek. St. Thomas, gifted with the subtle power of contemplating things invisible, was comparatively uninterested in the world of sound and colour. He is content to repeat what others have said about it. Aristotle the philosopher did not cease to be Aristotle the naturalist. When he describes the external appearances of things he takes his time over it and is not obsessed with the idea of obtaining an intellectual grasp of the underlying essence. St. Thomas, who was more of a metaphysician than a zoologist, is always thinking in terms of the essences of spiritual substances which are so limpid and transparent. Intellectually desirous of such diamonds, he does not take the trouble to assess the value of the copper treasure he believes he possesses, and which an attempted inventory would have scattered to the four winds as it would have also done to the " proper ideas " of " spirits and mysteries."

[61] *Spir.*, 8, 10. St. Thomas, of course, believed that each celestial body was unique, the only one of its kind.

CHAPTER III

KNOWLEDGE OF THE PARTICULAR : ART AND HISTORY

WHATEVER illusions may have been entertained by St. Thomas regarding the mental process involved in definition, these must not be allowed to obscure his principles, which affirm the exclusive existence of the particular and the necessity for an apprehension of the particular if we are to possess a radically "complete and true knowledge." These principles are not likely to displease those modern thinkers who insist most on the vagueness and poverty of general ideas and who place the perfection of human knowledge in a more exhaustive apprehension of the individual.[1]

From this it would seem to follow that the value of our cognitive life depends to a great extent on these apprehensions of the particular which are more " real " though less easily fixed, and which are more complete even though in themselves they are less certain. We are here in presence of what may be said to form the subject-matter of art and history. It would also follow, where the "faculty of being" is concerned, that an effort should be made by it to embrace its object as entirely as possible either by a deduction of the individual if that is possible, or by having recourse to inferior auxiliary faculties that are intuitive. For philosophy itself the obligation arises of instituting a critique of this new process and of determining the conditions under which it might be expected to reach its maximum value.

Such a study could scarcely have been expected from Greek philosophy. In the beginning science could not have asserted itself except as opposed to art and to practical

---

[1] We have already indicated the complex mental activity on our part which, according to St. Thomas, takes the place of the intellectual apprehension of the individual (p. 101). It has been already said also that he admits for every instant of conscious human life an intuition of the actual particular ego, that is of the human mind as informed by the idea of some material essence. It does not occur to him to raise the question of the speculative value of these perceptions of the ego.

knowledge. The enthusiastic efforts of the first Greek philosophers as well as the more sober attempts of Aristotle were turned exclusively towards the general. The Arabian philosophers had sensed the problem, but had found no good solution for it. Might it not be said that Christianity implied the existence of certain elements in the minds of Christian philosophers which were calculated to bring about a more exact appreciation of the particular in reality and in knowledge ? Its doctrine of Providence reaching down to the smallest insect, its respect for the most insignificant individual soul redeemed by the blood of a God, the Bible with its inculcation of ethical ideals by the example of living personalities, the mystery of the Incarnation which presents salvation as the acceptance of a Person rather than of a doctrine,[2] these were things conductive to a better appreciation of concrete knowledge. The philosophical utilisation of these new elements would have been a task not unworthy of the greatest minds. As regards St. Thomas it is well known how he looked upon the ontological aspect of the problem : his theory of the individual is his masterpiece. All that he had to do was to transfer to the plane of knowledge the same poise and balance that characterises his metaphysics, and this would have been entirely in accordance with that parallelism of reality and knowledge which he professed. As against Avicenna and many others he did succeed in establishing the rights of complex reality where the divine and angelic knowledge was concerned. When he came to human knowledge, however, he failed. The mentality of the Middle Ages was not as yet mature enough to lead science so far away from its origins ; the weight of the double tradition, Socratic and Mussulman, was too heavy, and the mystic contempt for the world of sense was not without its influence. It was a very delicate problem for this young civilisation, which as yet had not thought out its principles of art nor succeeded in transforming its life

---

[2] Or more exactly, as St. Thomas would have said, in the acceptance of a Person Who is the source and end of all doctrine. See his theory of the Word and his remarks on the judiciary power of Christ. Christ is the Man *veritate imbutus . . . unum quodammodo cum ipsa veritate, quasi quaedam lex et quaedam iustitia animata* (3 q. 59, a. 2 ad 1).

into æsthetic experience, to indicate the road along which mind was to regain the individual. It was difficult for it while remaining true to itself to engage in a very subtle renunciation which would help it to see the unfruitful character of pure abstractions in the life of man while affirming the pre-eminence of intelligence.[3]

The bringing together of knowledge and the concrete individual may be understood in different ways. One solution, that which is the most crudely intellectualist in form, would consist in holding that the individual in its particularity could be deduced by the human mind : such a view identifies the real not only with what is intelligible but with what is rational. It puts our representations of particular objects on the same plane as the abstract ideas that appear in our reasonings and imparts to them the same value. This solution is excluded by St. Thomas. Another solution consists in refusing an intellectual value not to what transcends man's intellect under the terrestrial conditions of its exercise, but to what he grasps uniquely by means of sense-faculties, that is to say, the material concrete individual. This is the solution which St. Thomas, following his masters, adopts. Finally, a third solution is possible, and it is the one that St. Thomas logically ought to have adopted. It consists in seeking in the data of sense, over which intellect presides as judge, everything that could lead to a representation and evaluation of what truly *is*.

I

The reduction of all reality to the rational is implicitly a denial of chance as well as of the intervention in the world

[3] It has been said that better-stocked libraries would have helped the Scholastics to grasp the interest of individual syntheses and of connected historical questions. But it was not really subject-matter which was lacking at all. With the Bible, the Fathers, and what they possessed of the classical authors, as well as the world in which they lived, which was the meeting-place of three civilisations, the Scholastics had enough to stimulate interest in the intelligibility of the concrete changing reality of things. What was lacking to them was the taste and aptitude for such a study. It is very remarkable that the spontaneous interests of the dawning intelligence of the children of Catholic parents are drawn to such questions as aroused the enthusiastic attention of the Scholastics, questions that have to do with the power of God, the terrestrial Paradise and the like.

of events of a true liberty of indifference. There is a twofold reason why St. Thomas could not have accepted such a solution. Chance exists. That does not mean that there is any particular effect for which human reason can assign no cause, but that there may be a coincidence of effects in the presence of which the human mind must remain silent. Hence to the extent that the concrete individual *is* and as such is determined by the simultaneous influence of many coincident factors, to the extent that actual reality is made up of many circumstances that are simply coexistent, to that extent will concrete reality elude deduction. I know, for instance, why such a man digs his field, I know why he finds therein a treasure, but I do not know why it is that *while digging his field he finds a treasure*. I know why Socrates is white and why Socrates is a musician, but I do not know what has determined the appearance at this particular point of time or space of a white musician. St. Thomas frequently recalls these examples of Aristotle in order to refute a " stoic," a " pharisaical," and Mussulman determinism which would place either all human acts or all physical phenomena under the necessary influence of the celestial bodies.[4] For him the system of various causal relations that comes under human observation is not one or unique ; there is room for many which may cross and intersect one another. Does that mean that the universe is unintelligible, or that even a single one of these eventualities is without purpose or meaning ? Emphatically not. The unity and intelligibility of the entire scheme of things lies with God, and this is true of the world of actual things as it is of the world of essences. Chance does not exist for God. In a single act God possessed a systematic view of all things, He knows all because He is the ultimate Cause of all, and it is He who unifies and harmonises the universe of things. *Nihil est a casu respectu universalis agentis, qui est causa simpliciter totius esse.* Such supreme perfection as this does not belong of course to the created intellect. Further, seeing that the contingent arrangement of the existing world depends on the free will of the Creator, even a mind who enjoyed an

[4] 3 *Contra Gentes,* 85 and 86.

intuitive vision of God and could see all the series of effects produced by Him could not deduce them from its vision of the divine essence. The divine essence cannot be regarded as a "middle term for the demonstration of contingent facts." [5]

These views ought not to cause any difficulty. The philosophy of St. Thomas may not be classified as a particular form of "panlogism." He does not suspend the universe from an axiom or axioms. For him the source and origin of things is a living Mind endowed with freedom.

II

On rational grounds, then, St. Thomas is convinced that the actual world eludes his syllogisms. Observation teaches him that it also outsteps his concepts, the object of which is the general. We have said that he saw in this disproportion between the idea and reality an imperfection inherent in the human form of intelligence.

In the case of man, as has been said, the direct intellectual knowledge of the individual is replaced by a composite apprehension. Reflecting on our acts, we unite the essence of a thing conceived with certain sensible qualities perceived and this serves to designate for us the external object.[6] What, it may be asked, is the speculative value of knowledge obtained in this way? Did St. Thomas entertain the idea that this co-operation of sense-faculties with intellect would succeed, at least under favourable conditions, in exhausting the cognitive content of the individual? And if this be denied, had he any thought of inviting us, by means of a greater co-operation of our heterogeneous faculties in an effort to obtain a more intimate grasp of the real, to seek a certain enjoyment of pure speculation in those composite images which no longer represent man in general but Callias, Peter and Martin?

The Arabian Peripatetics held that the individual was

[5] *Ver.*, 2, 12, 12.
[6] See p. 101.

radically unintelligible.   According to Avicenna the particular as such was knowable only as the effect of its cause.
The knowledge that intellect possesses of it was something
which resembled rather the astrologer's knowledge of an
eclipse obtained by means of calculations rather than that
which the peasant enjoys on looking at the sun.⁷   This is
also true of God's knowledge.   It is to be noted that such
an explanation does not touch the doctrine of providence.
When St. Thomas discusses it he attacks it on purely philosophical grounds.   On the one hand, his intellectualism
requires that nothing which has reality is out of all relation
to Mind, but, on the contrary, that Mind penetrates to the
very depths of being, laying bare and examining everything that could boast the slightest title to reality.   On the
other hand, the particular is something ineffable and is
not merely a conglomeration of universals, and therefore
the knowledge of the particular which absolute Mind
possesses is something quite different from any knowledge
of it produced by abstractions.   Granted that all the attributes that are common to an object and exclusively possessed by it are known, granted even that their co-existence
in the individual has been affirmed by mind, yet the intelligibility of the object would not be totally exhausted and
something would still remain to be known.   What is this
something ?   It is just the intellectual counterpart of what
the senses see in the object.   To see red is not the same as
knowing red : it is something more.⁸   " The knowledge of
the whole order of celestial phenomena does not impart
the knowledge of an eclipse as though actually present.
To know that such an eclipse will occur under such conditions of sun and moon and at such a particular moment of

⁷ See 1 q. 14, a. 11 and parallel passages. *Cf.* Carra de Vaux, *Avicenne*,
Paris, 1900, p. 225.
⁸ One of the reasons why knowledge of the particular is to be found in the
First Source of all knowledge is that this representation of the individual is
to be found in other cognitive faculties (the senses) (1 *Contra Gentes*, 65, 4).
More powerful and more exhaustive than any other faculty of knowledge,
the divine Mind " by a simple and unique glance perceives everything that
the human mind by means of its different faculties, intellect, sense and
imagination, comes to know (*ibid.*, 5).   For the angelic intuition of the particular see 2 *Contra Gentes*, 100.

time does not exclude the fact that there may not be recurrences of this same eclipse on different occasions." [9]

The particular essence must be here judged in the same way as a singular fact, and for that reason if I say " a white, musical, woolly son of Sophroniscus," and if I add as many other such formalities as I wish, still I shall never have exhausted all that the individual contains.[10] This conjunction of accidents remains subject to multiplication. We must admit, then, individualised matter has its own type in God which is something incommunicable and, like itself, incomplete and substantially distinct from the form which imparts being to it. We are here at the very antipodes of universalisation, and are in the presence of what may be considered the most difficult case for an idea which is at once subjectively spiritual and objectively particular. It is no rare occurrence to meet with minds accustomed to the study of Scholastic philosophy which fail to grasp the Thomistic system as something intelligible, for this very reason that their minds are under the tyranny of the intellectual habit which renders universal everything it touches. And yet the thesis we have just outlined follows necessarily once we have grasped the theses of the identity of the species and the individual in the angels and that of God's knowledge as the source and measure of all things. " The same would be true if the knowledge of the artificer of it were productive of the being of the whole thing and not merely of its form or disposition." [11] " All knowledge is the result of assimilation between knower and known : yet there is this difference,

[9] *De Anim.*, a. 20. According to St. Thomas, Avicenna and Algazel refused to believe that God knew circumstances of time (1 d. 38, q. 1, a. 3). But according to the doctrine of the saint himself it would not be sufficient to add the time-circumstance to a number of others in order to have a knowledge of the incommunicable individual as such. *Cognitis huiusmodi formis aggregatis, non cognoscitur Socrates vel Plato* (2 d. 3, q. 3, a. 3). A collection of accidents is not sufficient to mark off the individual since such a collection may be found in several subjects (*cf.* in 7 *Met.*, l. 14, 34 a). Strictly speaking, therefore, it would not be sufficient for individuation to possess, according to one of the formulæ employed by St. Thomas, *similitudines rerum etiam quantum ad dispositiones materiales individuantes* ; it would be better to add, as he does, *etiam quantum ad principia materialia*, since matter itself (and not only the accidents) possesses its own *similitudo, secundum quod omne ens, quantumcumque imperfectum, a primo ente exemplariter deductitur* (2 d., 1 c.).

[10] *De Anim.*, a. 20 ; 1 q. 14, a. 11 ; *Ver.*, 2, 5, etc.

[11] 1 q. 14, a. 11.

that in human knowledge assimilation is brought about by the action of sensible things in the human cognitive powers, whereas contrariwise in God's knowledge which arises from the action of the form of the divine intellect on things." [12] If direct intellectual knowledge, then, of the individual is impossible for the human mind, the reason for that is the receptivity which is characteristic of our knowledge. " It follows that the divine intellect can know particular things whereas the human intellect cannot." [13]

This much, then, is clear : when by reflex thought and with a word I try to cover a substantive idea such as that of man with a certain number of accidental perceptions given by the sense-world such as white or woolly or silent, such a synthesis does not help me to know the whole for which the particular Socrates stands. It may help to discern particulars in practice, to employ them in reasonings where propositions of a special form are reserved for them, but from the intellectual point of view all this is nothing more than a makeshift. Does it follow, therefore, that such a procedure is to be looked upon with contempt ? *Quod non potest fieri per unum, fiat aliqualiter per plura.* Here is an instance where this principle holds. We must see intellect as it engages in grasping as perfectly as possible the intimate harmony of individuals as it is found in art, in history and in life.

The intrinsic logic of the intellectualist position, however, had not force enough to lead St. Thomas to this issue. Authority impelled him in another direction and he allowed himself to be duped by the old ambiguity of the formula, *scientia est de universali.* For not only does he repeat the formula, which in itself would have been of no great significance if the concept of science had not been purposely restricted or at least left in a vagueness that might have prevented a hazardous meaning of the old formula, but, developing his thought, he goes to the extent of affirming that the knowledge of the particular is not to be looked upon as a perfection for the speculative human intellect. " To

[12] 1 *Contra Gentes,* 65, 8.
[13] When St. Thomas affirms that the individual is unintelligible not indeed as individual or particular but as material, he has in mind only human knowledge (*De Anim.,* 2, 5, etc.).

the perfection of the understanding belong," he says, "species, genera, and the reasons of things. . . . But to know the particular beings, their thoughts, their acts is not perfection of the created intellect nor is its natural desire turned in that direction." [14] "Because the knowledge of contingent things does not exclude that certain truth which excludes error it must be said, in regard to matters of pure speculation, that they are laid aside by mind in possession of truth." [15] It is clear that he treats particulars and contingents in the same manner, while elsewhere they are explicitly classed together and excluded from that domain of scientific certitude as belonging to that of sense. [16] Nor is the indetermination that belongs to sensible conditions the only reason for this exclusion. When there is question of the infallible knowledge of the separate substances and of their actions which may take place between them, we find observations identical with those already mentioned. [17] Finally we may refer to a curious passage of his commentary on the *Ethics* where St. Thomas declares that the study of applied or special moral theory presents only a very minor interest from the speculative point of view. [18]

It is not to be wondered at, then, that this great theorician of disinterested contemplation did not succeed in arriving at a perfectly consistent theory of art. Here and there the intellectual nature of artistic pleasure is clearly indicated, but more often poetry is conceived in a narrow and superficial manner whether it be numbered amongst the "mechanical arts" or placed amongst the means of attaining truth such as demonstration, dialectic or rhetoric, where of course it occupies the last place. [19] As for the "delightful

[14] 1 q. 12, a. 8 ad 4. *Cf.* 3 q. 11, a. 1. Certain affirmations made regarding the imperfection of universal knowledge are to be understood in regard to generic knowledge : it is necessary to reach *usque ad species* (In *Meteor.*, l. 1 *cf.* in 2 *Met.*, l. 4).

[15] In 6 *Eth.*, l. 3.

[16] In 6 *Eth.*, l. 5. *Cf.* 1 q. 2 ae, q. 57, a. 5, ad 3.

[17] *Ver.*, 9, 5, 6. *Cf.* 1 q. 107, a. 2.

[18] In 2 *Eth.*, l. 2.

[19] In 9 *Eth.*, l. 7 ; In 1 *Post.*, l. 1. The function of the poet is to stimulate thought and convince by means of a representation. But the pleasure of the representation is distinguishable from the utility of its effect (1 q. 1, a. 9 ad 1). *Cf.* 1 q. 39, a. 8 : *Videmus quod aliqua imago divitur pulchra si perfecte repraesentat rem quamvis turpem.*

visions of beautiful forms," just as for the "hearings of
sweet melodies" these are pleasures of sense knowledge :
speculative pleasures seem to be reduced to a "certain
contemplation of the true." [20]

The deep root of this slight esteem for art is a misunderstanding of the intelligible value of its object as contained
in a particular synthesis. *Album musicum non est vere ens,
neque vere unum.*[21] There is nothing stable about this conjunction of accidents, and the philosopher who believes that the
object of scientific reason is something independent of time
despises them. *Album musicum non est vere ens.* In our day
it is not difficult to sense the amount of potential irrealism
that is stored up in such words, and on the contrary all are
aware that true reality is not "man" in the abstract but
just precisely "Socrates, the white musician." *Neque
vere unum.* Unity is always the correlative of reality. The
progress of experimental and historical psychology, the
advance in literary criticism, not to speak of other sciences,
has taught us to what extent intellect is capable of discerning and re-creating that original and intimate harmony
which makes one man so profoundly different from another.
This it does because it is capable of bringing together
within its unity and of fusing the diversity of such and such
accidents. Quality does not exist apart from quantity,
figure may influence character, "climatic conditions" are
not without influencing "temperaments"; it happens that
we can cite the old example and say that where music is concerned a negro has not quite the same tastes as a white man.[22]

St. Thomas, however, is not to be judged in the light of
intellectual advances made in the last century ; his own
doctrines of Providence and of mind should have enlarged

[20] In 10 *Eth.*, l. 6. St. Thomas, however, unhesitatingly repeats that man
alone amongst the animals takes pleasure in the knowledge of sensible objects
for its own sake or (which is the same thing) for the beauty of these objects
(In 2 *Cael.*, l. 14 ; 1 q. 91, a. 3, ad 3, etc.).

[21] 1 q. 115, a. 6 ; in 11 *Met.*, l. 8, etc.

[22] Aristotle has wisely pointed out that amongst causes *per accidens* there is
a certain order to be established : συμβέβηκε τῷ ἀνδριαντοποιῷ τὸ Πολυκλείτῳ
ἶναι... ἔστι δὲ καὶ τῶν συμβεβηκότων ἄλλα ἄλλων πορρώτερον, καὶ ἐγγύτερον, οἶον
ἰ ὁ λευκὸς καὶ ὁ μουσικὸς αἴτιος λέγοιτο τοῦ ἀνδριάντος (*Phys.* B. 3). The explana-
ions given on this point by St. Thomas do not go beyond ordinary common
sense (1, 2 *Phys.*, l. 6 ; In 5 *Met.*, l. 2).

his logic.   Aristotle removed individual accidents from the
intelligibility of the world by excluding them from the
order of finality.   It is matter for astonishment that St.
Thomas admits these same exclusions : " We can speak of
final causes," he says, " when we are dealing with properties
that always follow the species.   The same cannot be said
of individual accidents which must be explained either by
having recourse to matter or to the agent." [23]   Elsewhere,
returning to the same thought of the Philosopher he links
it up with another dogma of peripatetic philosophy which
holds the subordination in the order of finality of the individual to the species.[24]

Here, doubtless, his Christian faith prevents him from
going the whole way with Aristotle.   Where his Master
spoke of an " intention of nature " which aims only at the
permanence of the species and abandons individual accidents to chance, Providence, according to St. Thomas,
must intervene and the knowledge of God must determine
everything.   But if he agrees that the divine idea is the proto-
type of the individual, he regards this as something secondary
and subordinate : the primary object of the divine idea is
the nature or specific essence.   This essence is something
more perfect and richer than the indetermined generic
essence and at the same time it is of greater being-value
than individual reality : it overcomes in itself the twofold
imperfection of matter and of the genus.   St. Thomas is
advancing here a metaphysical reason to which he sometimes adds another taken from the constant flux of individuals
as compared with the permanence which mind demands as
the " end of nature " : the individual passes away while
nature remains, and hence it is the species which is " willed
for itself."   If it were Socrates that nature primarily intended,

---

[23] In 2 An., l. 1 ; De Anim., 18. Cf. Aristotle, De gen. anim., 5, 1 (778 a. 30),
and elsewhere. It is obvious that another kind of science of what is accidental
may be conceived, a science which would treat of it in general and which would
find its place in the old logic and metaphysic. Δεκτέον ἔτι περὶ τοῦ συμβεβηκότος
ἐφ᾽ ὅσον ἐνδέχεται (Met., Ε. 2) and St. Thomas : Ratio huius quod est esse per
accidens, per aliquam scientiam considerari potest (In 6 Met., l. 2 ; also 4 d. 34, q. 1,
a. 1 ad 9).
[24] Ver., 3, 8.

then with the passing away of Socrates the end of nature would be defeated.[25] And this last reason seems to gain weight from the fact that in species where this does not hold as in the case of immortals and of the heavenly bodies, the general theory must yield : when individuals are incorruptible " they themselves become part of the principal end of nature." [26]

So strong a breach in the doctrine shows that it was not perfectly consistent with the rest of his system. To tell the truth, I think that ultimately he would have to renounce completely this Aristotelian idol. To maintain it would have meant going against his integral intellectualism, calling in question the identity of the real and the intelligible, and doubting the penetration of mechanism by finality. Fundamentally " the intention of nature " is always an ambiguous formula with St. Thomas. For what indeed is this nature ? In merely animal procreation it is not the animal's intention which counts but his pleasure. In human generation human intentions are as variable as the human will is changeable. Further, by what right can it be affirmed that the intention of a simple individual cannot fail of its end. If there is question of God, then it is false to say that His intention stops short at man in general and does not reach the individual Socrates. *Praedictum Providentiae ordinem in singularibus ponimus, etiam in quantum singularia sunt.*[27] Everything is much more clear and coherent and more satisfying for mind, which is the sense of the intelligibility of the world, if while affirming the intelligibility of each individual synthesis—this bird or rose or negro or white man—we maintain at the same time that this finality which lies hidden in the bosom of God, for whom it is identical with the finality of the species, must remain unknown for us, that God has reserved unto Himself to know the real depths of each individual while man must be satisfied to set out in quest of this garden enclosed by the two routes of art and history, which go on approaching each other

---

[25] *Ver., loc. cit.* ; *Quodl.*, 8, 2. *Cf.* 2 *Contra Gentes*, 45, 5 : *Bonitas speciei excedit bonitatem individui, sicut formale id quod est materiale.*

[26] 3 *Contra Gentes*, 93, 6 ; 1 q. 98, a. 1. *Cf. Ver.*, 5, 5.

[27] *Ver.*, 5, 4.

without ever reaching that point where they become one. In the light of these conclusions we see that the doctrine of St. Thomas avoids being a " panlogism " and must be reckoned for what it really is, a kind of " panæstheticism." Otherwise, it admits, with a concession to the Arab mind, an infidelity to its first principle, and on one point at least treats discursive reason as if it were intelligence as such [28] which is, in the eyes of St. Thomas, the $\pi\rho\hat{\omega}\tau o\nu$ $\psi\epsilon\hat{v}\delta os$ of rationalism.

Besides, on Thomistic principles the explanation of the value and imperfection of those complex acts which aim at an understanding of the individual do not present any insuperable difficulty.

Granted that the individual is an example of true reality, it is only natural that its perception should make us feel the presence of the non-self in a manner which is more conscious and more perfect than that given by any other intellectual operation. The experience that is given by art and by life especially is in agreement with the theory when, thanks to the artist or some incomparable poet, a dis-interested memory, the harmony of a concrete human individuality, or an instant of human perception resuscitated in its total complexity, charms and almost overpowers us. Such an enjoyment is as intense and as pleasurable as that given by any generalisation, and its practical utility is far greater.

On the other hand, reflection will convince us that in such precious instances of enjoyment our intellects are not fully satisfied. There is a feeling of instability and of change which disturbs the mind. Accustomed to rational theorems which are so satisfying in their own order, the human mind would wish to find in its artistic experiences the same clarity and stability that it finds in the contemplation of rational principles. To do this it would try in vain to

[28] On last analysis it is because his principles excluded the individual in its complexity from demonstrative *science* that St. Thomas places it beyond the pale of speculation. In *Met.*, l. 8, 160 b ; *cf.* 3 *Contra Gentes*, 86. He seems to have here confounded the value of pure speculation with the certitude of affirmation (*cf.* In 6 *Eth.*, l. 3 cited above, p. 119). In this he was not faithful to the principles given in his critique of the judgment : the simple affirmation of an existence has no speculative value.

stabilise what is essentially changing and to clarify what is obscure. This would be to deny itself, and if it ceases to be itself in such concrete experiences, there is every danger that it will slip down the slope that would reduce it from the rank of intellect to that of mere sense. It does seem that intellectual perfection depends on two elements that the human mind cannot fully unify.

All this is in agreement with Thomistic principles. As long as there is question of the perception of the individual *by man* it is Avicenna who is right. St. Thomas agrees with him that we have only the mere semblances of intuitions, that we do not grasp the individual in its particularity but that we conceive separately the essence and each of its determinations that go to form its concrete reality. This counterfeited idea is simply a rapid reflection which in virtue of the unity of the thinking subject brings together the sense seized by intellect and that which the senses have been able to obtain from its phenomenal manifestations.[29] In this there is an imitation of intelligible fusion and coincidence, but the real thing is not present. For that and to be fully intelligent it would be necessary to be able to perceive the *esse* as it is, that is, as actuating the essence. It would be necessary to be like the angel who in one comprehensive idea of the species is able to perceive the temporal unfolding of the individuals that it contains. Here we have the true handling of the *self*, where each thing is " known as it is in act " and where " the actuality of the object is its light." [30]

We do not enjoy this prerogative of intuitive intellects, but in our own way we can imitate it. For that we shall have to allow for our potential intellectuality and the necessity for recourse to a multiplicity of faculties : the elements of time and space become essential to our mental functioning. To arrive at these conclusions it was not necessary to add anything to St. Thomas ; it was sufficient to bring together some of his favourite affirmations. St. Thomas

[29] See p. 98.
[30] In *Caus.*, l. 6, 531 a. *Unumquodque cognoscitur per id quod est in actu ; et ideo ipsa actualitas rei est quoddam lumen ipsius.*

himself did not make this *rapprochement*, which is not surprising. But the explicit exclusion of all thought which has not to do with judgment of essence or the formation of abstract concepts from the domain of pure speculation authorises us to say that he has not followed out his principles, and that in this instance he was not sufficiently intellectualist to be here accounted an exaggerated upholder of discursive reasoning (*ratio*).

III

The *ratio* itself, that is intellect when engaged in discursive reasoning and in comparisons, suffers from this absolute pre-eminence that is ascribed to the quidditative concept. Once the general conditions that determine the general idea have been arrived at, it seems to be the destiny of mind to cease functioning abruptly. Once a knowledge of the fixed essence has been acquired, a gulf opens which limits the domain of pure speculation on the one hand and discloses on the other an abyss of the irrational and the haphazard. Order reigns in the harmonious series of essence ; there is order even in the revolutions of the celestial bodies ; but within each species, in our sublunary world, there are only accidental successions which have no interest for mind.[31] The reason for this static conception of the intelligible world is not far to seek. It is not to be found in a species of Eleatic monism which denies the reality of change, nor yet in a scepticism which declares change to be inaccessible to the human mind. "Nothing," says St. Thomas, "excludes the possibility of a stable knowledge of things that are subject to change."[32] The text of his Commentary on the *Physics* opens with the proclamation of Aristotle : " Not to take account of movement is to ignore

[31] 1 *Spir.*, 8. *Perfectius participant ordinem ea in quibus est ordo non per accidens tantum. Manifestum est autem quod in omnibus individuis unius speciei non est ordo nisi secundum accidens . . . differunt . . . secundum principia individuantia, et diversa accidentia, quae per accidens se habent ad naturam speciei. Quae autem specie differunt ordinem habent per se . . . In istis . . . inferioribus, quae sunt generabilia et corruptibilia, et infima pars universi, et minus participant de ordine . . . quaedam habent ordinem per accidens tantum, sicut individua unius speciei.*

[32] 1 q. 24, a. 1 ad 3.

nature." [33] He is well aware that everything here below is subject to change and fluctuation : *dicitur autem creatura fluvius, quia fluit semper de esse ad non esse per corruptionem, et de non esse ad esse per generationem.* [34] And this *Physics* itself is nothing else but a general philosophy of becoming.[35] If, then, he is more interested in things that endure than in the turmoil of the evolving universe, in ideas and eternal essences rather than in their contingent participations, the reason must be sought in his esteem and love for the world of immaterial things where the subsistent intelligibles are to be found.   It is there that truth principally resides and it is towards this horizon that what he calls the " gaze of the mind " will be turned.[36]

The modern mind, guided by the idea of development, and in so far as it retains the idea of species, claims that it finds within the species a certain intelligible succession, a rhythm of causes and effects which link up individuals and groups of individuals together.   This method has justified itself by brilliant results both in the domain of natural and human history.   Is this introduction of the intelligible into the sphere of things dynamic in conformity with, or opposed to, the principles of Thomism ?   Just as the individual is intelligible by its harmony, might it not be said that the continuity of the species in time would also render it intelligible ?   This question which is closely related to the previous one requires a similar answer in both cases.

It must be first noted that if we reply in the affirmative there can be no question on Thomistic principles of an exhaustive comprehension in either case.   The question here has to do with mind considered as *ratio*, and if it appears to approximate to the use of mind as *intellectus* in the measure in which the complexity of its object brings it close to the conditions of reality, still its rôle is to unite in one idea

---

[33] In 3 *Phys.*, l. i.   *Ignorato motu, ignoratur natura.*
[34] *Sermones festivi*, 61.
[35] The object of which is *ens mobile simpliciter.*
[36] 3 *Contra Gentes*, 75, 7 : *Cognitio speculativa et ea quae ad ipsam pertinent perficiuntur in universali ; ea vero quae pertinent ad cognitionem practicam perficiuntur in particulari ; nam finis speculativae est veritas, quae primo et per se et in immaterialibus consistit et in universalibus . . .*

things that are only roughly similar, granting that it strives to accomplish this as perfectly as possible. In view of this, can it be said that St. Thomas could find a place for such a rational operation ?

If we are careful not to allow our own preoccupations to obscure his thought we shall, I think, be obliged to admit it. It is very rare that an idea of this kind as entertained by St. Thomas goes beyond what ordinary common sense can furnish, in presence of the regular development of things, to a rather primitive reflection.[37] Besides, once we look to the really important theses, what may be called the most " architectonic " point of his finalist intellectualism, and not merely unimportant phrases of his, we shall be forced to admit that these tenets imply the idea of an intelligible and constant differentiation at the very heart of the species itself.

Let us suppose that we admit the theory discussed in a previous paragraph of the subordination of the individual to the species. It does not follow that by this admission we are forced to limit the domain of intelligibility to the species. The finality contained in the individual, it is true, is hidden from us. But there is another kind of causality which contains within itself intelligibility : we refer to the formal or quasi-formal cause. Did matter merely receive the form and uphold it, without in any way affecting or modifying it, then material multiplication would have no meaning whatever, and the idea of knowing the individual for the mere pleasure of it would be entirely vain. In this instance individual matter would imply nothing more than common matter. This twofold assertion is verified in the celestial bodies. If, on the contrary, matter according to its pre-existing dispositions in quantity and quality restricts and limits the virtualities that are contained in the form, if

[37] His theory of the " development of dogma " may be urged as an objection to this. But that really is an instance of positive indications that have not been systematised. These indications further are limited to the period covered by the Old Testament. " Everything invites us," it will be said, " to extend such observations to the New Testament." Assuredly everything invites *us* since Newman and the Council of the Vatican, but the question to be settled is if St. Thomas heard such an invitation and whether he would have considered it well to accept it (see 2a, 2ae, q. 1, a. 7 ; 3 q. 1, a. 5 ad 3, etc.).

when it unites with the form to constitute an individual it is
not confined to the mere production of an individual (an
aliquid) in the sense of *ens ratum in natura*, but an individual
in the sense of a *hoc aliquid*, which within the limits of the
species differs by certain qualities from another example of
the same nature (*illud*), then as a consequence and in virtue
of matter itself (which, as we know, for man is unintelligible)
an element has entered the world which is accessible to
our minds because it is conceived as subject to multiplication and which represents an intelligible value because of
its union with something different from itself. It follows
that the comparison of the *hocs* and the *illuds* within the
domain of the same species is not something which is totally
incapable of contributing to the perfection of the human
mind.

Everything in the philosophy of St. Thomas, we may say,
points to these differences of the *hocs* and the *illuds*, and the
qualitative multiplicity of what by nature is one and the
same as something which, if not a fact, is at least a postulate.

We have already seen what St. Thomas regarded as the
ultimate end of all creation. This final end is beauty which
may be identified with intelligibility because it is the likeness of creation to God and the representation by creatures
of the divine perfection. The universe, then, assumes the
proportions of a work of art which is the pleasure and the
delight of the divine creative mind. St. Thomas himself
concludes that merely material multiplication cannot as
such be an end wnich regulates the order of things. And
from this it may be inferred that such a phenomenon is
not to be met with in the world. " No agent proposes mere
material plurality as an end to be achieved because such a
plurality is indetermined essentially and tends to go on
indefinitely." [38] And if we take tnings that are absolutely

---

[38] I q. 47, a. 3 ad 2 : *Nulium agens intendit pluraiitatem materialem ut finem,
quia materialis multitudo non habet certum terminum, sed de se tendit in infinitum.*
The reason here given is a *sign* which indicates that the quality of the end is
not reconcilable with plurality as such. *Cf. ibid.,* a. 2 : *Distinctio materialis
est propter formalem.* Logically it will be also seen that the " necessity of permanence " as a reason for plurality in material essences is neither ultimate nor
exclusive : time ought not to be reduced to a category devoid of the elements
of intelligibility.

alike why should there be two rather than one ? *Eadem ratione . . . tres : et sic in infinitum.* Suppose we postulate an eternal recommencement of things, then the world would be devoid of meaning, seeing that movement is not in itself an end, and this would be tantamount to saying that the universe would be devoid of beauty. St. Thomas is of opinion that there is only one world : " If God were to make other worlds, then they should be either similar to the present one or unlike it. If He made them all alike, then they would be without meaning (*essent frustra*) and this is not in accordance with divine wisdom." [39]

In the foregoing we have a first reason for supposing the absence of mere material multiplication from creation which is the reflection of divine perfection. If two worlds could not be alike why should two tigers, or two butterflies, or two amœbæ be so ? To risk an *oportet* on such *rationes convenientiae* would not at all have been opposed to the intellectual habits of St. Thomas.[40] But there is another and a more proximate reason. If the form is to be considered as act relatively to the matter, the individual substance may be also looked upon as act and determination with regard to the specific essence. " Relatively to the individual the nature of the species is indeterminate, just as the genus is in relation to the species." [41] Nature is the source of the essential energies in the individual, but the individual is more comprehensive and complete than the essence. " In all beings the common element in them is the more intense, but there is more actuality in that which is proper to each. It is the perfection of that which is common to all to extend to what is peculiar to each, just as the genus is perfected by the addition of the specific difference." [42] Where the angels are concerned there is a coincidence of the common element and the specific difference because of their simplicity of nature. But this is not so in the case of terrestrial essences. The latter are of more extended potentiality, and it is impossible to conceive the simultaneous actuation of all

[39] In 1 *Cael.*, l. 19 end.
[40] See Ch. 5.
[41] *Opusc.*, 22, ch. 2.
[42] 3 d. 30, q. 1, a. 2.

possible determinations in one particular subject or even their successive actuation. That is a further reason for material multiplication, and this carries with it the necessity for diversity also. " Every individual in the case of natural things as we know them here below is imperfect since no one of them is capable of exhausting all the attributes of the species." [43] " Where inferior things are concerned we see that the same nature comprises several individuals. The reason of this is . . . the incapacity of any individual to show forth all the perfection that is contained in the nature as a principle of activity, and this is particularly manifest in the case of men where there is a mutual co-operation in their activities." [44]

With the perception of qualitative differences the intellect has attained its object. Even when it finds them scattered about and is forced to gather them from here and there it does not cease to be interested in such differences. In its perception of individuals it does not cease to be rational, and because the foundation of the rational is to be found in things, seeing that a similitude is a " real relation," it is natural to conceive that the perception of causal connections, and the comparison of similarities and dissimilarities as well of co-existences and successions, will be more satisfying for

[43] In 1 Cael., l. 19 end. Cf. also Opusc., 14, ch. 10, where many of the ideas here indicated will be found as well as the following precise affirmation : In his vero quae materialiter differunt, eamdem formam habentibus nihil prohibet aequalitatem inveniri.

[44] In 2 Cael., l. 16. When we saw that there is a greater amount of potentiality in men we did not mean to suggest that man enjoys less perfection than the brute. The reason of this greater potentiality is the fact that, being endowed with intellect, there is more room to modify his sense-organism and to adapt himself to different ends. Since he is a more complex being than the ant or the beaver, man is also capable of a greater specialisation of activity than such lower organisms. The " perfect specific activity " which is the end of the species requires in the case of man that one be cobbler, another king and so forth for the greater good of humanity. Man in the abstract, that Platonic monster, does not exist, but it may be said that society as a whole tends to represent this abstract man by the multiplicity and diversity of human types (cf. Opusc., 16, l. 1). The angel, on the other hand, contains within its limpid unity all the perfection represented by its essence, and therefore its activity is essentially specific. Somewhat like those instinctive beings, the bee and the eagle, the angel is ever ready, an intelligent being that is quite actualised intellectually and infallible. But in the case of the angel this unity is a unity of perfection while in the case of the brute it is a unity of imperfection : man occupies in virtue of his potentiality a middle place. In this we can recognise those principles of the In 2 Cael., l. 18 already frequently cited.

intellect and helps it in its effort to know the real. Suppose, for instance, that the racial connection of individuals is made the basis for an intelligible connection—and this idea would be accepted by St. Thomas either as an extension of the Dionysian concept of continuity or as a simple consequence of his theory of generation [45]—then, this arrangement being rational, each being would suggest by its own intelligibility a preliminary idea, as it were, of the individuality of its neighbour, and the general *ensemble* of accidents grouped about a common notion would help to enlarge the common idea while at the same time replacing it.   Now if it were possible to perceive all these rhythms within the species, if what floats before the mind as the mirage of an ideal were to become actual scientific knowledge, and if it were possible to follow the ordered trace of harmonious development (*explicatio*, in the terminology of St. Thomas) of all the determinations of the essence through its many types which represent and limit it at one and the same time, then in this panorama of a vast but vigorous unity, with its ordered undulations that go in all directions, we should have an image in miniature of the divine Idea, or better still a shadow of those angelic ideas which reveal the immense number of individuals that belong to a nature and constitute it.   In the idea of an ox, for example, would be arranged the big the little, the white the black, the red and all intermediate and mixed, and similarly for all other possible qualities.

In possession of such a humanly perfect knowledge we should resemble the least of the angels who perceive the individuals in their species (*specialissime*).   But it is important to note that even then an immeasurable distance would separate our knowledge from that of the angel. The sensible origin of all this knowledge of ours would prevent its being anything other than a patchwork of corresponding pieces, and as a consequence a system of abstractions, not of intuitions.   Inevitably we would conceive, before the reflex judgment of correction, each determination and individual synthesis as something communicable. So that we should still remain what we truly are, the lowest of created intelli-

---

[45] See *Pot.*, 3, 9, 7 ; *cf. Mal.*, 4, 8.

gences. There would simply be on the part of the *ratio* a cleverer and a more refined imitation of intellectual activity in its higher forms.

The very danger of self-deception and of believing we have reached intuition when we have merely pushed analysis, which is its very negation, to its limit, prevents us from regretting those rather absolute declarations of St. Thomas on the speculative value of anything that is not the quidditative concept. The important point to bear in mind, once we have seen the possessive perfection of intellect as expounded in Part I, is that the intuition of real external being in its individuality is wanting to human knowledge. St. Thomas was aware of this. Many who came after him failed to see the essential difference between intuition and discursive reasoning because they had no proper grasp of what is meant by intellectual possession of reality. These same Scholastics attributed discursive reasoning to the angels, and at the same time held that man had an intellectual intuition of the individual. This levelling of intelligence in its purity to the plane of intelligence in its discursive form was responsible for upsetting all philosophy and revealing mere puerilities where formerly there were depths. It suffices to have grasped the internal logic of the Scotist system to realise that once intellectualism has become " anthropocentric " it has also become self-contradictory.

CHAPTER IV

I

AFTER the process of intellectual knowledge in its purity St. Thomas considers human science as the best that our human speculations can offer in the form of knowledge. Science is for him at once universal and deductive, and it represents the specific perfection of the human intellect in its discursive form as *ratio*. Though this rational systematisation cannot be said to be of the same order of excellence as pure intuition, yet in the general philosophy of St. Thomas it occupies considerably greater space. Of that there can be no doubt. We pass on, therefore, immediately to the examination of rational science as the second substitute which we possess for knowledge by means of the intuitive idea. We shall see what St. Thomas expects from science, and what, consistently with his principles, he had a right to hope for from it as an instrument of pure speculation.

Science properly so called, in St. Thomas's view, may be defined as an intelligible, an autonomous system whose unity is due to the principle of deduction, and which is made up of a number of propositions logically subordinate one to another, these propositions descending from more general principles, by a process of increasing contraction, down to the laws which determine *specialissime* the proper characteristics of each species. The expression of truth in the form of propositions as well as the general form of the laws in question is an essential element in his conception of science. Further, if the whole in question is to form an intelligible system it is necessary that the different propositions be unified in virtue of a common principle. Seeing that the system as a whole belongs to the order of representation and that the ontological connection of things both among themselves and in God is hidden from the human mind, it follows that this unifying principle must belong at one and the same time to mind and to things ; it is consequently an abstract principle. For this very reason, as has already been stated, the approach to an intellectual conception of the entire universe which is opened up by science is necessarily blocked : what science can at the most furnish as a mental equivalent of reality is a logical skeleton of the scheme of things.

What, then, is that light which pervades our different judgments on any group of objects and gives them, as a whole, that appearance of the angelic idea ? What is the unifying principle of science ? St. Thomas replies that it is the principle of deduction. Applicable to all abstract ideas, including even that of being, this principle is capable of unifying all kinds of knowledge. It serves as a bond of unity not only for different propositions concerning one and the same object, but even for different systems of ideas that have to do with the most diverse objects. He rejected, as we have seen, the idea of a deduction of all being down to its concrete and particular embodiments. Here, however, he seems to entertain the idea of a deduction of all the laws that appertain to them. On the one hand, all reality that is knowable by reason must find a place in the ideal system of science.[1] Yet, on the other hand, in such an ideal system there is no legitimate, definitive, or official place except for such knowledge as can be obtained by a demonstrative deduction. The sciences enjoy their title to the name science in virtue of a syllogistic subordination to certain common correlative first principles upon which all depends, and it is in that way that they acquire, besides their absolute certitude, their value as instruments of speculation. That, in fact, is the purport of his theory of the " subalternation " of the sciences, that is, of their essential dependence among themselves and of all of them ultimately to metaphysics. Each subaltern science receives its principles from that science immediately above it. The physicist receives his principles

[1] Cf. In Politic. Prol. Omnium enim quae ratione cognosci possunt, necesse est aliquam doctrinam tradi ad perfectionem humanae sapientiae quae philosophia vocatur.

from the metaphysician, and he, in his turn, hands on to the botanist those principles that furnish a basis for the science of botany. Likewise, arithmetic which is itself subject to " first philosophy " brings under it music and botany, and the same is true of the other sciences.[2] Formal subordination holds between a subaltern science and its ruling science.[3] With such a conception of the sciences it is not difficult to see that the ideal Science, so vast and complete in its aspirations, transcends the capacities of the individual : no one human mind could hope to grasp it. As for the man engaged in some subaltern science, it must be said of him that, in his isolated position, he is rather a " believer " than a " knower." [4] There can be little doubt, judging by the frequency with which he returns to it, and the many allusions he makes to it, that this theory of subalternation was fundamental and incontestable in the eyes of St. Thomas. He gives us a rather peculiar exposition of his views in a lesson which he devotes to the question of the general division of natural philosophy. " Since the universal is that which is the most removed from matter," he argues, " the method of progress in natural science must be, as Aristotle pointed out, in the First Book of the *Physics*, from the more general to the less general. True to this principle he sets out in this science from certain general notions that are common to all natural beings, such as movement and the principles of movement. He then goes on, by way of application of principles and in a more concrete manner, to consider certain particular beings and the different moments that are characteristic of them, and these are again considered after the same method." Then, giving the results obtained by Aristotle, he shows that having first treated of soul in general, Aristotle proceeds to the con-

---

[2] In *Trin.*, 2, 2 ad 5, ad 7, etc.

[3] *Ille qui habet scientiam subalternatam non perfecte attingit ad rationem sciendi, nisi in quantum ejus cognitio continuatur quodammodo cum cognitione ejus qui habet scientiam subalternantem* (*Ver.*, 14, 9, 3).

[4] *Si autem aliquis alicui proponat ea quae in principiis per se notis non includuntur, vel includi non manifestantur, non faciet in eo scientim, sed forte opinio vel fidem* (*Ver.*, 11, 1). *Cf.* principles given in *Ver.*, 12, 1 and relate them to In 1 *Met.*, l. 1 : *Et si ea quae experimento cognoscint aliis tradunt, non recipientur per modum scientiae, sed per modum opinionis vel credulitatis.*

sideration of more concrete elements, and that " finally he goes on to examine each of the animal and vegetable species and determines what is characteristic of each." [5]   The final words, *determinando quid sit proprium unicuique speciei*, leave no doubt as to the direction of his thought.   St. Thomas supposes here that by some reasoned observation which runs side by side with science the scientist has obtained a " quidditative " definition.   Thanks to that, the scientist may hope to elongate the series of his inferences so that his final deduction will be characteristic of the ideal syllogism, the aim of which is to conclude from the definition given to a particular " property " [6] (just as from man as rational animal it is possible to conclude to man as a social being or as a being capable of laughter).

To doubt that this conception of the formal subordination of the sciences was that of St. Thomas would be to question one of the first principles of his epistemology, which says that certitude being a specific element in science there is increasing incertitude with a growing complexity of conditions. " The greater the number of particular conditions that are taken into consideration, the greater will be the possibility of error." [7]   This axiom harmonises with the principle which declares principles to be " more certain " than conclusions.   It follows not only that the simpler the object of knowledge is the greater is the degree of certainty possible, but also, seeing that all affirmations have a common basis

---

[5] In *Sens et sens.*, l. 1. *Cf.* Prologue to *de Caelo* : *In scientiis esse processum ordinatum, prout proceditur a primis causis et principiis usque ad proximas causas, quae sunt elementa constituentia essentiam rei.*   *Cf.* Aristotle, *De generatione et corruptione*, B. 9. Ρᾷον γὰρ οὕτω τὰ χαθ'ἕχαστον Θεωρῆσομεν, ὅταν περὶ τοῦ χαθόιου. St. Thomas adds to the explanation of these words (In 2 *Gen.*, l. 9) : *Discursus enim ab universalibus ad particularia est maior et universalior via in natura.*   To understand the sense of the word *concretio* as employed in the commentary on *de Sensu, cf.* those passages where *componere* is opposed to *resolvere* (for example, In *Trin.*, 6,1,3, where the words *resolvendo autem, quando e converso* must be expunged as a glossary). *Concretio* means the addition of more particular determinations by means of the definition of essences which are less abstract.   As an example of *a priori* deduction applied to natural sciences see In 1 *Cael.*, l. 4 (demonstration taken from Aristotle).

[6] In 1 *Post.*, l. 1, 1, 30 ; *Ver.*, 2, 7 ; *cf.* ad 5 ; In 2 *Post.*, l. 19 (285 b) : *Medium est definitio maioris extremitatis.   Et inde est quod omnes scientiae fiunt per definitiones.* For the function of definition in science see also 3 *Contra Gentes*, 56, 4.

[7] 1a, 2ae, q. 94, a. 4.

and that science ought to be unified knowledge, that all certitude which has for object something complex enjoys merely a borrowed certitude. " Those sciences that are superimposed on others (*quae dicuntur ex additione ad alias*) enjoy a lesser degree of certitude than those sciences which deal with fewer elements : thus arithmetic is more certain than geometry . . . so also that science which has for object, being, is the most certain of all since it is the most universal." [8] It is absolutely necessary to have a science " better known than all the others," a science that " ranks above all the others." Such a science is to be had in metaphysics, which is in a position to " prove all things and the truth of which cannot be established by any antecedent science." [9] Undoubtedly, St. Thomas is not so unfaithful to his rational psychology to the extent of forgetting that a distinction has to be made between objective certainty and subjective certitude. On the contrary, in one of his final works, where he emphasises the great certitude of mathematical theorems owing to the presence of images which serve to support the mind in its reasonings, he seems to reduce the value of judgments in metaphysics to the rank of " opinions." [10] His own practice, however, shows clearly that the theory of the sciences we have just given is the true one. The problems which he declares obscure belong to special metaphysics [11] ; as regards general metaphysics he believes it possible to find an absolutely certain basis for its principles. I do not now speak merely of those principles that are at the basis of logic, as for instance the principles of contradiction and identity ; I speak of those scholastic principles that have to do with ideas most remote from vulgar experience, principles that deal with the remote objects of philosophic abstraction and which are " common principles " or " analogical principles of all being," as

[8] In 1 *Met.*, l. 2.
[9] In 1 *Post.*, l. 17. *Cf.* 3 *Contra Gentes*, 25, where he says that all the speculative sciences receive their principles from metaphysics.
[10] In *Trin.*, 6, 1.
[11] There is no distinct human science having for object the separate substances (In 7 *Met.*, l. 15), nor have we a " natural theology " as distinct from general metaphysics (In *Trin.*, 5, 4, 538 a). For the limitations of our natural knowledge of God see p. 154.

Aristotle would have said. These principles concern being and substance, potency and act and they can be reached by a consideration of " effects." Though in themselves they are absolutely certain,[12] yet for the uninitiated they present considerable difficulty and obscurity. For the scientific mind it is such principles which are at the basis of everything, principles that " prove everything, and which nothing else can prove." The clarity that belongs to mathematics is not something more intense, rather is it something spread out uniformly over a greater number of objects. As regards the subordination of the other sciences, there is no difficulty. Uncertainty grows according as mind moves away from the general principles of ontology. The object of Physics is already more complex because its object

---

[12] In *Trin.*, 5, 4. The practice of St. Thomas, we hold, corroborates our view. Examine his proofs, for example, of the existence of God and it will be found that he declares these philosophic proofs " irrefragable " (*Ver.*, 10, 12 ; *cf.* 1 q. 32, a. 1 ad 2), notice the underlying principles of the celebrated " five ways " (1 q. 2 ad 3), which are of an abstract form and may seem philosophically very disputable. St. Thomas is never so victoriously certain of thesis than when he can introduce the abstract conception of *form*. See for instance, his judgment on the Averroistic doctrine of the unity of the *intellectus possibilis* (*De Anim.*, 3 ; *Spir.*, 9) or on the doctrine of the forms of the elements (*De Anim.*, 9, 10), or that of the celestial bodies (In 8 *Phts.*, l. 21). Likewise, his rigorous demonstration (*necesse est omnino*) of the immortality of the human soul is based on the same conception : *esse* cannot be separated from a form in which it inheres *sicut ab homine non* " *removetur quod sit animal, neque a numero quod sit par vel impar* " (*De Anim.*, 14). Here we are in presence of the *a priori* reason for incorruptibility, and that is followed by two signs or indices : the capacity for intellectual knowledge of the universal, and the natural desire for continued existence. A micrographical study of the uniqueness of the individual in the angelic species also brings out the fact that here he intends to deduce this characteristic of angelic nature as a rigorous geometrical consequence from the concept of form and not, as some have held, who base their contention on isolated texts, a mere *convenientia*. And all these strong affirmations take on a bold relief when compared with his hesitancy and shades of doubt according as he comes near to experience in dealing with subjects that are more complex and therefore more obscure, as when he treats of theses in psychology. Take the fundamental thesis on the origin of ideas : there is always a suspicion of doubt, as it were, regarding his accepted position, that of Aristotle ; just as a shadow of probability always seems to linger regarding what he puts forward as the doctrine of Plato. *Verius esse videtur*, says St. Thomas (2a, 2ae, q. 172, a. 1), or *Secundum Aristotelis sententiam, quam magis experimur* (1 q. 88, a. 1), or yet *Prae omnibus praedictis positionibus rationabilior videtur sententia Philosophi* (*Ver.*, 10, 6). *Cf.* the theoretical texts on the difficulty of rational psychology (*Ver.*, 8, 10, 8 and elsewhere). Still more evasive does the object of knowledge become according as we approach objects that are still more near us because their being is itself imperfect. *Illa quae habent esse deficiens et imperfectum, sunt secundum se ipsa parum cogniscibilia, ut materia, motus et tempus propter esse eorum imperfectionem.* In 2 *Met.*, l. 1.

is linked up with movement, and accordingly it is more " uncertain." There cannot be the same adjustment of its laws to reality ; they hold true "in a majority of cases," and they must be said to be " contingent " because of the possible exceptions to them.[13] Then we have the human sciences, the science of morals and politics,[14] and finally those sciences dealing with forms of activity " which are the most uncertain because it is necessary to take into account the many circumstances that govern the production of particular things." [15] The conclusion is evident : when St. Thomas declares those very things which in another place he recognises as *notiora nobis* as the most uncertain, it is clear that for him the method of science is just the inverse of that progressive knowledge which commences in sense, and that the whole stability of science rests on principles that are abstract and of a general nature. The science of metaphysics is the one which in point of time is studied last,[16] and yet it is the science which " establishes " the other sciences.

This way of viewing the matter finds confirmation in the Saint's theory of " demonstration." It is his views on demonstration that determine for him his concept of

[13] That is to say that because of accidental and unforeseen arrangements of things, or because of " indisposition of matter," there may happen to be monsters, as, for instance, men with six fingers or germs that do not fructify. This " contingency " in no way implies the presence of liberty (see 1 q. 115, a. 6) and the comparison with moral sciences (*e.g.*, 1a, 2ae, q. 96, a. 1 ad 3) has to do merely with results. It is not without design that I speak of " laws," for though admitting with M. von Tessen-Wesierski (*Die Grundlagen des Wunderbegriffes nach Thomas von Aquin*, p. 107) that the word "law" does not occur in St. Thomas, yet we must hold that the concept corresponding to it is to be found in his works since he discusses the value of propositions which express an *essential* connection between *distinct* phenomena (see, for example, 3 *Contra Gentes*, 86, and *cf.* the expression itself, *Verum ut in pluribus*, 1a, 2ae, 1 c).

[14] The employment of reasons that are only probable belongs to the moral sciences (In *Trin.*, q. 6, a 1 ad 3, 1st series ; *cf.* c.) History on the conception of St. Thomas does not rank as science since it does not allow of deduction of its facts. Though very doubtful about knowledge due to testimony (*Quantacumque multitudo testium determinaretur, posset quandoque testimonium esse iniquum.* 2a, 2ae, q. 77, a. 2 ad 1 ; *cf. ibid. corp.* and ad 3 ; 1a, 2ae, q. 105, a. 2 ad 8, etc.), St. Thomas nevertheless admits that it is possible to obtain certitude regarding an historical fact (see the function of history in the *præambula* to faith, 1 *Contra Gentes*, 6, and *Opusc.*, 2, *Ad Cantorem Antiochenum*, ch. 7).

[15] In 1 *Met.*, l. 2 ; *cf.* In *Trin.*, 6, 1 (542 b, *multo plus*).
[16] In 1 *Met.*, l. 2.

science.[17] It is true that there is a twofold kind of demonstration, one perfect and the other imperfect. Perfect demonstration sets out from principles that are " true, primary, immediate, antecedent, clear," and the causes of the conclusion with an essential definition as the middle term. Imperfect demonstration starts with principles that are *notiora nobis* and prove causes, for example, by effects.[18] Imperfect demonstration of a fact, which does not give the " why " of the fact, really falls outside true science, except in certain cases where a demonstration of fact is convertible into a demonstration by the cause. It ranks as a kind of auxiliary science when it helps in the preparation of a definition by indicating that a certain sensible substance, for example, may be classified as belonging to some genus already known. Properly speaking, however, definition is not the conclusion of any syllogism : it is rather the fruit of a wide induction based on repeated findings. Demonstration, therefore, of a simple fact, if it does not help us to get beyond the fact, must be excluded from the realm of science and relegated to that of the arts.

It would seem that it is amongst the arts also that St. Thomas would have placed the scientific induction of to-day,[19] had he before his mind any clear idea of what it implies. He would not have gone so far as to consider such work as unimportant from the scientific point of view. But for him, though it may be necessary for the man of science in its results, yet as a method and a procedure such induction could not appear in that ideal form of knowledge which science was for St. Thomas. Once " science " has been reached, the human mind sees nothing but the luminous and harmonious descent of deductions from first principles.

[17] In 4 *Met.*, l. 1 (471 a). In 2 *Post.*, l. 20 end ; In 1 *Post.*, l. 1, where demonstration is thus described : *Rationis processus necessitatem inducens, in quo non est possibile esse veritatis defectum, et per huiusmodi rationis processum scientiae certitudo acquiritur.*

[18] See *Opusc.*, 36, *De demonstratione*, the authenticity of which can scarcely be doubted. The same is to be had more briefly in the *Summa*, 1, q. 2, a. 2.

[19] He does not seem to have had this exact idea, however. See the opinion of M. Mansion in his excellent articles *L'induction chez Albert le Grand* (*Revue néo-scolastique*, 1906, pp. 115 and 246).

II

By a clever handling of texts, however, an entirely different impression from that which I have been striving to convey in the previous paragraphs might be given to the reader. In this new reading St. Thomas would be praised for having remained faithful to the experimental tradition handed on to him by Aristotle, despite his own great confidence in mind. Emphasis would be placed on the important place he assigns to observation in his theory of natural sciences. " Investigating truth in the natural sciences," he says, " some set out from rational ideas, as with the Platonists ; others from sensible objects and in this, as Simplicius says, consisted the originality of Aristotelian philosophy." [20] Besides, did not St. Thomas, like Aristotle, criticise the apriorism of the Platonists and their " inexperience " ? [21] Did he not declare that, in the natural sciences, the method of mathematics was excluded ? [22] Further, demonstration by sign or by effect is that which is not frequently employed in the sciences. [23] And in general the progress of knowledge is from that which is less clear *in se*, but *notiora nobis*. [24] The purport of all this seems unambiguous.

Then it would be possible to refer to the actual practice of St. Thomas himself. In his philosophy of movement, and particularly in his psychology, he always takes account of facts, and frequently appeals to experience as an unanswerable argument.

Likewise, appeal would be made to the experimental character of his theory of knowledge. In general St. Thomas seems to look on the opposition that hold between the *notiora priora quoad se* and the *priora quoad nos* as an absolute one. [25] That being so, how can we reconcile with it his almost puerile confidence in deduction ?

These objections, however, when they are not reducible

---

[20] *Spir.*, 3.
[21] In 1 *Contra Gentes.*, l. 3.
[22] In 2 *Met.*, l. 5.
[23] In *Trin.*, 6, 1.
[24] In 2 *An.*, l. 3.
[25] See 2 *Contra Gentes*, 77 ; 1a, 2ae, q. 57, a. 2 ; In *Job.*, 4, 3.

to a confusion of the order of discovery and the order of
exposition or system—a thing sedulously to be avoided when
speaking of mediæval philosophy—serve merely to show
that there was a certain vagueness in the mind of St. Thomas
regarding certain fundamental problems of epistemology.
They cannot prevent us from believing that the really
central thing for him, that which he has most frequently
reiterated and most systematically affirmed, was precisely
that " architectonic " connection of science which I have
been expounding. The whole difficulty in the Thomistic
view of the value of science lies in reconciling these two
diverging tendencies of his thought and in showing to what
extent there is an opposition, real or apparent, between
them.

III

In order to appraise the Thomistic conception of human
science as a shadow of the intellectual process in its purity,
it will be necessary to fix two conclusions that emerge
spontaneously from what has been said.

In the first place, it is evident that where we have in mind
a unitary intellectual grasp of reality an arrangement of
successive judgments is by its very nature imperfect and
unsatisfactory. The same defects which characterise the
ratio are also to be met with in science.[26] By the progressive
determination of its object, science tends towards that
unitary grasp of reality which is characteristic of the angelic
idea. Yet for science to attain to such a limit would mean
self-destruction, since the characteristic multiplicity of its
object would have entirely disappeared. It is true that the
principle of deduction brings unity, and makes it possible

---

[26] See 1 *Post.*, l. 35 for replies to those objections which attack the superiority
of demonstration that deals with the universal as against those which have the
particular for object and especially the following one : *Universalis demonstratio
ita se habet quod minus de ente habet quam particularis.* . . . St. Thomas replies
by distinguishing between the order of reason and of reality : *Quantum ad id
quod rationis est. . . .. Quantum vero ad naturalem subsistentiam.* . . . Still we
must look for a critique of science as an imperfect form of speculation in this
paragraph ; it is to be found, rather implicitly only, in the questions that deal
with the Angels (as, for instance, *Ver.*, 8, 15, where he distinguishes knowledge
n aliquo which is unified and possibly intuitive and knowledge *ex aliquo* which
is discursive and multiple).

for us to recognise conclusions in premises and premises in conclusions. *Oportet in conclusionibus speculari principia.* But even granting that attention be paid to this final act which may be said to contain a semblance of an integral and saturating vision, but which for St. Thomas is merely a logical operation, the very reduction of multiplicity to the unity of an *abstract* principle which is implied would only serve to emphasise the unreal character of the approach to reality that is possible in virtue of the deductive method. The nerve of deductive reasoning is simply the substitution of equivalents ; but on Thomistic principles there is no such thing as an equivalent in the world of purely intelligible objects, and in the material world it does not seem feasible to admit of their presence there seeing that finality holds sway. There is, therefore, no escaping the fact that there is a radical contrast between the typically intellectual process of knowledge and science even in its most perfect form. *Omnis scientia essentialiter NON est intelligentia.*

In the second place, no matter how crude and confused deductive knowledge may be, St. Thomas is perfectly consistent with his principles in admitting the possibility of a philosophy which employs the deductive method, and in asserting the relative superiority of such a philosophy. If it is possible to demonstrate a proposition, " no better knowledge of it can be had than that of scientific knowledge, while it must be admitted that we have a still better knowledge of indemonstrable first principles." [27]   The duality of the means of knowledge accessible to us implies that, since any information about a particular essence supposes work on the data of sense, a world-system must necessarily suppose the abstraction of general principles by means of a wide induction. And the unification of such a system is inconceivable without a necessary intersection of those principles among themselves or with quasi-definitions obtained in the same way. There is nothing to prevent the possession of such a scientific whole from being accompanied by perfect certitude. But everything goes to show that its extent will be extremely limited.

[27] In 1 *Post.*, 1, 32.

The error made by St. Thomas, then, would seem to have consisted in the fact that he wished to embody into his deductive philosophy every certain proposition for which the arts had no immediate use. It is sufficiently well known that once this method had been renounced it was found possible to undertake an autonomous systematisation of sensible phenomena, and that this undertaking succeeded. Its immediate value from a speculative point of view may have been meagre, but from a practical point of view it was extremely fecund. What St. Thomas is reproached with, then, is not precisely that he taught the possibility of a philosophy of movement, or yet that he wished it to be taught before the sciences of zoology and botany, but that he seems to have believed it possible to " deduce " botany and zoology from that philosophy, and to have regarded these sciences, both in their ultimate essence and as sciences of living beings, as merely " application " of a philosophy of being subject to movement. In his effort to make use of everything for his philosophical synthesis, St. Thomas was following out his own principles ; but in his desire to force into his system so many results of the ratio's activity there was just the danger of falsifying his principles. Had he not himself spoken of the *vis cogitativus*, comparable to the *sensus estimativus* of the animals, which, in the case of man, was strengthened by its contact with reason ? Had he not insisted on the continuity that contains amongst all knowing beings ? Would he not have suspected that, side by side with pure speculation which is a shadow of angelic knowledge, men might possess systems of laws and practical recipes, in this resembling the bees or higher beaver, which would help them to subject the world of sense to their respective needs ?

It is impossible to assert that he was unaware of such a simple idea. He was cognisant of the existence of arts side by side with science, and amongst them he places, for example, agriculture and medicine.[28] And the best way of

---

[28] In 2 *Post.*, l. 20. The assertion is even extended to all that is concerned *circa generationem, id est, circa quaecumque factibilia.* His thought here seems somewhat vague. In 2 *Phys.*, l. 4 (348 b) medicine is spoken of as *scientia artificialis.*

expressing his theory of knowledge in general would be perhaps to say that the sciences as we understand them to-day would have been classified by St. Thomas amongst the " arts," and that the term " science " properly so called would have been reserved by him to designate the synthesis of philosophy. To what, for St. Thomas, would the term " savant " have corresponded ? For him the " savant " is one who knows the essence of things. For us the man of science is precisely one who professes to know nothing of the nature or essence of things, and is interested rather in classi-fying the relations that hold between phenomena. To attribute heat to " God in presence of fire " and not to the proper " virtue " of that element would have meant for St. Thomas the abnegation of all science since it would render the knowledge of things by their causes [29] impossible. But what does the savant of to-day care for all that, provided that the constancy of relations between phenomena, in which alone he is interested, is left untouched ? And this attitude of the savant to the essence of things is likewise his attitude towards the ultimate " why " of things. The concept of finality is no longer for him something " received from without " which becomes an intrinsic constituent of science, but simply a direct hypothesis conceived, as it were, from within. St. Thomas, on the other hand, identified nature and the end [30] in his metaphysical epistemology.

Speaking, therefore, of Thomistic principles of science in relation to the theories of modern scientists, we must not allow ourselves to be deceived by superficial or verbal resemblances into believing that what on all sides is spoken of as " science " is to be identified with what St. Thomas had in mind when he employed the term. So to be deceived would imply, if not an identification of two contradictory things, at least a very rough treatment of Thomistic texts.

Physics, on the contrary, is looked upon as a necessary (*Ver.*, 15, 2, 3) and a demonstrative (2a, 2ae, q. 48, a. 1 ; In *Phys.*, l. 1) ; *naturalis* as applied to science seems to be a species of *speculativus* (In 10 *Eth.*, l. 15 end).

[29] 3 *Contra Gentes*, 69, 7.

[30] In 2 *Phys.*, l. 15, 380 a. According to St. Thomas physical philosophy employs all the causes (In 1 *Phys.*, l. 1) and preferably the final cause (In 5 *Met.*, l. 2, 518 b ; L. 1, 513 b *Praecipuae* to be read instead of *praecipue*. (*Cf.* 3 *Contra Gentes*, 69, 7).

A very precise distinction must be made between pure speculation and the systematised " arts." Assuredly that does not mean the abandonment of the peripatetic theory, provided it is admitted that the " arts " can supply materials for the purely speculative sciences and that certain generalisations provided by the sciences can be brought under general metaphysical principles. Besides, if we consult the practice of St. Thomas himself on those two points in order to clarify or correct his theory, we shall find that for the preparation of his materials he goes more often to vulgar experience for his facts than to his scientific theories, and that as regarding his ultimate systematisation of the facts observed he puts it forward more frequently as a possible arrangement than as a certain deduction.[31] These two facts explain the facility with which his biology (if the word is not too pretentious), his physics and his astronomy may be cut away from his ultimate metaphysical theories.

The really important point, however, is this : supposing the practical sciences to be as complete and as co-ordinated as possible, place them side by side with the deepest ontology in any mind ; as long as these sciences simply affirm facts, the two knowledges will be irreducible to one another. Further, granted that a fusion between the two were brought about by an intellectual grasp of the intelligible in the generalised sensible object, even then reality in itself would not be held by mind. Denying the possibility of knowing " all natural things," [32] St. Thomas might have also added, consistently with his principles, that even if all things were known *modo humano* man would still be very distant from the ideal of intellectual knowledge. The ultimate reason for all the imperfection of knowledge may be reduced to the duality of man's medium of knowledge as contrasted with the ineffable unity of the real with and in itself. The essence and law as grasped by a mind which has not an intuitive vision of matter exists, after all, only in matter. So it is that in our perceptions and in our propositions *multum inest de natura indeterminata*.

[31] See following chapter.
[32] In 1 *Meteor*, l. 1 ; In *Job*, l. 11 ; 1a, q. 88, a. 1.

CHAPTER V

THIRD SUBSTITUTE FOR THE PURE IDEA : SYSTEMS
AND SYMBOLS

I

DESPITE his rigorous conception of science and the fact that he saw in philosophy the embodiment of this conception, St. Thomas admits, both in theory and in practice, that it is lawful to combine arguments of merely probable value with philosophically certain ones. The most exact way of describing this process of combination, from the Scholastic point of view, would be to affiliate it with that part of Logic known in the Schools as " dialectic." [1] The characteristic argument of dialectic is the " enthymeme." By this it is not implied merely that one of the premises of the argument is left to be understood. What we intend to convey is that, omitted altogether or included expressly, this premise is lacking in the certitude required for demonstration. Here we have an example of the employment of the deductive method characteristic of the mind as *ratio*, even though the knowledge which serves as the principle of the argument is too vague to be applied with certainty to the matter in hand.

We see the nature of this procedure best when the major premise is of very wide application and when the conclusion is far removed from its premises. It may be said to reach its peak-point in such arguments as the following, which are not rare in the writings of St. Thomas. He starts with one of these high-sounding phrases that seem to contain the supreme expression of the coincident laws of reality and

---

[1] For *dialectic* as opposed to apodeictic reasoning see In 1 *Post.*, l. 1 and l. 33 ; 2a, 2ae, q. 48, a. un. ; in 4 *Met.*, l. 1 (471). *Cf. logice* or *rationabiliter* as opposed to *demonstrative*, *e.g.*, In *Cael.*, l. 2.

mind (*Bonum est ut in pluribus. Natura semper ad unum tendit.
Natura semper meliore modo operatur*). He, then, goes on to
postulate the application of this so-called principle to some
particular detail ; that the middle term is missing or at
least insufficient does not seem to matter. All arguments of
the *conventientia* type, or of analogy, come under this heading.[2] Nothing could be more ingeniously naïve than the
argument he bases on the " sufficiency of combinations." [3]
Adam was created *sine viro et femina ;* Eve, *ex viro sine femina ;*
all others *ex viro et femina.* It was " appropriate," therefore,
ad completionem universi that Jesus should have been born *ex
femina sine viro.* Such a method of argument we may well
designate as " artistic " ; it is employed apparently for the
pleasure of it, and it would seem to have satisfied needs in
the mind of that epoch for which art caters at the present
day.

It is not difficult to notice that such a method of argument
bears a certain relation to the development of the Thomistic
theory of knowledge as we outlined it. Were the human
mind to remain fully faithful to its own rigorous methods of
scientific knowledge nothing better than a duplicate and
disordered vision of the world would be the result. Once
the general laws of reality have been established we seem to
possess the essential structure of the universe in outline. But
it is only an outline, and the temptation to fill in the picture
is enticing. The aspiration of the human mind to grasp the
totality of things, no matter how, in the unity of a single idea
cannot be stifled : the whole rhythm of its movement from
act to act, from lesser perfection to greater, is determined
by this more generic tendency to equate reality. If certain
portions of the universe are unknown it will supply for its
lack of knowledge by having recourse to imagination guided
by analogy. Because the practical or industrial applications
of knowledge fall outside the sphere of pure science, there
will be a tendency to discover certain relations between
propositions *propter quid* and propositions *quia.* Endowed

---

[2] 3 d. 12, q. 3, a. 2, sol. 2 ; 3 q. 31, a. 4.
[3] This is the argument of " equilibrium " of the Ancients (*cf.* Cicero, *De
natura deorum*, 1, 35). *Cf.* In 2 *Cael.*, l. 4, 116 a ; In 1 *Post.*, l. 11.

with senses that bring it into contact with the particular and living being, the human mind, one might add, will be tempted to fill in its outlines by pressing into service its singular apprehensions. In this way it has recourse to sensible symbols, so that with their aid, as well as with the help of system, it will be able to unify the universe as thought. The word " art " as employed here must not deceive us. We are really in presence of a philosophical procedure. It was precisely because of its intimate conviction of the intelligibility of the entire universe that Scholasticism in its effort to beautify and integrate its vision of the world was ready to add to what was certain knowledge that was only possible and so on *ad infinitum*.

To turn one's back on the rigorous laws of science, and to accept this new collaboration of the senses with philosophy, is to admit into one's conclusions that flexibility and uncertainty which is characteristic of sense-knowledge : it is to sacrifice the rigour of absolute precision to a desire for unity. And if it be true that there is something disordered about all assent that is not infallibly grounded, we must confess that something other than rational conviction becomes the ideal.[4] With this introduction of sense-knowledge and opinion the question is no longer one of simulating the pure idea : it falls into a lower level, that of an artistic complexity which strives to simulate the rational. The fruits of this new collaboration which makes room for the intervention of imagination are the System and the Symbol which are thus seen to be substitutes for complete and integral scientific knowledge. When what is merely probable is poured into the same moulds with what is certain, hoping thereby to provide a unitary impression, and when reason in its avowed incapacity to deduce everything seeks to console itself with the illusion of a complete deduction, it becomes imperative for the philosopher to distinguish within himself the dual personality of the poet who is content with dreams and the philosopher dissatisfied with anything less than proofs. Many of the mediæval minds

---

[4] See text already cited from *Ver.*, 18, 6.

possess sufficient pliability to engage in this sort of thing,[5] and where St. Thomas is concerned it is certain that his reason was not duped by the intellectual pleasure that such exercise afforded him.[6]

It is a rare thing for St. Thomas to stop to determine the exact proportions of certainty that he ascribes to his assertions. We believe, however, that it would not be difficult, at least within the limits of pure philosophy, to determine what he considered certain in his doctrine and what he looked upon as merely probable. Such an investigation of course would take us too deeply into the material content of his system to allow of our giving even an outline of it here. Neither would it be sufficient to instance the fragmentary theories that are to be found here and there in order to have an accurate idea of the subjective co-existence of these two methods. Nothing less than a study of the very body of his expositions could give an adequate idea of the place and meaning of artistic logic, and in these expositions it would be necessary especially to pay attention to those of the theologian, for theology is the favourite *terrain* for this particular method. I select three examples taken from the domain of natural knowledge.

The first example will serve to show that, notwithstanding his exalted ideal of science, St. Thomas was well aware of the large part played by hypothesis in the natural sciences, which for him went beyond the mere enumeration of phenomena to their explanation. There is a text from the Commentary on *De caelo* which is so well known that we must excuse ourselves for quoting it, but it is of such value that it cannot be passed over. " The hypotheses put forward by astrologers are not necessarily true ; they seem to explain the facts but we are not obliged to admit that those who framed them have said the last word : perhaps another explanation, as yet unknown, will one day be put

---

[5] This is in keeping with the Greek tradition both in its Platonic and Aristotelian form. A typical example of the procedure is to be found in the second book of the *De caelo*, where astronomical hypotheses are accompanied by this neat suggestion : εἴ τις διὰ τό φιλοσοφίας διψην χαὶ μιχρὰς εὐπορίας ἀγαπα περί ἄυ τας μεγίστας εχομεν ἀπορίας (B.12).

[6] See declarations such as 4 d. 40, a. 4 ad 4.

forward which will explain all the appearances of the side-real world." [7] It is important to notice that this judgment affects the very system he himself accepts and in terms of which he writes in his own works. A similar doubt arises in his mind treating in meteorology of the suggested explanation of comets. It is there declared that the hypothesis adopted enjoys less certainty than mathematical theorems or even propositions framed to express sensible facts ; its only merit consists in furnishing an explanation that satisfies the mind.[8]

The second example would be much more significant were it expressed in the same clear and unambiguous terms. The question at issue is that of the separate substances. There can be no doubt that the whole Thomistic system would lose something of its apparent solidity if we were to regard this piece of it as purely hypothetical. But here faith comes to the aid of philosophical conjecture. There is no question, then, of mere opinion here. Nevertheless there are several points of interest that may be indicated. Thus the arguments put forward in the philosophical part of the *Summa Contra Gentes* to prove either that angels exist or that the sensible world is under their control are simply *argumenta convenientiae* drawn from the general arrangement of the world and from the plan that seems to have presided over creation.[9] It would be true, indeed, to say that many

[7] In 2 *De cael.*, 1, 17. The same doctrine is again explicitly taken up in lq. 32, a. 1 ad 2, and is even more strongly affirmed in *Job*, 38, 2 : *Per certitudinem via motus luminarium cognosci non potest ab homine* . . . (*cf.* context).

[8] In 1 *Meteor.*, l. 9. At the outset of this treatise we are told explicitly that the author's intentions are not ambitious.

[9] 2 *Contra Gentes*, 91 ; 1 q. 50, a. 1 ; 1 q. 51, a. 1. Notice the presence of *necesse est* and *oportet* in these different passages. In general, it is impossible to base oneself on such words for the degree of assent that St. Thomas gives to a conclusion. Sometimes *oportet* alternates with *exigere videtur* (4 *Contra Gentes*, 79, 1) ; at other times *videtur* is employed concerning matters where the author is certain though the phrase might be translated as " It would appear that . . ." Account must also be taken of the character of certain works. It is possible that the technical value of certain expressions, elegantly written, is less weighty. In the *Sentences* the mass of doubtful expressions may simply translate the modesty of the beginner. Everywhere he had many reasons for treating Augustinianism with respect ; in the works edited by Brother Reginald particular expressions that are strongly worded are due to the unmitigated zeal of the disciple (In *Cor.*, 13, l. 4 : *omnino faesum et impossibile*). All this goes to show the futility of discussions that have no other basis than such fine points ; it would have been useless to refer to them were it not that even still they are to be met with too often.

theses of the treatise on the angels are independent of the fact whether angels exist or not. But there are others which presuppose the existence of angels. The more convinced we are of the necessity for stressing the autonomy of philosophy in its relation to the data of faith, the more likely are we to appreciate the daring of some of his conjectures and to realise that in momentous questions he was not at all adverse to accepting a probability where certainty was out of the question.

His theodicy, in fine, affords us the best example of all, and it is well worth our closest consideration. Take, for example, the logical development of his demonstration of the attributes of God either in the *Summa Contra Gentes* or in the *Summa Theologica*. Does it seem possible to doubt that here we are in presence of a reasoning process that has all the appearance of absolutely proving its point ? Would anything remain standing in his system if these great theses are allowed to totter ? And then, what is our surprise to hear him declare that the unity of God, understood as covering God's omnipotence, His universal providence and similar attributes, is the object of faith and not of demonstration. Seeing the constancy with which this assertion is repeated as well as the character of the works where such repetition occurs, there is no question of saying that it is an assertion thrown out by chance, or in answer perhaps to some old trifling theological difficulty. Granted even that such assertions do not represent the mature thought of Aquinas, yet the facility with which they are uttered and his apparent indifference to striking a blow in defence of an elaborately built up demonstration is a more eloquent proof that St. Thomas had not that naïve confidence in his metaphysical reasonings that is sometimes attributed to him. Recall at the same time the complete absence of restrictions when he puts forward elsewhere a rational proof of providence and you will have granted all that I wish to say.[10]

[10] The problem touched upon in this paragraph is sufficiently important to justify a more detailed consideration of it. Amongst the attributes of God that reason can demonstrate St. Thomas mentions several times that of " incor-

We may now pass on to purely theological questions, where the use of " artistic " logic is much more conscious and undeniable just as it is also the least contested.

II

The way in which St. Thomas defines and understands the task of theology is likely to come as a shock to those who know nothing about Scholasticism except what they have been accustomed to hear about its rationalism.

It is true that theology is presented first and foremost as a speculative science with the articles of faith as its first principles and its conclusions in the form of propositions deduced by reasoning from these principles. In regard to divine knowledge theology is a " subaltern " science, as it receives from God certain truths much in the way as the medical man receives his formulæ from the physicist, *sicut medicus credit physico*.[11] The certainty of dogma, as well as of the truths derived with evidence from them,[12] is absolute and unchangeable. In this way he safeguards the funda-

---

poreity " and " intelligence," to which he assigns primacy of place. In addition he also mentions incorruptibility, volition, a certain unity or uniqueness of excellence, and the prerogative of being the final cause of the world (3 d. 24, q. 1, a. 3, sol. 1 ; *Ver.*, 18, 3 ; *Comp. Theol.*, 35 and 254 ; In *Rom.*, l. 1, 6 ; 2a, 2ae, q. 2, a. 4, arg. *Sed contra*). What seems to him to be exclusively an object of faith is unity conceived as enveloping omnipotence, immediate and universal providence, and the exclusive right to adoration (*Ver.*, 14, 9, 9 ; *Comp. Theol.*, 254 ; *cf.* 2a, 2ae, q. 1, a. 8 ad 1) ; and to these he adds the attributes that belong to God as Remunerator and Judge (3 d. 25, q. 1, a. 2 ad 2 ; see, however, In *Rom.*, l. 1, 8). With regard to divine causality in relation to the world, reason must affirm it in general, but it does not seem able to determine if it is exercised according to the Christian idea of creation (3 d. 25, *loc. cit.* ; In *Rom.*, l. 1, 6 ; *Comp. Theol.*, 68 ; *cf.* 36 ; *cf.* the vague expressions of 3 d. 2, q. 1, a. 3, sol. 1 and the reference to Aristotle, and also notice the frequent mention of the emanation-theories. This problem differs from that of the creation *ab aeterno*, which is treated elsewhere by St. Thomas). It is difficult to recognise in this distinction of two classes of attributes the exclusive work of *a priori* reflection ; St. Thomas has certainly before his mind the peripatetic and Arabian philosophers. It is to be noted that if reason is too feeble to affirm the attribute of omnipotence it is even less capable of denying it (In *Rom.*, l. 1, 7). In the *Summa Contra Gentes* (3, 75) and in the *Compendium Theologiae* (123) a philosophical form of the proof of Providence is to be found.

[11] In *Trin.*, 2, 2 and ad 55.

[12] See 1 q. 32, a. 4 (*Utrum liceat contrarie opinari de notionibus*) and more emphatically in the *Sentences* (1 d. 33, q. 1, a. 5) : *Pertractata veritate et viso quid sequitur, idem, judicium est de his et de illis quae determinata sunt in fide, quia ad unum sequitur alterum.* . . .

mental needs of reason ; St. Thomas could not have com-
promised on any of these points without being untrue to
himself. Yet an examination of the object of theology and
of the manner of its formation convinced him that its results
were of very unequal value. He saw that it depended to
no small degree for its existence on what we have called
System and Symbol.

God is above and beyond all categories. Supernatural
realities are likewise transcendent, and it is only by a rough-
and-ready form of classification that they can be " reduced "
to any form of arrangement. The natural categories of
Aristotle are not fitting receptacles for these new realities.
Grace, for example, does not enter any of the four known
classes of *quality*, and among the eight ways of inherence of
one thing in another none can be found to suit the Trinity.[13]
Any idea that we can form of them must be in the highest
degree analogical. It follows that the expression of dogma
in terms of a philosophy which is supposedly adequate for
things here below is neither exhaustive nor exclusively the
only one conceivable. This last point is to be borne particularly in mind. St. Thomas, though he employed the
peripatetic and Scholastic formulæ in theology, was far
from " canonising," if the expression may be employed,
any one form of philosophy. " Sacred doctrine," he says,
" can receive something from the philosophical sciences,
not as if it stood in need of them, but simply with a view
to making its teaching clearer. . . . That it does have
recourse to them is not due to any defect on its part, but to
the defects of our intelligence which is more easily led by
what is known to natural reason (from which proceed the
other sciences) to matters above reason which are expounded
in this science." [14] Obviously this statement implies that
if we possessed a direct intuition of supernatural realities,

---

[13] *Ver.*, 27, 2, 7 ; 1 q. 42, a. 5 ad 1. It is here that the whole doctrine of
" proportionality " appears. *A propos* of the Hypostatic Union see *De Un.
Verbi Inc.*, 1, and *Pot.*, 1, 4, 4 (2nd series) and note the general principle :
*Secundum consideratione theologi, omnia illa quae non sunt in se impossibilia, possibilia
dicuntur.* As regards the doctrine of Transubstantiation see 3 q. 75, a. 4 and
for that of the sacramental *character*, 3 q. 63, a. 2, etc.

[14] 1 q. 1, a. 5 ad 2. *Cf. Prol. Sent.*, q. 1, a. 1 : *Utitur in obsequium sui omnibus
aliis scientiis quasi vassallis ;* In *Trin.*, 2, 3, 7 : *quasi famulantes et praeambulae.*

of grace for example or of the infused virtues, we should not be under the necessity of classifying them or reducing them to some known natural category. Furthermore, it is also suggested (*ad maiorem manifestationem*) that the ordinary common concepts of people who are unacquainted with Aristotle suffice to give them a general and approximate idea of the whole of theology. These ideas, it is true, may not be as clear or as adequate as those of learned philosophers, yet the difference would not be radical or in nature but simply one of degree. The question of employing some philosophy which does not coincide with the true one in the elucidation of theological matters is left untouched. The practical solution offered by St. Thomas may be seen in his frequent allusions to the Platonism of certain Fathers, and this seems to imply the possibility of divergent theological explanations which have their source in different philosophical systems.[15]

The introduction of philosophy, then, into theological discussions makes for a greater clarification of dogma, but this introduction is not unaccompanied by a certain multiplication of views amongst believers which reflect divergencies in their philosophies. This serves to indicate the distinction, both from the view-point of expression and of domain, that must be recognised between theology and faith. The influence of human opinions in matters of faith is seen from the fact that some accept one conclusion and others a different one. "And here," says St. Thomas, "we have an application of the dictum of St. Paul to the Romans 'that each may abound in his own sense.'"[16] This affords a true sample of theological *system* in its formation.

[15] See *a propos* of Dionysius, 2 *Contra Gentes*, 98. For St. Augustine see *Ver.*, 21, 2, 3 ; *Spir.*, 10, 8. Even where a doctrine is commonly held by philosophers we must beware of identifying it with faith (*Opusc.*, 9, Prolong.). In the exposition of the Scriptures exclusive adherence to an opinion which may prove anti-scientific is to be avoided : *Ideo multis exitibus verba Scripturae exponuntur, ut se ab irrisione cohibeant litteris saecularibus inflati (ibid.*, n. 18 ; *cf.* 1 q. 68, a. 1). This fear of the *Irrisio infidelium* is as strongly felt by St. Augustine as by St. Thomas.

[16] *Quodl.*, 3, 10. The article is entitled : *Utrum discipuli peccent sequendo diversas opiniones Magistrorum.* Since, on the other hand, there is room for sin when an *evident* consequence is not accepted, systematic propositions are very clearly marked off from what to-day are called " theological conclusions."

That theological reflection which is concerned with the logical deduction of consequences from dogma will imply a certain amount of uncertainty cannot be denied. But it is important to remember that this was not the sole, nor perhaps the principal, concern of the theologian as St. Thomas and his contemporaries viewed the matter. Their ambition was to return to dogma in the newly found strength of their philosophical findings in order to obtain a clearer " understanding " of its content. No doubt the doctrine of *fides quaerens intellectus* was clearer by the time of St. Thomas than it had been for St. Anselm or for Richard of St. Victor. The proper sphere of mysteries has been delineated ; that these mysteries completely transcend the powers of human reason is generally admitted. And yet the incurably ambitious Scholastic theologian will speak as if he hoped to comprehend them. No attempt, of course, is made to prove the articles of faith, but something very like proof is frequently offered. An attentive reading of those passages in which St. Thomas treats of the method of theology clearly indicates that it was of this he was thinking. The majority of the dangers indicated by him seem to point in this direction. Sometimes, it is true, he warns us that nothing new is to be added to the truths imposed on us by the Church. But what he most frequently insists upon is that no one must have such confidence in reason or in individual genius as to think it possible to comprehend these mysteries imposed. They must be defended, he says, without wishing to prove them, much in the same way as Aristotle defended first principles in the Fourth Book of the *Metaphysics*. What needs to be done is to show the absence of contradiction in them and to refute the objections of the adversary. And then one may engage upon a quest for certain " illustrations " or " similitudes " for the mysteries such as St. Augustine found for the mystery of the Holy Trinity. This last remark is not without significance.[17]

To a great extent, then, the efforts of the mediæval theologian centred around the indemonstrable element of mystery. His modern successors, for the most part, are

[17] In *Trin.*, 2, 1 ; *ibid.*, 2, 3.

interested rather in indicating the conclusions that follow from dogmatic premises, while he, faithful to that imperious instinct which shaped his conception of an integral synthesis, built up his theological system as he did his system of science and was not beyond feigning a certain deduction of the Trinity and of the dogma of the Beatific Vision. As a first result there was uncertainty in deductions : by trying to explain the inexplicable. The world of nature accessible to the human reason, it is true, may be in outline a rough image of the world of faith, but as it does not furnish our abstractive intellect with a law that is common to created essences and to God as He is in Himself (seeing that He is above and beyond all categories), this image can never be more than a very imperfect one.[18] Quite consciously the mediæval thinker puts forward at one and the same time his ideas in a form that seems strikingly probative and refuses himself to believe in the probative force of these so-called demonstrations. His work takes the form of a logical poem which is more charming for a mind already endowed with faith than it is useful for controversy. Before we enjoy the vision of God it is legitimate and reasonable to embellish *toutes nos pièces*, as Pascal would have said, with our ideas of God and to exercise our minds and so stir up our hearts. *Ad consolationem fidelium*, remarked St. Thomas. And, allowing for a slight difference of meaning, his words may be illustrated from Plato : χρὴ τὰ τοιαυτα ὥσπερ ἐπᾴδειν ἑαυτῷ.

Two examples, taken from the two great dogmas of Christianity, the Trinity and the Incarnation, will suffice as illustrations. Nothing is more systematic than the exposition of the *rationes convenientiae* for the Incarnation of the Word, taking the Word as the Idea of God, the Image of the Father, the creative exemplar of the universe.[19] But the classical example, and the one that is principal from every point of view, is that of the apparent demonstration of the Holy Trinity which is taken from St. Augustine. This is based on the presence in God, as in us, of thought and

---

[18] In *Trin.*, 2, 3 ; *ibid.*, l. 4. *Aliquales rationes non necessariae, nec multum probabiles nisi credenti.*

[19] 4 *Contra Gentes*, 42.

love. The opinion that St. Thomas attributed to this kind of proof anything like a probative value could not be sustained for a moment : his assertions to the contrary are too clear. A perusal of the passages where he treats the argument *ex professo* does not give the same impression of rationalism and of evacuation of all mystery as in the case of St. Anselm, yet what is there in these passages to tell us that we are not in presence of probative arguments but simply analogies the aim of which is to illustrate and to clarify the matter according to our human standards ? Only a few scattered remarks hidden away in the *Sentences* and in the two *Summa*'s, for the most part in replies to objections.[20] As regards the abstract explanation of the matter, we come across it developed at a stretch in the Fourth Book of the *Summa Contra Gentes*, and there it is punctuated with *oportet* and *ergo*, and there is a daring combination and fusion of certainty and probability which astonishes those who know and which is calculated by the equality of its tone to deceive the uninitiated. One can well imagine that, reading these pages, some theologians have had those uneasy and impatient feelings of a scientist in whose presence scientific law and scientific theory are identified. It is remarkable that here the " Book of the Master " is more explicit,[21] but then is it not the disciple that needs to be put on his guard against the presumption of having demonstrated the indemonstrable ?

The value of St. Augustine's explanation of the Trinity can best be understood by putting it back in the context of the intellectual history of its author and by taking account of the immature spirituality from which it arose. It is based on the possibility of a certain multiplicity that can have place in an immaterial unity. Thus, my thought, or my act of love, is identical in some way with me, it has its life in me and, like me, it is incorporeal, and yet there is also a certain opposition between it and me. But such an illustration certainly fails to establish that the distinction

---

[20] 1 q. 32, a. 1 ad 2 ; q. 42, a. 2 ad 1.

[21] *Pot.*, 2, 1 ; 8, 1, 12 ; 9, 9, 7 ; 10, 5. But side by side with this see those easy phrases that seem to give the whole of the comparison as an exact representation of reality. *Pot.*, 2, 3 (*corp.* end and ad 11) ; 2, 4, 11.

in question is a personal one, and also it fails to explain the equality of the different terms. Its value as an illustration is inseparably bound up with its futility as a proof. The quaintness of this combination, so it seems to me, is less striking in the somewhat oratorical developments of St. Augustine than it is in the syllogistic exposition of it given by St. Thomas. At the same time it serves excellently as an illustration of his method, since it goes to show that St. Thomas, fully aware of what he was doing, enriched his theological faculty with both truths and symbols.

St. Thomas has somewhere epitomised the function of rational theology in this short phrase : *ad cognoscendum fidei veritatem . . . veras similitudines colligere.*[22] Whether there is question of an assemblage of material and coloured images as in the symbol proper, or of logical constructions as in systems, there is ever question of a mere approximation to defective images of truth.

III

Just as science is demonstrative reason's substitute for the pure idea, so system is a substitute on the part of intellectual imagination for science. In this systematic construction there are many degrees, and the more general the analogies selected the less certain will be the conclusions ; since so much room is made for subjective considerations. At one and the same time mind is moving away from both science and the pure idea.[23] According as the sequence that holds such vague conclusions together loosens there will be increasing lack of intellectual rigour until it finally dissolves altogether in the indetermination of sense-impressions.

Symbol lies at the very limit of systematic construction.

[22] 1 *Contra Gentes*, 8.
[23] Amongst the systems the last place falls to such arrangements as are undertaken for the pure pleasure of systematisation, as, for example, the five-fold classification of the sacraments (4 d. 2, q. 1, a. 2), the detailed adaptation of the gifts to the beatitudes in 2a, 2ae, the divisions of the virtues, etc. There is nothing so futile in the whole of Scholasticism as these awkward attempts to simulate the science of the particular. Instead of attempting to give rise to an intuition the spiritual, on the contrary, is materialised in order to satisfy quantitative imagining.

There is no change of method, and all symbolic philosophies conceal a dialectic enthymeme. The major premise is furnished by the principle current in the Middle Ages that the world of sense somehow represents the world of spirit ; in the minor some sensible thing is taken for its power to represent in a particular way the reality of the spiritual object in mind. *Per iridem significatur Christus, per quem protegimur a spirituali diluvio.*[24] Obviously the certitude imparted by a " symbolic " proposition is small in the extreme. This bringing together of sensible objects and spiritual ones and the linking up of appearance with truth is largely an affair of arbitrary choice determined by preconceived ideas. The pure idea, however, is excellently simulated by such a process since the most spiritual objects are brought down to concrete realities which are objects of intuition.

Every possible shade between a very probable system and pure symbolism are to be found in the theology of St. Thomas. The essential relativity of a symbolic minor premise can only lead in this way to philosophically fantastic results. As employed in the realm of natural science it serves St. Thomas simply as a method of comparison.[25] Naturally it could attain to much importance in the sphere of religious thought since it is quite possible for a free intelligence to pre-establish certain harmony between sensible appearances and to reveal that pre-established relation to man. As a matter of fact, however, it is not so. The value accorded by St. Thomas to the religious symbol is not epistemological but simply æsthetic. *Symbolica theologia non est argumentativa.*[26]

It is true that on certain occasions there is room for hesitation between symbolic and systematic interpretations. Even in the judgment that it is " appropriate " that spiritual creatures should not have been formed after corporeal

[24] We must not confound the theory of universal symbolism with the doctrine of theistic exemplarism ; according to which the most spiritual beings themselves have their archetypes in the bosom of the Word.

[25] *Exemplum est quaedam inductio imperfecta* (In *Post.*, l. 1). The *intellectus agens*, for example, is compared to a cat's eye, which is at once the source of light and the organ of vision : here we have an analogy, not a proof. *A priori* it could be also compared to the eye of a dog, which sees but is not the source of light.

[26] *Ver.*, 22, 11, 18 ; *Quodl.*, 7, 14, 4.

bodies because of the unity of the universe there is a certain amount of reasoning.[27]   But what shall we say of such *minutiae* as the following : " It is not improbable that the moon was created full just as plants were created in their perfect form, carrying already their seeds, and likewise animals and men.   For although natural development goes from the less to the greater perfection, yet, absolutely speaking, it is the fully perfect which comes first." " The terrestrial atmosphere is a fitting habitation for the demons.   Its transparency accords with the beauty of their nature, its wildness with their sinful will, and its position in the universe with the office assigned to them of trying us."   Again, " It is likely that at the hour of the resurrection of the dead there will be a certain twilight in order to allow of the sun's being present at this great event." [28]   Here the limits of both symbol and system are reached.   Nowhere else do we come so directly upon the co-mingling of deductive reasoning and poetry which is so characteristic of artistic logic.   Some modern partisans of Scholasticism are considerably disturbed by such little pearls of Scholastic philosophy.   There is no occasion for this, however, as such examples are of inestimable value : they have a necessary place in the whole psychological content of these mediæval Scholastics.   Without them how could we represent to ourselves the compenetration of the two orders in the mind of St. Thomas, and see to what extent he detected the flow of the rational in the most intimate veins of the real ?

In the majority of cases there is no room for doubt.   Symbolic adaptation is frequently put forward in the form of an *argument*, but from the view-point of either science or opinion its value is nil.   " By the red cow Christ is typified : the feebleness that He was pleased to take upon himself is represented by the sex which is feminine ; the blood that he was to shed by the colour."   " The two doves of the Presentation at the temple signify the divinity and the humanity of Christ."   " To the blue tunic of the priest little golden

---

[27] *Pot.*, 3, 18.   *Unius . . . totius una videtur esse productio*, etc.
[28] 1 q. 70, a. 2 ad 5 ; 2 d 6, q. 1, a. 3 ; 4 d. 43, q. 1, a. 3, sol. 4.   Artistic reasoning concludes here from the rational principle to sensible fact : elsewhere it proceeds from sensible facts to general laws (1a, 2ae, q. 100 ad 3).

bells were attached to signify the knowledge of things divine
which in him should be united to celestial perfection of
life." [29]   St. Thomas himself has explained, à propos of
religious symbolism as well as in connection with what may
be called " poetic science," the significance of these images
for his philosophy.   " It is necessary to elevate towards
divine realities the dual composition of man, and for that
reason Dionysius employed corporeal figures in order to
reach the divine through the sensitive part of man's
nature." [20]   Unable to impart demonstrative proof, poetry
" charms the reason with its images."   And theology, the
principles of which are not accessible to reason, could likewise employ images the better to hold the imagination.[31]
The whole question is to introduce harmony into man, to
evoke his belief by means of images and to reach his mind by
reasons aided by the grace of God.   Even if the speculative
value of the symbol is negligible, and not adequately distinguished from its usefulness for man (it is really not unlike
those rites intended " by means of sensible impressions to
intensify our convictions regarding the things of God "),[32]
even if it is primarily intended to influence the animal part
of man and prevent it from warring against the spirit, yet
it is natural to link it up with system and with our other
instruments of knowledge, the aim of which is to simulate
the Idea.   The symbol, as it were, forms a kind of appendix
to rational speculation in so far as it is intended to realise the
unity of the thinking subject and this unity of the thinker is
Idea.   It is not impossible that it will be looked upon as of
greater importance than those logical arrangements which
undoubtedly St. Thomas himself preferred to symbols, and
of which we must now say a few words.

[29] 1a, 2ae, q. 102, a. 5 ad 5, ad 7, ad 10.
[30] 1 d. 34, q. 3, a. 1.
[31] *Prol. Sent.*, a. 5 ad 3. *Poetica scientia est de his quae propter defectum veritatis
non possunt a ratione capi ; unde oportet quod quasi quibusdam similitudinibus ratio
seducatur ; theologica autem est de his quae sunt supra rationem ; et ideo modus sym-
bolicus utrique communis est, cum neutra rationi proportionetur.* Cf. 1a, 2ae, q. 101,
a. 2 ad 2.
[32] 3 *Contra Gentes*, 120, 1 ; and In 1 *Post.*, 11, where it is said that poetry
does not convince the mind, but rather is calculated to influence the *sensus
cogitativus*, " just as a man experiences a strong dislike of a certain meat which
has been spoken of in such a way as to sicken him."

IV

It was the most natural thing in the world for St. Thomas to evince this extreme desire, which is evident in the examples we have given, to bring order into the universe, since he was so strongly convinced of the intelligibility of reality. A system is simply an attempt to reconstruct the plan that was worked upon by the divine artist. In every part of Thomistic philosophy the effort is apparent to reconstruct and to complete the order of things. Nowhere, perhaps, is this so strikingly manifested as when St. Thomas undertakes the analysis of a human product. From the depths of subtle intentions and the micrographical rationalisation that he ascribes to the human artist we may gauge to what extent he was likely to seek out in the universe traces of the divine creative Reason. It may not be out of place to stop for a moment to consider this aspect of his work, and it is here that it must be approached. For, by a remarkable verification of what we have just been saying, when St. Thomas comes to analyse the products of human genius, he is content rather to charm his reason than to convince it : his remarks savour more of system than of science.

Take, for example, that work of art created by humanity at large, language. The argument " from predication," as is well known, plays a large part in the philosophy of Aristotle : it appears therein as the mirror of thought, which, in its turn, is the reflection of reality.[33] The successors of Aristotle, and particularly the Scholastics, went beyond the Master. Leaving aside the serious history of the relations between Logic and Grammar, let us take up some isolated words. Isidore, the tutor of the Middle Ages in etymological matters, admits as a certain fact that " ancients " named many objects " according to their nature," while others selected names arbitrarily, and he goes on to record his own opinion that " the knowledge of all things is facilitated when the etymology of words is known." [34] The Scholastics then, and St. Thomas is no

---

[33] Ὁσαχῶς γὰρ λέγεται, τοσαυταχῶς τὸ εἶναι σημαίνει.   Metaph., Δ 7.
[34] Isidore of Seville, Etymologies, 11, ch. 29.

exception, pass from the etymology of a word to the nature of the object for which it stands. An intimate relation is supposed to exist between the name and the reality, and in the name they find the key which supposedly will open the box which contains the essence of the object stated.

There would be no point in multiplying examples of this kind of procedure. They are to be met with on every page and phonetic materials are turned and twisted into every shape in order to provide some modicum of intelligibility. The most typical examples are of the following kind : " The word heresy in Greek signifies choice according to Isidore . . . election being called *prohaeresis*. . . . It is also applicable to the heretic who is Latin and who may be said to have just adhered (*haerere*) to an idea because such a man tenaciously holds to his own idea." [35] If such an explanation is taken seriously, it cannot escape our notice that many hypotheses are taken for granted by it. Every argument that sets out from etymological data in order to arrive at the essence of an object presupposes, in the first place, that the " author of the word " has chosen that particular word which expresses precisely that characteristic marked out by conceptual abstraction as the essential thing in the object. In the second place, it implies that since the word was first framed it has remained faithful to its original meaning and has undergone neither restriction nor extension nor variation of any kind, that the name and its object, in fact, are as inseparable as essence and its property. But in the example just given a third hypothesis which is stranger still has been introduced : a root has been consciously chosen which in two—or several—languages happens by chance to express different and important attributes of the thing to be named.

Is it possible to say that St. Thomas allowed himself to be the dupe of such puerile considerations ? It does not seem

---

[35] d. 13, q. 2, a. 1 ; *cf.* 3 d. 25, q. 1, a. 1, sol. 1 (*articulus*, Greek and Latin). In *Cor.*, 5, 2 (*Pascha*, Greek and Hebrew) ; In *Rom.*, 1. 1 (Paul, Hebrew, Greek and Latin. Here when the author has given this explanation in virtue of a quasi-formal causality he passes on, as to an entirely distinct question, to indicate the real circumstances which explain the fact that Saul received the new name of Paul). Needless to say this is not peculiar to St. Thomas. It is already to be found in Plato (*Cratyle*, p. 405).

so, since when he comes to criticise the etymological argument, which he does practically on every occasion that the argument goes against his own thesis, he denies explicitly each of these presuppositions. He rejects complicity on the part of different languages,[36] he repudiates the chimerical idea of a natural language,[37] he excludes the idea of a language which is perfectly logical,[38] and he introduces a distinction between etymology and meaning.[39] In accordance with his own empirical principles he says that we name things according to our manner of knowing them, that is, by setting out from external and accidental characteristics of the object to be named.[40] He admits, in fine, certain transformations of language, declaring that " it is customary for words to vary in their meanings leaving behind them primitive meanings for newer ones." [41] Both at the starting point and all along the way the history of language is dominated by facts of the sense-order and subject to the influence of circumstance.

Such a sharp opposition as this between theory and practice brings out clearly the principle underlying artistic logic. The very same method that as a whole is condemned is employed on occasion. Its value from the point of view of demonstration is declared to be negligible. But in practice it is not without its own attractiveness. The conclusion is obvious. St. Thomas, in the majority of those instances where he has recourse to etymology, has no idea of a scientific demonstration ; it serves simply as a method of arranging his data. Underlying the whole process is the vague and far-reaching principle that a certain correspondence subsists between language and reality through the intermediary of thought. But the certitude of its application varies *ad infinitum*, at one time being as certain as the rock of divine

[36] 2a, 2ae, q. 45, a. 2 ad 2.
[37] 2 d, 13, q. 1, a. 3 ; *Spir.*, 9, 9, etc.
[38] Like Aristotle he is of opinion that the wise man speaks in the common language of everybody and is not to disturb himself about the use of words. In 1 *Post.*, l. 3.
[39] 2a, 2ae, q. 92, a. 1 ad 2, etc.
[40] In 5 *Met.*, l. 1, 1, 4 ; 3 d. 26, q. 1, a. 1 ad 3 and a. 5 ; *Ver.*, 4, 1. For examples see the explanation given of *spiritus* (4 *Contra Gentes*, 23, 1) and that of *nature* (*ibid.*, 35, 3), etc.
[41] 2a, 2ae, q. 57, a. 1 ad 1.

authority,[42] at others as inconsistent as human testimony. At times, in fact, no attempt whatever is made to suggest the truth of the affirmation put forward ; it is simply a question of putting together certain fluid and badly melted elements apparently for the pleasure of seeing how they unite. Thus between arguments truly probable and a simple rapprochement or *jeu d'esprit*, or even a mere mnemo-technical arrangement, the " etymological argument " may assume a thousand different forms. At all times, however, an ideal thread holds together particular applications and the general psychological principle mentioned, while not unfrequently the syllogical form is introduced to remind us, as it were, that such phantasies belong to a philosophical system, and that the artist is engaged in an attempt to give the appearance of solid constructions on the part of the human reason to his castles in the clouds.

Similar considerations arise out of literary criticism and textual exegesis as St. Thomas understood them. It might be shown that in his exposition of an author, be it Aristotle or St. Paul, he proceeds by way of a minute logical analysis which seems to postulate the application rather of a certain rational finality on the part of the author than the principles of concrete psychology : he seems to imply that this finality is perfectly conscious on the author's part and that it ramifies into all the details.[43] And yet here and there we find assertions to the contrary, as when he says that a text is to be expounded psychologically rather than rationally justified, and just then, after this announcement, he puts before the reader a sample of those arrangements which he had condemned.[44] Always, then, it is the same conclusion to which we are forced. In spite of his excessive employment of systematic arrangements, St. Thomas was persistently aware, though at times only dimly, of their futility. It was not for him so much a question of incapacity to

---

[42] 3 q. 37, a. 2 and *ibid.* ; the general principle : " Names should correspond to the properties of objects.

[43] For the logical plan that St. Thomas discerns in the metaphysics of Aristotle see the opening remarks of the different books of his *Commentary*. This conception is judged by Werner to be *sehr natürliche und ungezwungene*. See also 1a, 2ae, q. 108, a. 3 for the plan of the Sermon on the Mount.

[44] See In *Gal.*, 5, l. 5 and l. 6 end (wording of Br. Reginald).

criticise as a disinclination to exercise his critical faculty in
their regard.   What difference did it make to him?   The
essential thing, did it not consist in the simulation of the
Idea?   And for that purpose, as he thought, he had no
better instrument than that of reasoning.

CHAPTER VI

THE VALUE OF HUMAN SPECULATION

" Weariness and the many occupations of daily life necessarily interrupt that contemplation wherein consists human happiness, if there be any in this life ; errors, doubts, and the various misfortunes to which the present life is subject all go to show that human happiness, especially in this life, can bear no comparison to the happiness of God." [1] In our opening pages we laid down the principles that under-lie a rigid and intrepid form of intellectualism. To such an extent did intellectual activity appear to be of the very essence and purpose of nature that it was difficult to see what value was left for voluntary action. All kinds of precisions and suppositions had to be made so as to safe-guard that pre-eminence which love and moral life enjoy for human consciousness. Coming to the analysis of intellectual activity under human conditions, it appeared so crude and limited that even a greater space was devoted to showing the vanity of the very primacy we had been previously establishing. Eventually it seemed as if on such a philosophy men were like the owls who find all their happiness in staring at the sun.

The solution of this antinomy is rendered difficult for the reader of St. Thomas by the overlapping of two questions, one an abstract question and the other a question of fact. The gratuitous elevation of man to a supernatural destiny and the theological complement that it implied solved the problem in a way that Aristotle could not have foreseen, and dispensed St. Thomas from elaborating a purely philo-sophical solution. He has written enough, however, to enable us to see what was in his mind. In the first place, he seems to have regarded a kind of æsthetic beatitude as

---

[1] I *Contra Gentes,* 102, 6.

absolutely speaking possible in the purely natural order. Secondly, this beatitude which he considered satisfying in its own order would not to his mind exhaust man's full capacities for love and knowledge. The value of human speculation, then, may be considered with reference to the two domains, that of the possible order of " pure nature " and that of the actual order of grace which prepares man for the vision of God.

I

St. Thomas sometimes takes account of the hypothesis of a pure state of nature wherein man would have been left to his own resources without any question of God's intervention to raise him to a participation in the intimacy of his own divine life. On such a supposition man's beatitude would not be supernatural, though it would be intellectual, since intelligence is that which is highest and noblest in man. It is to be remarked that such knowledge would not have been exclusively abstract in form, even of things other than the actual self, but it is true that the theory of natural felicity is less liable to instil a disdain for abstractions than is the promise of a higher ideal. In this way the ambitious principles we have been expounding can be reconciled with a felicity that is only relatively satisfying.

As understood by Aquinas this natural beatitude would require a life of immortality for its completion. After a period of intellectual and moral preparation on earth where by " study and especially by merit " the soul would have prepared itself for a knowledge of the separate substances death would intervene to introduce the soul to another world. Once here, the soul would undergo not only the reception of a more abundant light than it could have sustained on earth, but in addition God would provide it with infused ideas which would help to enrich and perfect its acquired knowledge. Ideas gathered on earth would enable it to apply or render more precise its present perceptions. After a certain period perhaps the body would be restored to spirit in order to complete man's natural perfection. The idea of God, now simplified and purified by its liberation from the opacity of human phantasms, would still remain obscure and analogical. By this time also the soul would have denied more things of God, even things more beautiful, than was possible for it in this life.[2]

In these few lines we obtain an idea of what St. Thomas saw in this other-worldly natural beatitude. But more frequently St. Thomas speaks of that disinterested speculation which belongs to the wise man of Aristotle on earth. With the exception of the intuition of the actual ego he regarded all such knowledge as essentially abstract. It is not for that reason, however, devoid of all delight or pleasure, especially in the eyes of those whose horizon is bounded by the frontiers of this world. This felicity is constituted by such knowledge as the human mind, working on philosophical principles, can glean of God and of separate substances. A general and even vague knowledge of such sublime realities, thinks St. Thomas, is of greater value than a more detailed and more perfect knowledge of things less noble. This knowledge will be relatively poor and thin, of course, and cannot be said to reach the level of intuitive knowledge despite the principles of Alexander and Averrhoes. "It is in such knowledge that man's supreme beatitude consists in so far as he is left to his natural resources."[3] Elsewhere, speaking of the opinions of the "philosophers," St. Thomas speaks of "divine things"[4] instead of the "separate substances," while in yet another place he adds a certain panoramic view of the entire order of things.[5] The acquired virtues are looked upon as a preparation for this felicity, and though the activity of the practical intellect is implied they do not rank as constitutive elements. Bodily well-being as well as the presence of friends is required.[6] In a word, those ideas familiar to all acquainted with the writings of Aristotle find their place in the Thomistic view of this terrestrial beatitude.

[2] De Anima, q. 17–20. In these articles he discusses *natural* beatitude as it exists in the other world (17 ad 11, 18, ad 14, 20, ad 11). *Cf.* 4 Contra Gentes, 79.
[3] De Anim., a. 16 and ad 1 ; 1 q. 62, a. 1 and q. 88, a. 1.
[4] Ver., q. 27, a. 2.
[5] Ver., q. 2, a. 2 ; q. 20, a. 3.
[6] V. i. C., 9, 6 ; 1a, 2ae, q. 3, a. 5 ; 94, a. 6, a. 8 ; In Job, 7, 2 ; 8, 2 ; Ver., 1, 2, etc.

What interests us here is the precise value to be ascribed to human speculations on this hypothesis. Confining our outlook to the present world, it must be admitted that these speculations rank rather as an instalment of human felicity than as a mere preparation for it. We notice that consistently with this St. Thomas ascribes to intellectual activity in the abstract certain prerogatives that belong to something that is essentially and radically good. Two things are implied in this. In the first place, intellectual activity as such cannot be evil, and, in the second, intellectual activity has something absolute about it in virtue of which it is willed for its own sake, without reference to any ulterior ends.

When the dilettante is described as one who would make of life entire a work of art " without distinguishing between his pleasures " we have put our finger on the very root of his outlook on the world. But at the same time we have come very near putting our finger on one of the sources of Thomistic intellectualism. For St. Thomas it is an indisputable principle that intellect has power to transmute the things it touches to good. It would follow that as far as thought is concerned and in *so far as things have been subjected to the transforming influence of thought* there is no room for a distinction of pleasures from the point of view of good and evil. It would undoubtedly be futile to look for a deliberate and explicit application of these principles to the three domains of religious contemplation, of science and of art. But it is not by dismembering a principle that we may hope to see the universality of its application. The principle itself is frequently proclaimed by St. Thomas, and then he goes on to apply it in a haphazard fashion, as it were, to all orders of intellectual knowledge. But this procedure is significant as indicating that he wishes to apply the principle all round. " Every kind of knowledge by its nature belongs to an order of things that are good." " Evil in so far as it is known is good because it is good to know evil." [7] He goes even further than that. He admits that because every act of intellectual knowledge, whether found in man or in

---

[7] *Ver.*, 2, 5, 4 and 2, 15, 5.

God, is intrinsically so excellent that the pleasure derived is itself of the same high order of excellence. Absolutely speaking all intellectual pleasures are in accordance with reason. Only in one instance can there be question of limiting them, and that arises only when directly or indirectly one form of intellectual pleasure interferes with some higher or better form of the same kind of pleasure.[8] This holds good for scientific studies as well as for those more intimate and nearer joys that come from personal reflection or philosophical research. Every objection urged against this view of things arises from a confusion between the pleasures of appetitive activity which draw their value from the objects pursued, and those essentially good pleasures that accrue from intellectual activity as such. " The pleasure of thought may have a twofold source. There is the pleasure that comes from thought, and the pleasure that is derived from the object thought about." [9] " The pleasure which arises from thinking as such is of an entirely different order from that which is derived from external action. Nor is the pleasure that arises out of the thought of the most evil objects in any way a sin ; it is a praise-worthy pleasure such as may be derived from the knowledge of the truth." [10] To those theorists in æsthetics who deny artistic value to things because of certain pleasurable impulses aroused, and who subordinate art to morals, St. Thomas would have certainly replied that they judge the value of a form of activity by a feeling that follows only *per accidens* from it, and not by that which is proper to it as artistic activity, and that therefore their arguments are false. He would have denied that the value of æsthetic impression is to be measured by the result produced in the practical will, just as in the same way he would have con-demned anybody who, comparing the respective merits of two alchemists, would decide *a priori* that one of them was the less learned because he employed his art to poison rather than to cure.

[8] *Cf.* 4 d. 44, q. 1, a. 3, sol. 4 ad 4.
[9] *Quodl.*, 12, 33.
[10] *Ver.*, 15, 4.

Would he, however, have been for that reason less severe when it was a question of the practical ordering of one's intellectual life ? Would he have condoned the procedure of the æsthete who makes pleasure the sole end of all his actions ? To think so would be to ignore one of the commonest distinctions of his system, a distinction which he explicitly mentions in this precise context. Science and art are independent of morals in their own orders *quoad specificationem*, but in actual practice they are subordinate *quoad exercitium*. It would be wrong for an architect to build a house in order to satisfy some base passion, but he does not cease for all that to be a good architect.[11] A young person who reads forbidden books indulges in an evil practice, but he nevertheless acquires a knowledge of new truths. Thus in virtue of the close connection that may exist between certain studies and impulses aroused by them curiosity may be a particular vice and magic a forbidden art. There are certain delicate matters where speculative thought quickly becomes an intermediary between us and evil. Experience of such accidental connections between speculative thought and evil practice must lead to a kind of moral hygiene which will help us to avoid such thoughts as lead us into sin.[12] Science, art, even religious meditation itself must be regulated in practice according to the exigencies of final happiness. But this doctrine (which is only a systematic development of the dictum of Aristotle that in certain circumstances it may be better to acquire riches than to philosophise) does not affect the primacy of contemplation in the order of essences, nor does it diminish its intrinsic value in all instances.

Some actions are intrinsically evil, such as blasphemy and lying. Other actions, though good in themselves, are liable to be rendered evil by the corruption of one of their intrinsic elements as may happen in the act of generation.

[11] 1a, 2ae, q. 21, a. 2 and q. 57, a. 3 ; 2a, 2ae, q. 71, a. 3 ad 1. *Cf.* In 6 *Eth.*, l. 4 ; In 1 *Pol.*, l. 11. The incidental dangers of knowledge are all enumerated in 3 d. 35, q. 2, a. 3, sol. 3 ; 2a, 2ae, q. 167, a. 1.

[12] 1 q. 22, a. 3 ad 3 ; *Ver.*, 15 4 : *Eo quod propter corruptionem concupiscibilis, statim sequitur motus in concupiscibili ex ipsis concupiscibilibus causatus.* Theatrical representations are blameworthy in as far as they promote luxury and cruelty. 2a, 2ae, q. 167, a. 2 ad 3.

But the speculative idea is always pure and it is only the presence of some extrinsic factor which can render it blameworthy.   Another prerogative of the speculative idea, correlative with the former and indicative of it, is the intrinsic attractiveness of the idea.   Always pure, the speculative idea is always loved, and in this it bears a resemblance to the ultimate end itself.   St. Thomas explains this generally by saying that the speculative idea " has no contrary."   The idea as such is the perfection of mind in action.   Because it is not limited by spatial contraction to one particular form, mind is naturally superior to the need of temporal transformation and inaccessible to all corruption :   it belongs to another order of things altogether. That which is subject to substantial and successive changes, such as matter, is capable of being transformed so as to become other than it was.   But even such changes cannot affect the object of mind which is essential truth and they are as incapable of touching mind as the dog which bays and leaps at the moon is incapable of grasping or biting the moon's rays of light.   Such changes, then, leave the pleasures of mind intact, and if at times to think spells sadness that can only be as the result of some far-off consequence, *per accidens valde remotum*.   Even in such cases, if we are anxious to speak correctly, we shall have to say that it is not the idea as such which is the cause of sadness.   The objections that seem to rise to mind in view of ordinary good sense and the common uses of language are disposed of one by one. Speculative activity is so pre-eminently good and appropriate that we need only isolate it from the apparent wrappings that clothe it in practical life to be convinced that it is on all occasions something essentially attractive.[13]

It seems clear, then, that activities that belong to the purely intellectual order are such as will appeal to the will. " The speculative sciences are lovable for their own sake precisely because their aim is knowledge and because there

---

[13] 4 d. 49, q. 3, a. 3, sol. 2 ; 4 d. 50, q. 2, a. 4, sol. 1 ad 2 ; 1a, 2ae, q. 35, a. 5 ; *Ver.*, 26, 3, 8, etc. See also those passages where St. Thomas rejects the explanation given by St. Gregory the Great as to the way in which the demons suffer from fire : the simple perception of fire, he objects, could cause only pleasure.

is no other form of activity which is not directed to some extrinsic end, with the exception of speculative contemplation. For even playful actions, which would seem to be done without any purpose, have some end in view . . . else we should always have to be playing if play were an end in itself, and this cannot be admitted." [14] This familiar example of play and the difference it emphasises serve to bring out the fact that all speculative activity is intrinsically something more than a means to an end and that it is already an instalment of the absolute end itself. "For even playful actions in their own order are not subordinated to any other end, yet the pleasure that accrues from them is intended to relax the mind and to bring rest." "The end of playful actions is something according to reason since we indulge in play in order the better afterwards to engage in serious occupations." [15] Now thought ranks as one of the highest forms of serious occupations, and the neglect of thought for a time may be looked upon, consistently with his principles, as a preparation for a more perfect thinking in the future. On occasion it may be necessary to devote oneself to money-making and abstain from philosophy, but the ultimate reason for this is the necessity for not being harassed by more immediate preoccupations when there is question of lengthy excursions in thought.

Combining the specific value of speculation with its independence in the order of ends, we have the most perfect image of what is implied in beatitude.[16] Conformably with these principles, it may be remarked, the intellectual life appears in the context of man's present life as the better part to be chosen. But in the perspective of a future life the intellectual vocation may appear either as the most dangerous of temptations or as the most suitable form of preparation for it. Nothing in fact is more calculated to turn away one's attention from true beatitude than that which gives a deceptive counterpart of it, and, from another

[14] 3 *Contra Gentes*, 25.
[15] 2a, 2ae, q. 168, a. 2 ad 3 ; 3 *Contra Gentes, loc. cit.*
[16] 3 *Contra Gentes*, 63. *Hujus autem perfectae et ultimae felicitatis in hac vita nihil est adeo simile sicut vita contemplantium veritatem, secundum quod est possibile in hac vita.*

point of view, nothing is more likely to lead us to true felicity than that which gives us a foretaste of it.

II

This logical working out of the Aristotelian theory of happiness, however, will scarcely impress humanity. Is it possible that these abstract ideas, which merely deceive our hunger, will bring full satisfaction to man and appease all his aspirations ? Do not the lower faculties, so immediately in touch with reality, suggest to reason a form of possession infinitely superior to its own ? Have we not before our eyes the constant spectacle of the majority of men deciding for a life of pleasure and thus giving the lie to the philosopher of abstract essences ? [17] We see a majority apparently going against what nature indicates for them. Is there not in this an appeal to the philosopher either to moderate his exigencies in this matter or else to elevate them to the extent of seeking happiness in some unknown form of intellectual knowledge which would be more intimate and pleasurable, or at least different from those dry abstractions on which he himself is nourished ?

Did this general uneasiness express itself with the precision of a formula instead of in the vague form of an appetitive tendency, then it would be comparatively easy to reply to it in accordance with Thomistic principles. It could be done by invoking the distinction that obtains between terrestrial abstractions and those pure ideas which the separated soul would enjoy after death even in the purely natural order. But would such a solution on purely classical lines fully satisfy ? It would still be true that man's lower faculties, with their own full and complete satisfaction, as well as that modicum of intuition which man enjoys in the actual perception of the ego, might possibly suggest the idea of a similar possession of the First Intelligible, God : the ape in us seems to lord it over the man, just as

[17] I q. 49, a. 3 ad 5 ; 1a, 2ae, q. 71, a. 2 ad 3. Elsewhere, in addition to composition of man's being, original sin is mentioned as cause (1 q. 23 a. 7 ad 3, 2a, 2ae, q. 136, a. 3 ad 1).

the egotistic æsthete would seem to render the religious being in us envious.

That at least seems to have been the thought of Aquinas. Without following the circuitous route demanded by an exact logic or observing cleverly delineated shades of meaning in expression, he arrived in one leap, as it were, at the conclusion that *somehow* the intuitive vision is postulated by the nature of intelligence.   It would seem that we are so constituted that peace will never be ours except in the possession of God, and this possession is brought about by mind.   Whether we like it or not, such was the procedure of St. Thomas.   For my own part I am convinced of the Saint's full and entire orthodoxy on this point, and I think that without modifying a single line of his thought he could have replied convincingly to any questions that arise out of his method of procedure.[18]   But I must be here permitted to close my eyes to the many theological aspects oɪ the problem and to follow his development of the question simply as it is given in its context side by side with dogma. One precaution, however, is necessary : we must not project back to St. Thomas heresies that followed after his time, we must read him in relation to the philosophies that preceded him.   We must not think of Pascal or Baius any more than St. Thomas himself thought of them ; those who presented him with the materials for this problem were Augustine and Aristotle, Alexander and Averroes.

The logic of the system is very clearly indicated in a chapter of that lucid opuscule, the *Compendium Theologiae*.

[18] It is beyond all question that St. Thomas safeguards the strict supernatural character of the intuitive vision of God. 2 d. 29, q. 1, a. 1 ; 3 d. 23, q. 1, a. 4, sol. 3 ; 1a, 2ae, q. 114, a. 2 ; 1 q. 62, a. 2 ; *Car.*, 2, 16. Likewise when Rousselot himself speaks of the Beatific Vision being somehow postulated by the nature of intellect he has no intention of compromising the supernatural character of the Beatific Vision.   This is also to be borne in mind when he employs such words as *exigence* or, as I have translated it, "need" in regard to this vision of God.   Obviously there can be no question of *need* or *exigentia* in the real order, since the supernatural is precisely what is undue to man and beyond his natural forces.   For what follows see my book, *The Desire of God in the Philosophy of St. Thomas*, pp. 138 *sqq.*, where the absolutely transcendent character of the supernatural vision of God is stressed, and pp. 155 *sqq.*, where an attempt is made to see how the supernatural order, though transcending nature, ultimately is in harmony with it.   In this discussion the pivotal point is that of a *desiderium naturale* on the part of intelligence to see God.—(*Translator's Note.*)

" When the ultimate end is reached natural desire is appeased. And yet no matter what progress has been made in that kind of knowledge which is obtained from the senses, there is still a desire to know something more. There are many things that the senses cannot know and of which we obtain a very poor idea by means of the senses : we can perhaps know *that* such things are, but not *what* they are because the essences of immaterial things are not of the same kind as those of physical things, but rather incommensurably transcend them. Within the province even of sensible things there are some whose nature we cannot know with certitude, some of which we do not know at all and others only slightly. The desire to know, to have a perfect knowledge, is always present with us ; it is something inborn, and a natural desire cannot be vain or aimless. We shall, therefore, reach our ultimate end only if a higher agent than our natural faculties actualises our intellect and satisfies our natural desire of knowledge. Now this desire to know is such that when we know effects we desire to know their causes, and no matter what the thing in question be, even when we know all its circumstances, our desire does not rest until we know the essence of it. Hence our natural desire to know cannot be appeased until we know the first cause, and not in any haphazard way, but in its essence. Now the first cause is God. Hence the ultimate end for an intelligent creature is to see God in His essence." [19]

The rapidity with which St. Thomas towards the end of this passage arrives at the conclusion will not have escaped the attention of the reader. He will also have noticed the apparent strength and rigour of the argument as it takes shape beneath his pen. But it must be further observed that the whole argument arises out of an analysis of the rhythm of human knowledge as such and that no appeal is made to Revelation, nor is there an allusion to the order of grace.

Such a text would seem sufficiently clear to suggest that it is to the very nature of intelligence we must look for the root and source of the " need " for that supernatural com-

[19] *Comp. Theol.*, 104.

plement that takes place in the Beatific Vision. There are other implied assertions in the text, however, which seem to envisage man in the concrete, and this fact alone is decisive as against those who see man's whole orientation towards the Beatific Vision as due to some secret transformation of man brought about historically by grace. It was in this sense that Cajetan interpretated the view of St. Thomas on this problem, and theologians commonly have gladly borrowed from Cajetan. It suffices to examine the development of the whole argument as it appears in the *Summa Contra Gentes* to be convinced that this interpretation is not justified. St. Thomas advances the same proofs there for angels as well as for man and recognises for both the same probative force. Now how can we be aware of the presence of such a desire in the angels if it is something contingent and not the result of their intellectual nature? *Omnis intellectus naturaliter desiderat divinae substantiae visionem.*[20] These words are taken from a chapter in which St. Thomas is dealing *ex professo* with the distinction between the separate substances and man, and in which he holds, as against certain Arabian philosophers, that all forms of intelligence, that of man included, enjoys a receptive capacity in regard to the *lumen gloriae.* The whole question then of the capacity of intelligence for the Beatific Vision is one that must be raised above the plane of man historically redeemed and subject to human observation. Two chapters are entitled : " That to know God is the end of every intellectual substance," and " That the natural desire of the separate substances is not set at rest in the natural knowledge they possess of God." [21] The arguments contained in the first mentioned of these two chapters do not all conclude to the intuitive vision—some stop short at the abstract form of knowledge—but it is clear that the principal and fundamental arguments are applied both to angels and to men. The other chapter can leave no doubt since it deals chiefly with the separate substances of whom we have no experimental knowledge, man being only incidentally mentioned.

[20] 3 *Contra Gentes*, 57, 3.
[21] 3 *Contra Gentes*, 25 and 50.

This recourse, then, to sanctifying grace as an excitant of the desire in question must be resolutely excluded, at least if it is put forward as an integral solution of the whole problem. It is in the intellectual nature itself that St. Thomas finds a certain inclination towards vision and a desire of God as He is in Himself. And it may be said that St. Thomas bridges the chasm between the lowest form of intelligence and the plenary possession of God by vision, by the ideas of potency and act : possession of intelligence in the lowest degree is the foundation for the possibility of this supernatural possession of God. " Whatever is in potency tends towards the perfection of act, and as long as a being is not wholly in act it cannot be said to have reached its ultimate end." [22] This argument put forward to prove that it is impossible for the human intellect to realise its ultimate perfection in this life may be looked upon as an epitome of the reasoning process we have just been indicating. Clearly, such an argument holds good for every kind of intellect alike.

There is, however, a second group of arguments that refer more directly to man. Once these are grasped they lead us a little further in the understanding of this mysterious " need " on the part of the intellectual nature for the Beatific Vision. Let us once more return to the *Nicomachean Ethics* and to its ideal of human happiness. A close analysis of these celebrated pages reveals a certain incoherence and lack of balance in the Aristotelian anthropology. Aristotle is anxious to base everything on nature and on what is commensurate with nature, but while he starts from this idea he soon asks his reader to renounce it somehow. We must not listen to those who say that man must be satisfied with merely human ideals, for he who is truly happy is so not in virtue of the human part of him but by that which precisely makes man divine. On the one hand, man is μάλιστα νοῦς, while, on the other, contemplation is something " superhuman." [23] This paradox is reflected in his

---

[22] 3 *Contra Gentes*, 48. *Omne quod est in potentia intendit exire in actum. Quamdiu igitur non est ex toto factum in actu, non est in quo fine ultimo. Intellectus autem noster est in potentia ad omnes formas rerum cognoscendos.*

[23] Aristotle, *Eth. Nic.*, K. 1177, b. 32 : οὐ χρὴ δὲ κατὰ τοὺς παραινοῦντας ἀνθρώπινα φρονεῖν ἄνθρωπον ὄντα. *Ib.* 27 : οὐ γὰρ ᾗ ἄνθρωπός ἐστιν οὕτως

ontology. It is true that as against the Platonists he holds
that the soul is the form, not merely the director, of the body.
But in view of his theory that the activity of the intellect is
"separate" or "from without" : ἡ δέ τοῦ νοῦ χεχωρισμένη ?
what becomes of his doctrine of the commensurate relation
of nature and its activity ? Is there not here an admission
of the Platonic idea that the natural instruments are unworthy of nature : τὴν δύναμιν ὀυκ ἀξίαν τῆς φύσεως ἔχον ?
Have we not here also the beginnings of an antinomy that
can be solved by a philosophy that would be "mystical"
in its principles, ascetical in the means employed and
reducible to a formula that seemed radically absurd to
the adversaries of the Stoics : *Id est convenienter naturae vivere,
a natura discedere ?* [24]

It is certain that the same antinomy is felt in the anthropology of Aquinas and that it is consciously accentuated.
We cannot now expound the doctrine as a whole with its
curious ramifications into pure metaphyics. [25] In a general
way it may be said that man is conceived as a strange and
paradoxical being : his natural means of protection seem
insufficient for him in his struggle for a happy life. Such a
being is, of course, conceivable, for though the world is
essentially good that does not mean that it is equally favourable to all kinds of essences or natures : the existence of
giraffes, for instance, requires more complicated conditions
than are required for their existence by mice. But between
such extremes there is the extremely sensitive being of man,

βιώσεται ἀλλ'ἡ θεῖόν τι ἐν ἀυτῷ ὑπάρχει, hence the trace of a doubt, *ibid.* 26 :
ἄν εἴη βίος κρείττων ἢ κατ' ἄνθρωπον. St. Thomas would appear to have
sensed this internal lack of consistency in the Aristotelian doctrine, for proving
that beatitude is not to be found on earth he goes on to add, after referring
to the Arabian theories : *Quia vero Aristoteles vidit quod non est alia cognitio hominis
in hac vita quam per scientias speculativas, posuit hominem non consequi felicitatem
perfectam, sed suo modo. In quo satis apparet quantum angustiam patiebantur hinc
inde eorum praeclara ingenia ; a quibus angustiis liberabimur . . .* , etc. (3 *Contra
Gentes,* 48 ult.). Regarding the question of extraterrestrial felicity, he says
elsewhere, Aristotle has nothing definite either in affirmation or denial (4 d. 49,
q. 1, a. 1, sol. 4).

[24] Cicero, *De Finibus,* IV, Xv, 40–42.

[25] These theories have only an indirect interest for intellectualism in so far
as they emphasise the fluidity of the rigorous concept of *nature* as well as the
room they make for variation in those apparently rigid relations that link up
nature with its end (see 3 q. 9, a. 2 ad 3 ; 2a, 2ae, q. 2, a. 3 ; 1a, 2ae, q. 113,
a. 10).

so easily disturbed and warped that it does seem difficult
to see how his history could enjoy an even tenor in the
exercise of his activities without some kind of adventitious
help. " Besides the help of grace another preternatural aid
was necessary in the case of man because of his composite
nature. Man is composed of body and soul, of sense and
intellect. Such a nature if left to itself alone would imply
the weighing down of intellect by the body and there would
be certain obstacles to impede it from rising to the heights
of contemplation. This aid was original justice which had
the effect of submitting the lower faculties to reason and the
body to spirit, thus allowing the human mind to tend
towards God." [26]

The ordination of man to the Beatific Vision, however, is
not implied in these words. The question of primitive
justice, like that of original sin, is logically independent of
the supernatural strictly so called. But such words mark the
introduction of a new idea into the peripatetic system of
thought. They put us in presence of the idea of a duality
of ends thinkable for one and the same nature, and indicate
an incapacity on the part of some beings of attaining their
end because of the very perfection of their nature. From
that it is but a step to the further idea of the extreme appropriateness of the intuitive vision of God as the ultimate end
of all intellectual natures. Undoubtedly, the reasons put
forward for man do not admit of application to the angels.
Being based precisely on man's composite nature, they imply
the paradoxical pre-eminence of the senses over intellect, for
the senses, though of a lower order, are nevertheless intuitive,
whereas intelligence is more sublime but is also more unreal
in its presentation of reality. It is this fact which also explains
the comparative rareness of success where mankind is concerned.[27] Man is the subject where the multiple holds
greatest sway. Just above man, in accordance with the
Thomistic laws of continuity, a new cycle commences where
perfection corresponds to an increasing simplicity of nature.
But the example of man suffices to show that the created

[26] *Mal.*, 5, 1. *Cf.* 1 d. 39, q. 2, a. 2 ad 4.
[27] See texts cited above, p. 184.

mind as a potential form of intelligence introduces into the order of nature an indetermination of a new kind which implies the possibility of different solutions for beings of one and the same species. As a capacity for being, intellect, *nata omnia fieri*, is more elastic and comprehensive than other forms that are tied down to matter. And no matter how determined the angel is from an intellectual point of view and specialised in its forms of activity, still the angel has the capacity for emerging out of its relative darkness into the purer light of the separate subsistence. The " obediential capacity " of intellectual natures, according to St. Thomas, is not something independent of their natural capacity ; it is rather to be identified with the intellectual nature as such. Granted, then, the knowledge of the supernatural ordination of intellectual natures, there is nothing impossible in the supposition—or at least the *post factum* supposition—that some trace of this capacity be recognisable in that conscious-ness of self that such natures enjoy as well as in certain blind impulses of their being. What in the absence of the divine offer would express itself in some mysterious appetitive form might with the light of faith be formulated in a series of luminous syllogisms. It is in that way that a probable synthesis is constructed so as to link up reason and revelation, taking as middle terms such things as the insufficiency of human speculations and the desire of possessing the First Object of intelligence in the immediacy of vision.

III

St. Thomas believed that as a matter of fact this supple-mentary addition had been offered to man in its very highest form, that of the vision of God. Viewed in the light of the whole intellectual movement of man so transformed, such a gracious gift from heaven came as the very crowning piece of his intellectualism. But from another angle, when we examine the exact conditions under which this gift is offered, it will be seen that this invasion of the natural order by the supernatural has for effect the reversal of philosophical values, a lowering of human speculation, and a bringing down of human thoughts from their high position to the humbler rank of means and instruments.

In view of the promise of the Beatific Vision the beatitude of abstractions diminishes in value necessarily. As a preparation for " felicity as such " they might have retained their position on earth. But as a matter of fact if the paradise opened for humanity by Christ is incomparably more beautiful than the natural felicity of the separate substances, its acquisition is also more difficult. It is held out to a nature wounded by sin, and one of the first effects of the loss of original justice is that reason is weakened and the senses strengthened, and thus the human mind finds itself impeded by many obstacles.[28]   Thus humanity as we possess it (and the philosopher like the theologian can only observe this) offers the spectacle of a continued struggle and a real natural discomfort. Further, this is precisely the state in which man used to prepare for supernatural vision. It follows that for human speculation we may expect conditions that are definitely unfavourable. There is no question of intellectual occupation being for the sons of Adam redeemed by a suffering God an unimpeded vocation, *operatio non impediti.*

To come down to specific details, it is to be remarked that a more or less free giving of oneself to a life of speculation is out of the question for the majority of men. But taking even those actually engaged in speculative pursuits, those who know for themselves the difficulties in view of man's unconquered sensitive energies, what objects are likely to attract them ?   It would be wrong, of course, to exaggerate the thought of Aquinas by reducing natural knowledge to something entirely insignificant from the Christian point of view. St. Thomas was capable of regarding even the lower forms of scientific knowledge as something essentially worthy of human research : to disdain them would be to disdain man himself.[29]   He differs from other saints of the Middle Ages in this respect by the very moderation of his expressions. But he never hesitates to subordinate every

[28] 1a, 2ae, q. 85, a. 3, etc.
[29] In 4 *Meteor.*, l. 1.   *Cf.* In *Trin.*, 6, 1.

form of human activity on earth to the intensity of the religious life, and I do not think that he would have been shocked by the opening lines of the *Imitation of Christ*. As his thought grows more mature we notice a corresponding increase in the growth of his mistrust of mere earthly knowledge, and as his mystical life becomes more intense it is easy to see that merely earthly science falls from its high estate : the knowledge of such things is good, but it must be abandoned when it prevents one from giving oneself to better things. " Since we are unable to take part in the holy solemnities of the angels," he writes to Brother Reginald, " the sacred time must not be wasted. Let us consecrate to study what cannot be given to psalmody. Anxious then to have some idea of the holy angels let us begin with the image formed of them in ancient times by human conjecture. What harmonises with faith we will retain and what is opposed we shall reject." [30]

It is right, then, on earth that the life of the spirit should gravitate around that knowledge which will serve as a preparation for vision and which teaches us concerning it. But it is here indeed that the lack of adaptation between intellectualism and man's present state comes most clearly into light. The knowledge in question is that of faith. Now faith for St. Thomas is a peculiar kind of act and one that is essentially imperfect. It is in fact an intellectual proposition which has for object something as yet unintelligible. It is intruded [31] among our concepts, and the very *raison d'être* of faith is that it brings us into contact with a Being Who transcends our concepts. The Apostle defined it well when he said that it was the *argumentum non apparentium* and the *substantia rerum sperandarum*. With reference to one and the same object it is impossible to possess faith and knowledge,

---

[30] *Opusc.*, 14, Prol.

[31] *Mal.*, 5, 3. *Supernaturali cognitione, quae hic in nobis per fidem plantatur.* The extrinsecism that this word suggests must not be understood out of relation to the *rationes convenientiæ* above mentioned. On the essentially instrumental character of faith see *Ver.*, 14, 2. Faith is subordinate to the moral life, but moral life is not itself the final end : *action may be looked upon as the end of the knowledge conveyed by dogma, but the Thing expressed by dogma is the end of action.* It is because vision is the ultimate end that St. Thomas places faith not amongst the practical but the speculative forms of knowledge (3 d. 23, q. 2, a. 3, sol. 2, *Cognitio dirigit in opere, et tamen visio Dei est ultimus finis operis . . .*),

and faith is also distinct from opinion, but least of all is faith a composite of both. Faith is essentially provisional, passing, and unsatisfying. This explains both its obscurity and its freedom for it is an imperfection on the part of a proposition when it cannot compel our assent, and it also accounts for the simultaneous presence of objective certainty which is absolute and its subjective instability. What best explains its hybrid or " monstrous " (in the mediæval sense of the word) character according to St. Thomas is the fact that while faith is situated in intelligence [32] it is not the product of purely intellectual factors ; both in its exercise and in relation to its proper object faith is under the empire of will.[33] " We are impelled to believe what we hear because there is a promise of eternal life if we do believe, and it is this recompense which moves the will to accept the revelation even when the understanding of no truth has intervened to move the intellect . . . " [34]   " In knowledge there is besides the assent of mind the movement of thought, but these two things are not merely parallel since the result of thought is the assent given and the peace that accrues from this assent. In faith, however, assent and thought remain parallel because assent is not finally produced by thought but is brought about by the intervention of the will, as has been said. Hence, since intellect by its own intrinsic movement has not reached the natural term of its activity, which is the comprehension of an intelligible object, there is still room for instability : intellect begins to work again and busies itself with the objects of belief even though it has given strong and firm assent to them. Intellect is not fully satisfied in its own order because it has been brought to give its assent not by the intrinsic laws of its thinking but under the influence of an extraneous factor. And it is for that reason that the intellect of the believer is spoken of as ' captive.' " [35]

[32] *Ver.*, 14, 4 ; 2a, 2ae, q. 4, a. 2. *Credere autem immediate est actus intellectus, quia objectum huius actus est verum, quod proprie pertinet ad intellectum. Et ideo necesse est quod fides, quae est proprium principium huius actus, sit in intellectu sicut in subjecto.*

[33] *V. i. C.*, a. 7 : *Voluntas imperat intellectui credendo, non solum quantum ad actum exsequendum, sed quantum ad determinationem obiecti.*

[34] *Ver.*, 14, 1.

[35] *Ibid.* St. Thomas further adds : *Quia tenetur terminis alienis, et non*

A number of *obiter dicta* scattered throughout the works of St. Thomas help to the completion of this picture. Thus the life of faith has two aspects. Looked upon as a preparation for vision, it marks the dawn of the supernatural triumph of intellectualism, while if it is taken as actual knowledge it seems to reduce intellectual knowledge to the very minimum that could be sustained by the life of mind. " In the knowledge of faith intellectual activity may be most perfect from the viewpoint of the object, but in its subjective nature it is most imperfect." [36] This is a point of fundamental importance and cannot be over-stressed when there is question of a critique of intellectual life from the Thomistic point of view. In this respect the only exaggeration possible would be that of sacrificing the intellectual character of the *praeambula fidei* in order to safeguard the obscurity of faith, and that is excluded by St. Thomas and the intellectual character of these *preambula* must be accorded under pain of rendering the act of faith immoral. We would not believe, says St. Thomas, did we not *see* that we must believe. [37]

propriis. The metaphor seems to me to have been borrowed from "physics" : intellect has not found its proper *locus ;* it is, as it were, suspended in mid-air. On the other hand, it is the will which is at home in faith and at rest because " it commands assent to a truth as its own proper good " (2a, 2ae, q. 11, a. 1).

[36] 3 *Contra Gentes,* 40. *In cognitione autem fidei invenitur operatio intellectus imperfectissima quantum ad id quod est ex parte intellectus, quamvis maxima perfectio inveniatur ex parte obieti.* This imperfection on the subjective side prevents us from designating faith as an " intellectual faculty " (3 d. 23, a. 3, sol. 3).

[37] 2, 2ae, q. 1, a. 4 ad 2. The rôle of the *preambula fidei* (or the reasons for believing) is to justify our assent intellectually. Since all our acts must be reasonable there is a strict duty of examining the reasons for belief. But the " articles of faith " and the reasons for believing taken together do not form a homogeneous series of rational propositions. The " articles of faith " are not brought under the first principles, though they may not be in contradiction with them. Somewhat like the judgments of direct experience in matters of virtue to which it is compared (3 d. 23, a. 3, aol. 2 ad 2 ; 1 q. 1, a. 6 ad 3 ; 2a, 2ae, q. 1, a. 4 ad 3) faith is itself a *habitus* that is not subordinated to anything but is comparable to the *habitus* of first principles and like it is inherent *per modum naturae.* It is seen, then, why we can assent to it with greater certainty than to first principles or to demonstrative sciences (*Prol. Sent.,* a. 3, aol. 3 ; *Ver.,* 12, 2, 3), and why faith may be found in the little child after Baptism as well as the cleverest theologian. Faith is not produced by nature as happens in the first principles, nor by habit as in the case of the virtues : it is produced by grace. If speculative reflection is capable of engendering a kind of " acquired faith " which is an *opinio fortificata rationibus* (*Prol. Sent., loc. cit.*), this new knowledge is not to be confounded with infused and theological faith : both kinds of faith are independent of one another just as experimental judgments in matters of chastity are independent of the abstract knowledge of chastity that can be obtained from instruction (*cf.* 2a, 2ae, q. 1,

Thanks to his ideas on demonstrative science and on certitude that is free, St. Thomas was able to show that faith as a whole had a voluntary character and yet was intellectually justified. But when it is a question of finding a place for St. Thomas amongst the Catholic theorists of faith it is rather on the shadows and on the insufficiency of faith that we must insist. From the point of view of knowledge I know of none of the great Doctors who are so outspoken on the imperfection of the act of faith. Compare him with his successors and it will be found that this comparison is best calculated to bring out the falling off in metaphysical and intellectual ambitions among Catholic Schools since the thirteenth century. Among his predecessors the difference is striking even compared with St. Augustine, the fervent apostle of the *crede ut intelligas*. Not indeed that St. Augustine was easily satisfied with earthly obscurities. On the contrary, he was an enthusiastic seeker after the true end of intellect which is that of Vision. Yet the same serenity and indifference is not to be found in his denunciation of knowledge that is the result of simple faith as is seen in St. Thomas, and the reason is that his theory is less deliberately founded on an ultimate metaphysic. Even after he had clarified the notion of Christian philosophy St. Augustine still complacently insists on the natural appropriateness of belief for the human mind. He looks upon it as something that is at the basis of all society, that prepares all minds for the acquisition of knowledge and so forth. St. Thomas was aware of all these considerations of the Master, but he recalls them only very briefly.[38] His aim is rather to insist on the tension of mind against simple belief : intellect wants to see, and nothing else will satisfy it.

In the life of mind on earth, then, the two ideas implied by *imperfection* and *preparation* are correlative. We must make up our minds to the fact that as long as intellect is in its

a. 3 ad 3). Further, this " acquired faith " is not *necessary* for the conservation of infused faith. What is essential is the practical judgment *hoc est tibi credendum*, which is produced under the influence of grace and is justified by the intellectual knowledge of the motives for believing (*Quodl.*, 2, 6 ; In *Trin.*, 3, 1, 4).

[38] *Opusc.*, 7, *Exp. super. Symbolum.*

present state it cannot have peace. There will always be present to it, if not an unreasonable sense of risk,[39] at least the discouraging consciousness of darkness and obscurity. On the other hand, seeing that Vision has been offered it will be the duty of reason to direct all human efforts towards the acquisition of that Vision, and not tarry by the way or entertain itself with things that may compromise its attainment, and for that reason knowledge must be appraised at the actual value that it possesses in the present order of things. The whole mass of human ideas, comprising that which is believed by Christians and known by theologians, constitute the " rudiments proposed on earth to mankind in order to enable it to reach its destined goal." [40] Without the slightest alteration of his metaphysic, then, without transmuting appetitive into acquisitive forms of activity, without subscribing to the idea of making tendency or movement as such the ultimate end, there is quite a natural modification on the side of his moral theory. Now that the goal of human life is something transcendent and superior to the forces of nature, the primary object that will interest man is less the End itself than the means to be employed in the attaining of that End. These means which are within man's reach will measure exactly his future share of happiness. In anticipation of final felicity all man's efforts in this life must be concentrated on the achievement of sanctity. And even logic will demand the further corollary that whereas the intellectual knowledge contained in the

[39] Since St. Thomas admits that faith is compatible with " evidence of credibility " (2a, 2ae, q. 5, a. 1).

[40] *Ver.*, 14, 11. An understanding of the helps offered to philosophy by Revelation needs a rather delicate distinction. It is true that, like all other Christian Doctors, St. Thomas appreciates the magnitude of the gift of faith and speaks of it in the same way as do the other Apologists (*Opusc.*, 7, *Exp. super Symbolum*, c. 1 : *nullus philosophorum . . . potuit tantum scire de Deo . . . quantum post adventum Christi scit vetula per fidem, cf.* 1 *Contra Gentes*, 5 end). Still bearing in mind his theory of science and of demonstration *propter quid* it will be seen that in his eyes faith can help knowledge only *per accidens*. It is this which explains assertions like the following : If to the questionings of an inquisitive spirit you reply only in the name of faith with a dogmatic assertion, the person will leave quite certain that the matter is thus, but his intellect will not have gained any knowledge : *certificabitur quidem quod ita est, sed . . . vacuus abscedet* (*Quodl.*, 4, 18). From the intellectual point of view faith is of a lower order than that of science, and it is this imperfection precisely which marks off faith by its opposition to science (*Ver.*, 12, 12 ; 2a, 2ae, q. 1, a. 5).

speculative sciences might previously have been, even as instruments, a vital stage in the advance towards the final End itself, they may now become mere ghosts of true felicity if they do not form part of one great movement that carries onward the human spirit towards a greater degree of grace : without this deep movement of the soul as a whole speculative knowledge as a mere shadow of the reality may be merely harmful and the time devoted to it a mere waste of time.

IV

For everyone present duty is both the instrument and measure of final beatitude. It does not follow, however, that it is impossible by reasoning on nature, with a view to practice, to determine which of man's good actions are most apt to lead to fullness of love and grace. Here again the ontological order comes into its own, and, faithful to his principles, St. Thomas affirms the superiority of the contemplative over the active life. Of all forms of activity that which best unites the human spirit to God is that of contemplation. It follows, then, that contemplation is to be preferred to external activity. Contemplation contains the really intense life for man since it is the most intimate form of application to the highest object. On earth, then, human perfection consists in this : *ut mens actu feratur in Deum.*[41] We cannot but notice how naturally " mysticism " appears as the crowning part of " intellectualism " of which it is in reality the fruit. No matter how legitimate the opposition of mysticism and intellectualism may be in other respects and for other thinkers, no opposition is more superficial or more false when it is a question of orthodox mysticism and of the classical philosophy of Catholicism. There is only one thing in St. Thomas which surprises us and that is that he did not bring out into even greater relief the exquisite intellectuality communicated to the life of mind by such mystical states as ecstasy and infused contemplation. In

---

[41] See the admirable theory of the evangelical counsels worked out by St. Thomas in the Third Book of the *Summa Contra Gentiles*, particularly ch. 130. Notice also ch. 133, which contains on religious poverty ideas so unlike those of the Franciscans (not indeed by opposition but by difference).

the simple life of faith and in the ordinary graces of prayer St. Thomas was able to discern those direct, rapid and delightful acts that are made possible for the ignorant by grace. Further he was also able to relate them to " intelligence." [42] How then is it possible that he did not make more of those infused intuitions which pierce through the opaqueness of images and go beyond the confusion of reasoning to lead the contemplative to a certain participation in the angelic mode of knowledge? The fact cannot be doubted, however. Whether it was because of his attachment to traditional classifications or to his unwillingness to admit too many exceptions to the principles of Aristotle, he makes only a few rapid allusions to such superhuman forms of intellectual knowledge and it would be impossible, without doing violence to his texts, to extract from them a complete theory of " mystical prayer." [43] Such a lack in

[42] See, for instance, 1 d. 15, q. 4, a. 2 ad 4, where it is said that there are uncultivated people who possess a certain knowledge of God as final End and as *profluens beneficia*, love being the necessary condition of such knowledge. *Cf.* also 3 d. 27, q. 2, a. 3 ad 2 : *Caritas habet rationem quasi dirigentem in suo actu, vel magis intellectum* ; In *Trin.*, 6, 1, ad ult. and 3 d. 35, q. 2, a. 2, sol. 1 : *Intellectus donum . . . de auditis mentem illustrat, ut ad modum primorum principiorum statim audita probentur.*

[43] The question is not as to whether St. Thomas admitted the existence of certain types of knowledge that are experimental and possessed of delight or savour : there can be no doubt on that point (1 q. 43, a. 5 ad 2, etc.). The question rather is whether he has expressly mentioned obscure, infused, and mystical contemplation properly so called, that form of contemplation devoid of imagery and reasoning which had been so expressively described by some of the Franciscan writers of the Middle Ages before it found its classical Doctors amongst the Saints of Carmel. It is with great caution that we must look for light here from second-hand authors. Vallgornera allowed himself to be carried too far in his desire to discover in St. Thomas the doctrine of the Mystics. Thus in his Q. 11, disp. 3, a. 1, *De Contemplatione supernaturali et infusa*, he writes : *D. Thomas 2a 2ae q.* 180, *a. 3 diffinit contemplationem infusam hac ratione : simplex intuitus divinae veritatis, a principio supernaturali procedens.* The four last words are simply added on by himself. Further, he cites opuscules that are either apocryphal or doubtful. In the more recent work of P. Maumus, *La doctrine spirituelle de S. Thomas d'Aquin* (Paris, 1885) other *rapprochements* will be found that are also to be taken with caution (p. 380, on the passive purification of the senses ; p. 401, on the gift of intelligence brought into relation with mystical union ; p. 454, on the prayer of union). Reading St. Thomas himself we find that he admitted the possibility, and in certain cases the fact, of this contemplation without images, though he regards it as essentially falling short of the intuitive vision which is " natural to the Angel but beyond man " (see *Ver.*, 18, a. 1 ad 1, ad 4 ; a. 2 ; 2 d. 23, q. 2, a. 1 ; and for a fuller psychological explanation 1 q. 94, a. 1). Yet, where St. Thomas treats the question *ex professo* he has in mind rather what man is capable of by his own efforts aided by ordinary graces and also that form of

his system is to be regretted. It cannot, however, be brought forward with the idea of diminishing the value of the contemplative life as he understood it. No matter how imperfect it is presumed to be, there are two prerogatives, I notice, which ensure a more certain primacy for it than for pure speculation in the natural order. For St. Thomas religious contemplation is more calculated to attract man than philosophical contemplation because the love of such contemplation is not distinguishable from love of the object to be contemplated.[44] Further, he ascribes more liberty to religious contemplation since he regards religious obedience as a sacrifice of practical and comparatively unworthy scientific pursuits, those namely which are concerned with things of the body and with the regulation of everyday affairs, in favour of a complete giving of oneself to the highest part of the soul to union with the One Thing Necessary.[45] "The great symptom of love is the desire for contemplation." "The sovereign perfection for human life is freedom of the human spirit to withdraw and be with God."

It must be remarked, however, that it is not precisely as

contemplation which even in the case of " intellectual vision " does not take place without images (2a, 2ae, q. 174, a. 2 ad 4 ; q. 180, a. 5 ad 2 ; *De Anim.*, a. 15 ; In *Trin.*, 6, 3, etc.). *Cf.* admission of Vallgornera (*loc. cit.*, art. 7, n. 2 : *Aliquando datur contemplatio supernatualis sine conversione ad phantasmata. In hanc sententiam videtur inclinare D. Thomas, quamvis non omnino certum sit in doctrina illius*). Very characteristic also is the exegesis given by St. Thomas of the *patiens divina* of the Pseudo-Dionysius and the other classical Fathers, which he explains as a phenomenon of the *affective* order antecedent to knowledge (*Ver.*, 26, 3, 18 ; 3 d. 15, q. 2, a. 1, sol. 2 ; In *Div. Nom.*, 2, 4), or as a kind of experimental knowledge without saying whether it goes beyond ordinary grace (2a, 2ae, q. 45, a. 2 ; q. 97, a. 2 ad 2). In the whole Commentary on the *De divinis nominibus* it is impossible to find anything that can be related to mystical knowledge with certainty even where the text to be explained seems to invite such an interpretation. All that seems to me the more remarkable since in his treatment of the knowledge of separate souls what he has to say of their indistinct kind of knowledge might naturally be associated with what the mystics have to say of the obscurity of their contemplation (*De Anim.*, a. 15, corp. ; *cf.* ad 21, etc.).

The most remarkable thing written by St. Thomas regarding this question of illumination that belongs to an order beyond the ordinary is what he has to say on the gift of prophecy (*Ver.*, q. 12 ; 2a, 2ae, q. 171 *sqq.*). Here he makes room for subjective conditions, and the way he envisages them is evidence of a great breadth of view and a constant desire to maintain contact between speculative theology and psychological experience.

[44] See 3 d. 35, q. 1, a. 2, sol. 1, sol. 3 on the difference between the contemplative life of the saints and that of the philosophers. And compare the two concepts of σοφια and *sapientia*.

[45] 3 *Contra Gentes*, 130.

a foretaste of heaven that contemplation is to be regarded as good and desirable, but rather as a preparation for heaven. To arrive at this and to place contemplation in the forefront as a means of preparation it was necessary to invoke the reflex principle that amongst means to an end the most efficacious is that means which most resembles the end itself. In the light of this it will be seen that the primacy of the contemplative life is not so absolute.[46] Much room is left for the intervention of divine designs, place is made for diversity of Providence, and there will be a greater variety of saints than of sages, and finally the ideal of the Christian will be very different from that of the happy man of Aristotle. But this last remark does not prevent the practical identification of the contemplative form of life with that which is the most perfect in the system of Aquinas. In conclusion it might be said that on the principles of St. Thomas Christianity implies the reconstruction of the moral world on its essential basis but according to a more embracive plan. The natural relations still hold, but what had been a closed and perfect system in itself has been taken up and made part of a larger movement and a vaster universe. The subordination of the older to the newer explains the fact that here and there minor deformations of the original structure may be noticed.

[46] 2a, 2ae, q. 182, a. 2 end ; V. i. C., 7, 4. St. Thomas agrees with all the Saints of Catholicism that it may be sometimes expedient to leave "Rachel for Lea" (Opusc., 2, De perfect. vitae spiritualis, c. 25 ; Quodl., 1, 14, 2), but there is nothing in his writings to suggest that extreme mistrust of the delights of contemplation and the desire to detach souls from them which we find in the ascetical writers of succeeding centuries. The great symptom of love is contemplation : if he seems to doubt it in the Sentences (3 d. 35, q. 1, a. 4, sol. 2), he affirms it in the Summa (2a, 2ae, q. 182, a. 2 ad 1). On the higher life of " illuminators," see Appendix, p. 224.

PART III

INTELLIGENCE AND HUMAN ACTION

I

HAD our study of the problems that arose in the preceding pages been sufficiently profound and thorough, the views of St. Thomas on the essential value of intellectual activity, which consists in its aptitude to know the real and to be an *end* in itself, would need no further elucidation. Since, however, in the final pages we have been reducing intellectual activity, like all other forms of human action, to the level of means in regard to a higher end, a new problem arises. Seeing that intellectual activity in man is so different from the intellectual process as such, seeing that it is destined ever to tend after a more stable, more refined, and purer form, and that it cannot attain to this without stirring into action and utilising man's other natural faculties, then the question of its precise place and value in the passive and progressive life that man leads on earth demands our consideration. We shall have to see if, in its new and for it secondary sphere, intelligence retains that pride of place it undoubtedly occupies when we view things in the abstract. Moreover, the necessarily provisional and paradoxical form—an intellectual activity which is not an end itself—calls for a close study of those human perceptions that enjoy only an imperfect and an analogical value, if we are to have a true perspective for the whole system.

There is no question here of unfolding all the principles that go to constitute the ethical system of St. Thomas as a form of moral intellectualism. It will have been already clear from previous developments that for St. Thomas reason does not merely serve as a subjective light in a virtuous life, the eye, so to speak, which sees the duties to be performed, but that it constitutes rather the very end of moral action since it is by reason or intellect that man

reaches his final end.[1] And because the " intellectual part "
of man is his final end it may also be looked upon as a formal
cause, so to speak, where morality is concerned. The direction imposed on human efforts by divine prescriptions is not
something indifferently or arbitrarily imposed, compelling
man to act in a non-human manner : rather, the dynamic
movement implied in human action is conformable to the
nature of man as a rational animal whose chief glory is the
intellectual part of him. This explains man's effort to
subordinate everything to his spiritual instincts and to
impregnate reality and action with mind. The whole
moral system of St. Thomas is reducible to the conquest of
the body by spirit, and the penetration of opaque matter
with the light of mind. " The good of man is to live according to reason," [2] and " considering things sanely virtue as
predicated of the appetitive side of man is nothing else but
a certain impression or form imprinted on appetite by
reason." [3] That is the central principle which explains his
whole theory of vices, virtues, sins and precepts.[4] Once
again, however, it must be remarked that this conception
of morals, though it is perfectly consistent with the ontological principles already laid down, does not affect the
value of intellectual activity *in statu viae ;* and it is in that
precisely we are interested for the moment.

[1] We have only to recall how St. Thomas identified intellectual activity
and pleasures of an intellectual order with that which is desirable *simpliciter*.
Even in regard to this life St. Thomas held that : *Sed delectationes spirituales
appetuntur secundum seipsas, quasi homini connaturales . . . et ideo delectationibus
spiritualibus nullam mensuram praefigit ration, sed quanto sunt maiores, tanto eligi-
biliores* (4d. 49, q. 3, sol. 1 ad 4). It is unnecessary to delay over the objections
that might be urged against this or with the reply that St. Thomas would
certainly have made by distinguishing intellectual activity *quoad exercitium* and
quoad specificationem. Those acquainted with the development of moral theory
and of Catholic asceticism after the Middle Ages will recognise the significance
of this prominence accorded by St. Thomas to such ideas.
[2] We find this principle repeated constantly. When St. Thomas employs
the phrase *secundum rationem* it seems to have suggested to him the two conceptions of reason at one and the same time. He thought of reason as a light or
measure and also of it as nature. But what is important to notice is that the
concept of reason as nature is the more important one and that the other is
merely a consequence of that.
[3] *V.i.C.*, 9.
[4] See, for example, 2a, 2ae, q. 123, a. 12 (the hierarchy of moral virtues
according to their relation to reason) ; in 4 *Eth.*, l. 15 (the theory of lying :
a lie is always and essentially evil in itself, and not merely because it injures
the neighbour).

We had just reached the point where we recognised that human values, identically intellectual ones in the definitive state of our final destiny, underwent a certain reversal in man's present state where values belong essentially to the order of volition. In heaven the perfection of the blessed is measured by the clarity of each one's Beatific Vision ; but on earth the only criterion of moral rectitude we possess is to be found in each one's capacity for love. The idea of progress is essential to the concept of man *in statu viae* and what is of prime importance consequently is man's capacity for action : " simply speaking, a man is said to be *good* according to the disposition of his will." [5] It follows necessarily that the value of intellectual activity must be gauged by the extent of its influence over will. In this world of practical needs the value we accord to reason and the estimation in which we hold it comes, not so much from its final or exemplary causality as from its efficient causality, if such a thing may be spoken of in regard to intellect. It is as an aid to action that intellect is productive of good, and it is in this way that it must pursue its own perfection and strive to " gain " itself and to " gain " God. " The sovereign good," writes St. Thomas, " is man's beatitude, which is his last end : and the nearer a thing approaches to this end, the higher must it be placed as a good for man. The nearest thing to that end is virtue . . . and after this comes the right disposition of reason." [6] That amounts to saying that when everything has been taken into account and when the present life has been esti- mated for what it really is, the question : " What is the value of the idea ? " is in practice reducible to this other question : " To what extent is the idea a *force* for action ? " and " To what extent does it bring about good conduct ? "

II

We need not delay here to prove that St. Thomas recog- nised that the idea could be a force or influence for action.

[5] *V.i.C.*, 7, 2 ; In 3 *Eth.*, l. 6, etc., *cf.* S. Augustine, *Enchiridion de fide, spe et caritate*, c. 117.
[6] 3 *Contra Gentes*, 141.

The difficulty, rather, is to show how his doctrine escapes being the merest form of psychological determinism.

He looked upon will as a tendency towards the good in general, and consequently he had to find in knowledge the determining principle for each concrete human action. Seeing that man's ideal was to realise himself intellectually, it followed that the only way he had of acting voluntarily was by recourse to intellectual motives. Will is something derivative : it springs from mind and acts for mind. And just as liberty has its root and source in the amplitude of intellect's proper object (*Ex hoc enim quod ratio deliberans se habet ad opposita, voluntas in utrumque potest*),[7] so each particular human act must be traced to an intellectual perception, and voluntary decisions take their rise therein. So true indeed is this that one is inclined ultimately to identify freedom of the will with that lucidity of vision which is characteristic of mind.[8] It would not be difficult to gather together certain texts, seductive in their apparent simplicity, which would go to indicate that St. Thomas was a " determinist." " Because it is intellect which moves the will, the act that proceeds from the will is the effect of knowledge." [9] " The proximate moving cause of the will is the good understood, which is its object, and it is moved thereby as sight is by colour." [10] " In all things the appetitive power is proportionate to the faculty of apprehension, by which it is moved." [11] Passages of this kind, as well as the interpretations given of them by Henry of Ghent and Duns Scotus, are too well known to be insisted upon.

It will be sufficient to indicate briefly in what sense St. Thomas understood these texts in order to be convinced that, while he did not abandon his theory of freedom, neither did he take away from the idea that influence for action which he had accorded to it. The metaphor of movers, applied to the idea as a motive-force of action, is

[7] 1a, 2ae, q. 6, a. 2 ad 2. See especially *Ver.*, 24, 1.
[8] Hence such strange expressions as *Voluntas libere appetit felicitatem, licet necessario appetat illam. Pot.*, 10, 2, 5. *Cf. Ver.*, 24, l. 20.
[9] In *Rom.*, 7, 3.
[10] 3 *Contra Gentes*, 88, 1.
[11] 1 q. 64, a. 2.

capable of different meanings, and St. Thomas employs it expressly in the sense of a final causality which does not exert a constraining influence over will. " The good perceived moves the will in the same way as a man who counsels or persuades, that is to say, by pointing out the goodness of an object." [12]

Unity of doctrine is apparent amidst certain divergencies, and indeed curious inconsistencies, of expression.[13] To grasp it all that is necessary is to bear in mind the many senses in which Scholastics employed the word " cause." Scotus, least of all, should have restricted the meaning of the term, seeing that he himself employed *movere* as St. Thomas had employed it.[14] The really important point in the explanation given by St. Thomas, though sometimes it has been responsible for the impression that he sacrificed liberty to his intellectualism, is to be found in his affirmation of an indestructible concord between the practical judgment and action. " The judgment which decides that a certain action is to be placed can never be out of harmony with appetite." [15] " Just as natural tendency springs from nature and is in accord with it, so does the tendency which corresponds to sensitive and intellectual nature follow knowledge . . . there is no room for evil in the appetite as arising out of a discrepancy between appetite and perception seeing that appetite (on the contrary) follows knowledge." [16] In all this there is no renunciation of his views on the part of St. Thomas, but, by an unexpected subordination of intellect to liberty, he succeeds in avoiding psychological determinism. Human liberty, springing from the diaphanous nature of mind, is essentially due to the capacity for " judging one's judgment " (*libertas in arbitrium*). In this man differs from the animals, for in them spontaneity does not exclude the most rigorous psychological determinism (*Agunt*

[12] *Mal.*, 3, 3.
[13] *Quamvis intellectus non secundum modum causae efficientis et moventis, sed secundum modum causae finalis moveat voluntatem.* 1 *Contra Gentes*, 72, 6.
[14] *Cf.* Minges, *Ist Duns Scotus Indeterminist ?* (*Beiträge zur Geschichte der Philosophie des Mittelalters*, Bd. V., Heft 4, Munster, 1905, pp. 105, 107).
[15] *Ver.*, 24, 1.
[16] *Mal.*, 16, 2.

quidem arbitrio, sed non libero),[17] that among the many things
desirable which are incapable of being simultaneously
possessed he can choose one or other object in virtue of his
power to choose one or other of his judgments.   This
doctrine might be roughly stated by saying that St. Thomas
carries forward liberty to the instant which precedes final
apprehension ; or, more accurately, since the temporal
duration of an act has nothing to do with its liberty, it
must be said that St. Thomas admits a reciprocal causality
belonging to two different orders, of the deciding will
(efficient cause) and of the idea (quasi-material and dis-
positive cause).[18]   What is to be borne in mind, then, is that
there are two different orders, one of determination without
any possible antecedent provision or necessity, and the other
of liberty ; in this way no break is introduced into the
continuity of being, and no magical power of making something spring from nothing is invoked.   This doctrine satisfies
the requirements of an intellectualist psychology, since
without a judgment there is no movement, and it safeguards
the independence of will since it is man himself who is
responsible for his own judgments.   It is the literal illustration of the Gospel-dictum so dear to the heart of Christian
Voluntarists : *sui facit veritatem*.   That is why in all sin the
lapse on the part of " intellect goes hand in hand with that
of will," [19] which goes to show that " evil desire is always
linked up with some error of practical knowledge." [20]

The mediæval adversaries of St. Thomas [21] were not slow
to point out to him that he was reviving the Socratic
identification of virtue and knowledge rejected by Aristotle.
As a matter of fact, the refutation of the Socratic thesis was
one of the favourite themes of St. Thomas.   It was when
treating of this question in relation to Socrates that he
brought full light to the discussion by distinguishing two
kinds of knowledge.   On the one hand, there is a universal
knowledge which may be " overcome by passion," and, on

[17] *Mal.*, 16, 5.
[18] Cf. *Ver.*, 28, 7.
[19] *Mal.*, 16, 2, 4.
[20] *Mal.*, 16, 6, 11.
[21] Henry of Ghent, *Quodlibetum*, 1, q. 16.

the other, there is a concrete or particular knowledge which is never out of harmony with the act performed.[22]   In this the reader will recognise a celebrated explanation given in the *Nichomachean Ethics ;* St. Thomas accepted unreservedly the theory of his Master contained in the " syllogism of the incontinent."   The originality of St. Thomas in relation to Aristotle consisted in this that he linked up this particular case with his whole system of rational psychology and insisted explicitly on the necessity for a judgment of reason as the necessary precursor of all action ; before desire could be a force for action it had to be intellectualised, so to speak. The mechanism of sin, when habitual knowledge failed because of the simple absence of actual reflection, more complicated in the presence of co-existing affirmation and negation, always presupposes the collaboration of that which is most " subtle and divine " in us, of reason itself.[23]   It is of decided importance to bear in mind the very marked distinction that obtains between the two kinds of knowledge. The first kind referred to is general in its nature and may be identified with science properly so called ; of that St. Thomas says that it is relatively unimportant for moral life.[24]   The second is particular, or practical, knowledge ; it alone is of decisive influence for action, and it is with the value of that kind of knowledge that we are here concerned.

III

The value of the practical idea in human action, such as it appears in the philosophy of St. Thomas, is exactly the reverse of the value accorded by him to the idea that belongs to the pure intellectual process as such.   It is all the more perfect in its sphere as its immanent character diminishes

---

[22] 1a, 2ae, q. 77, a. 2 ; *Mal.,* 3, 9, etc.

[23] See 1a, 2ae, 1c. ad 5 : It is all very well for man in a passion to condemn his sin by word of mouth, *tamen interius hoc animo sentit quod sit faciendum.* His particular and deep judgment *is* independent of vague and verbal assertion ; he resembles the drunken man who pronounces words full of meaning without being able to weigh the meaning his words contain.   Likewise the proud man does judge in the abstract and speculatively *aliquod bonum esse quod non est a Deo.* 2a, 2ae, q. 162, a. 4 ad 1.

[24] In 2 *Eth.,* l. 4 ; 3 d. 35, q. 1, a. 3, sol. 2 ad 2.

and according as its grasp of things distinct from it is less direct and immediate.

Immanence implies the capacity to penetrate to the depths of a reality independent of space and time. It includes also the idea of a gathering together, a unification, which is perfect only when there is complete identity of intelligible object and knowing subject. It would be possible to go down the hierarchy of intelligences, as we did at the outset when showing the growth of immanence with increasing immateriality, and we should find that the efficaciousness of the practical idea (in which its value consists) would grow and extend with increasing immateriality in the animal realm. Living things belonging to the lower orders perform " very few actions," a small number of innate images suffices for their reactions to the simple conditions of their existence. In the higher animals a certain " conditional liberty " and a " semblance of free-will " is recognisable. Sensitive to impressions that come to them from external objects, their power of reaction is more supple, the empire of that innate system of ideas which constitutes their instinct over them is less rigorous and absolute. " They can act if they judge that it is necessary to act, and if they do not so judge, they need not act. But because their judgment is determined to be such and such, so, in like manner, their tendencies and their action are determined ; perception or emotion wields a necessary influence in determining either their flight or their pursuit. Thus, a sheep on seeing the wolf takes fright and in virtue of a necessary impulse it will seek to save itself from him, just as the angry dog will bark and start off in pursuit of its enemy." " Because they are not aware of the reason of their judgment they cannot be said properly speaking to judge ; they simply follow the impulse God has given them, they are not responsible for a decision which they carry about with them so to speak, and they cannot be said to enjoy freedom." In addition because they lack the light of reason " the judgment which is theirs does not extend to the ideal range of all being, but only to certain determined objects." Just as the sphere of their perception is restrained and limited, so also is their sphere of action which covers the possible extent of their practical idea : " All swallows build the same kind of nests and the industry of the bee does not go beyond the formation of honeycombs to attempt any other form of art." [25] With liberty, however, and the power to judge one's judgment, the field of action is extended according as the restrictive empire of the practical idea loosens its hold. We must be careful, though, not to imagine that we can find full and complete liberty outside of God, since in all other intellectual beings we have not that divine identity of nature and intelligence. Man, no doubt, is free, but just as in the actual order of things his knowledge is limited to the intelligible that we find in sensible things, so also is his freedom hampered. The power of the practical idea is restricted to a circle traced for him by his limited corporeal nature. He cannot, for example, communicate his thoughts to others without taking account of space and time, nor can he think without having recourse to images : such purely spiritual actions do not fall within the sphere of his choice. What is true of the species holds also for the individual ; in the species general principles govern the form of activity, and in the individual there are particular principles that exert their influence. [26] Thus, the uninitiated rustic *cannot hic et nunc* think the principles of abstract geometry, and the intemperate man *cannot*, even if he so wished, act like the man of virtue, [27] and yet such actions are not beyond the powers of men in general. This principle still holds true as we ascend

---

[25] *Ver.*, 24, 1 and 2. *Cf.* 1 q. 55, a. 3 ad 3 for the idea of *prudentia*, which in man is universal and in the fox or lion merely particular, because in them it is restrained to acts of circumspection or magnanimity.

[26] *Pot.*, 2, 2 end.

[27] See the almost determinist expressions that he employs when speaking of the force of habit (*Comp. Theol.*, 174 ; *Ver.*, 24, 12 ; *cf.* ad 13). The capacity for the formation of habits is one of the great differences that separates man from angel in the philosophy of St. Thomas. Man, subject to duration, constantly re-makes and transforms himself. In the case of man it would not be sufficient to study one instantaneous and definitive decision (as happened in the sin of the angels) in order to have an adequate idea of the value of his practical idea ; rather it is necessary to remember that man arrives face to face with each particular moral problem in a state where previous decisions and conditions still hold sway, and that he is more or less apt to know the good simply and that he is more or less free.

the series of intellectual beings ; there is a direct relation between their free capacity for action and the universality of their ideas. Only in God, however, do we find unlimited power regarding all things *simpliciter* because of the identity of His Essence with the divine Idea ; in Him the Word, corresponding to what we have called the practical idea, comprises the whole world of intelligibility, infinite in extent like His Nature with which it is identical. His liberty is consequently perfect and unlimited.[28] The reason of this is to be found in the identity of the divine idea with the divine nature, while at the opposite extreme liberty is lacking to crude bodies because there is no room for a distinction between their tendency and idea and their nature ; but in the case of God idea is taken in its active sense, and, in the other, idea represents the thought of God taken passively and as realised in matter. In those beings that range between God and matter there will be a greater or less degree of liberty according to the distinction they can make between their ideas and what they are. In the whole series of corporeal things the more limited and rarer their ideas, the more these ideas exert a constraining influence, and this restraining influence will have for effect a greater impulse towards action. In the world of pure spirits the less limited and the less numerous their ideas, the less restrictive is their influence, but with this loosening of restraining influence there is a consequent loss for efficaciousness of action.

Such is the general schema which illustrates the constraining influence of the practical idea in different orders. When we come to examine this influence of the practical idea more in detail where man is concerned, it will be found that practical ideas are all the more powerful according as they are more subjective, less immanent, spread throughout the whole organism, more animal so to speak, and less typically human in the sense of being intellectually unified. Abstract moral knowledge may be a necessary condition for virtue,

[28] (*Naturale agens*) *secundum quod est tale, agit ; unde quamdiu est tale, non facit nisi tale. Omne enim agens per naturam habet esse determinatum. Cum igitur esse divinum non sit determinatum, sed contineat in se totam perfectionem essendi, non potest esse quod agat per necessitatem naturae*, etc. (1 q. 19, a. 4).

but it is not a cause of virtue ; the idea, in fact, ceases to be pure light and becomes rather a force precisely at the moment when it ceases to be a purely intellectual reaction. " Our acts and our elections are in reference to particular things ; wherefore, the sensitive appetite, being a faculty that has to do with the particular, has a great influence in disposing a man so that something seems to him such or otherwise in particular cases." [29] It is in that way, when the sense-faculties succeed in colouring intellect with their own tints, that tendencies of the sensuous order succeed in moving the will.

The peripatetic theory of the virtues, as adopted and developed by St. Thomas, throws a very clear light on this doctrine. Every man by an act of will, aided by the light of natural moral principles, can, if he so wishes, perform an act of virtue. Yet no human act is virtuous in the true and fullest sense which does not proceed from moral intuition (*prudentia*). Now this intuition is exclusively a personal and a practical one : it regards *my* acts, its object regards particular things and happenings, and it may extend to, and include, the internal senses. [30] What is yet more characteristic, it presupposes necessarily the presence of moral virtues in the sensitive faculties, and is not without implying also a certain virtuous disposition on the part of the body. [31] This pervasion of the whole organism by good habits is absolutely essential to the Thomist conception of virtue. [32] The " irascible " and " concupiscible " part of man must first be impregnated with fortitude and temperance before a man can be said to have " prudence " and with it all the other virtues. St. Thomas is certainly aware of the necessary

[29] 2a, 2ae, q. 9, a. 2, ad. 2. *Cf. Ver.* 22, q. 6.
[30] 2a, 2ae, q. 47.
[31] This is constantly affirmed by St. Thomas : *Ad prudentiam requiritur moralis virtus, per quam fit appetitus rectus* (1a, 2ae, q. 5a, a. 4) ; *Ex necessitate habet secum adiunctas virtutes morales tanquam salvantes sua principia* (In *Eth.*, l. 4) ; *Quod autem habeat rectam intentionem finis circa passiones animae, hoc contingit ex bona dispositione irascibilis et concupiscibilis* (1a, 2ae, q. 56, a. 4 ad 4).
[32] 1a, 2ae, q. 56, a. 4, etc. *Cf. Eth. Nic.*, 13, 1117 b. δοκοῦσι γὰρ τῶν ἀλόγων μερῶν αὗται εἶναι αἱ ἀρεταί. As long as violent struggles have to be sustained a person cannot be said to be truly virtuous (1a, 2ae, a. 3 ad 2 ; *Virt. Card.*, a. 1 ad 6, where the temptations of St. Paul are treated). The basis for virtue formation in man must be looked for in the amenability of the irrational part of man to be " persuaded " by reason (*Ver.*, 25, 4, etc.).

limitations of this doctrine which, if pushed too far, would land moral science in the subjectivism of mere material conditions. He is at pains to multiply his formulæ and to make them precise in order to break through, at its very source, the vicious circle wherein the mutual conditioning of virtues and intuition seems at times to enclose Aristotle.[33] But when the distinction between the abstract idea which affects consciousness and the practical idea which alone is a force for action permits him to avoid the vicious circle, he develops the consequences of his system with fearless logic. An action which results simply from an abstract idea and emanates from the naked will is not to be qualified as " virtuous " in the strict sense of the word. But in as much as it tends by force of habit to influence the organism and give rise to an inclination for its repetition, then according as this disposition spreads to the whole man it will favour the advent of prudence in the reason itself. In other words, it is possible that ideas which are definite, forceful and spontaneous may result. Prudence is almost entirely absent from a soul that reacts tumultuously to strong emotions simply

---

[33] Zeller, for example, reproaches Aristotle with " *eine unverkennbare Unsicherheit über das Verhaltniss des sittlichen Wissens zum sittlichen Handeln.*" " *Die Tugend soll ja im Einhalten der richtigen Mitte bestehen, und diese nur von dem Einsichtigen bestimmit werden können*" (*Philosophie der Griechen*, 1113, pp. 804 and 658). St. Thomas says, on his side : " *Scire praeexigitur ad virtutem moralem . . .*" and " *Prudentia praesupponit rectitudinem voluntatis ut principium*" (1a, 2ae, q. 56, a. 3 ad 2 et 3. Compare *Virt. Card.*, a. 2, etc.). A purely static psychology could not avoid contradiction here ; but this disappears, if one considers the origin and development of virtue, in the potential being of man. From the beginning, and all the way through, the general principles of morality are present as abstract ideas (synderesis). On their origin, see *Ver.*, 16, 1 ; 1 q. 79, a. 12 : on their clarity, *Ver.*, 17, 2 ; *Quodl.*, 3, 26). These great principles do not assume virtues (1a, 2ae, q. 58, a. 5 ad 1 ; 2a, 2ae, q. 47, a. 6). Obtaining virtues consists in first acting forcibly in accordance with these principles, in order to obtain the obedience of physical appetites and the accuracy of moral intuition, which are co-relative. Moral intuition is not, in fact, directed towards ends but towards means (see the texts quoted above). So the sovereignty of the intellectual element, properly a whole, is only divided by nature, and completed by liberty. *Principium primum, ratio est.* And because light, however dim it is, always remains, so long as responsibility remains, blind inclinations are always capable of justice. "*Sic igitur qualis unusquisque est secundum corpoream qualitatem, talis finis videtur ei ; quia ex huiusmodi dispositione homo inclinatur. . . . Sed istae inclinationes subiacent iudicio rationis.*" This is as true of acquired habits as it is of innate dispositions (1 q. 83, a. 1 ad 5). But, as is afterwards said, bad habits, becoming natural, place obstacles in the way of the actual consideration of principles, and gradually diminish their clarity.

because the body has not been brought under control. There is no prudence properly so called without some degree of developed virtue, and there is little real security or moral sensitiveness where virtue has not spread from the will to the passions of the body. Morality then must be deeply engrained in the whole man ; one must be holy not only in spirit but in the body also. In this conclusion we have the principle, which he constantly employs, of the necessary subordination of parts to the whole for the plenary perfection of a being capable of progress. It is the practical idea, in its dual capacity as efficient cause and result to be obtained, which binds thought and action together : *Qualis unusquisque est, talis finis videtur ei.*

It is not easy, in the case of the virtuous man, to mark off the effect of his character on his intuition since for him the function of intuition is to light up the obscure mass of things to be done, *agibilia*, which are almost indefinite in number and always of a relative character.[34] It is quite different

[34] St. Thomas has scarcely studied in detail the *progress* of the virtuous individual with the increasing docility of his body. The explanation is probably to be sought in the modifications of the moral ideal introduced by Christianity. In the lives of the saints which he could have read St. Thomas did not find a virtuous moral development in accordance with the rules of Nicomachean Ethics. In them grace had been more efficacious than intelligence and will, and the imitation of Christ Crucified was sufficient to make them rejoice in works where it was necessary to be " insensitive "—a vice according to Aristotle (see St. Thomas himself, 2a, 2ae, q. 142, a. 1, etc.)—if they were not to hate. St. Thomas has roughly sketched the fundamental principles of specifically Christian asceticism, but these principles do not seem to have commanded an adequate philosophic appreciation. In the matter of supernatural psychology I should refer to a conception which seems parallel to his idea of prudence and its dependence on subjective conditions, that of " intelligence," one of those gifts of the Holy Ghost compared by St. Thomas to the " heroic virtues " spoken of by Aristotle (2a, 2ae, q. 159, a. 8 ad 1 ; 1a, 2ae, q. 68, a. 1 ad 1. The gift of intelligence is treated in 2a, 2ae, q. 8. In art. 6 St. Thomas retracts explicitly his teaching of 1a, 2ae, q. 68, a. 4 on the exclusively speculative significance of this gift). The gift of intelligence brings with it a kind of experimental and personal perception of the Final End ; it is both speculative and practical because of the individuality of its object ; its activity is not one of judgment but rather a " penetration to the intimate essence of things " wherein the identity of the ultimate End with the God of Revelation and the Church, the God " of Abraham, of Isaac, of Jacob," is perceived. Faith in this context would correspond to abstract science since it can exist in a soul devoid of habitual grace, though precariously ; whereas the apperception of the ultimate End by means of the gift of intelligence ceases with the advent of sin and the disappearance of grace. Like the practical idea, then, it depends on good will, and is, says St. Thomas, the object of the sixth Beatitude : " Blessed are the clean of heart for they shall see God."

with the vicious individual who is deeply sunk in vice. In
him the very darkness of his mind allows him to follow clear
and general principles, and it is less difficult to mark the
stages of this invading darkness which overtakes his mind.
There is a certain analogy between the spiritualisation of the
organism in the one case and the degradation of intelligence
in the other. Just as the body of the virtuous individual
does not become entirely spirit, so neither does the mind of
the vicious man become completely materialised and
degraded. There is a subjugation of one by the other rather
than a complete transformation of one into the other. It is
always an *idea*, a practical idea, which is in power and its
influence is the more assured and insolent according as the
members are the more disposed to fall in with its commands.
The mind of the vicious individual takes on his character,
engages all its energies in the pursuit of bodily pleasures,
and the minimum of speculative enquiry that is left is tinged
with a metaphysic that is materialistic. When one leaves
behind that uncertain state which characterises the " con-
tinent " or the " incontinent " (of both of whom it may be
said *Quia duplex est, duplex finis videtur ei*), there is a tendency
to find a certain equilibrium in evil not unlike the poise and
balance of the perfectly virtuous or " temperate " man.
The mind of those who are divided in their allegiance to
good or evil may be represented by a quasi-syllogism of four
propositions, whereas in the confirmed intemperate person,
as in the perfectly virtuous man, unity of desire succeeds in
bringing about a certain unity of outlook : *Intemperatus . . .
totaliter sequitur concupiscentiam, et ideo etiam ipse utitur syllogismo
trium propositionum.*[35]

When the good of the body alone becomes the first
principle in life we are in presence of the power of the
practical idea in its most intense form. This influence can
be gauged by the fact that the acceptance of such a principle
can succeed in banishing from the field of actual consciousness all thought of ends or values. This applies not only to
such values as are acquired in the exercise of virtue, but
extends even to such as might easily suggest themselves as

[35] *Mal.*, 3, 9, 7.

immediately evident or as direct conclusions from evident principles. The influence of the practical idea has so invaded the entire man that even his higher faculties, in their oblivion of principles, are affected and surrender their very birthright. True, this systematic influence is never completely and radically efficacious precisely because the organism does not cease to be itself and is distinct from the idea. The impenetrability of matter asserts itself even here, and on last analysis it is only spiritual principles that can unify. It is impossible that every sense-appetite of the body should at one and the same time find complete expression. " To commit sin does not imply an ascent from multiplicity to unity, as happens in the unifying of the virtues by prudence, but means rather the descent from unity to multiplicity. Self-love is a disintegrating factor, for it sends man's love out to the things of time which are many and diverse." [36]   Probably it is this inherent contradiction amongst the diversity of sins themselves which prevents the entire suffocation of conscience (synderesis). But in the end these unbridled inclinations induce a certain *modus vivendi*, and gradually there is a fusion between a number of practical decisions the result of which is a sinful conscience where the domination of concupiscence is undisputed. " The ignorance of the intemperate man extends to the ultimate end itself ; he ends up by thinking that for him the good lies in the unrestrained following of his desires and impulses." [37] The opposing principle of duty, which implies responsibility, can become so effaced that it has no longer any power, even in speculative matters, to prevent him from constructing a purely animal philosophy. " Man is above all a spiritual being. But that does not prevent certain people from looking upon themselves particularly as creatures of flesh and blood and such people love themselves for what they think themselves to be." The inversion of things is then complete and it is speculation which, in the ends of action, overcomes the judgments of value that belong to psychological metaphysics. But the being who so subdues intel-

---

[36] 1a, 2ae, q. 73, a. 1 and ad 3.
[37] 2a, 2ae, q. 156, a. 3 ad 1.

ligence could have done so only by means of knowledge.
The triumph over abstract reason is the great history of the
practical idea.[38]

IV

The practical idea gains in efficacy according as it is more
subjective and more widely spread over the whole man.
Accordingly, its value in its own order is enhanced by the
imperfection of its grasp of the intelligibility of things as
such, distinct from the subject. The mind in fact is properly
speaking the *habitat* of ideas, whereas it is concrete sense-
impressions on the other hand that precipitate the whole
organism in the direction of action.

It would be necessary in fact to say, according to the
explicit principles of St. Thomas, that if from the beginning
the idea embraced reality simply and directly, then there
would be no room for action as the realisation of potentiality.
On such an hypothesis the intelligent nature would be
already in possession of its end, and the distinction of means
and ends would have no meaning. This, for instance, would
hold for the Angels if we confine ourselves to the natural
order and take no account of the supernatural ultimate end.
From the very beginning the Angel is in intellectual possession of its nature and liberated from shadows and obscurity.
Contemplative progress consequently is a thing unknown
for him.[39] It is quite different in the case of man who is
under the necessity of realising himself in contact with
matter and duration by the discursive activity of his higher
faculties. It is only when this life shall have come to an
end that man will cease to fabricate images of spiritual
reality and of the Absolute out of the stuff presented to him
by the relative. Then he will behold reality *sicuti est*.

Meanwhile the utility of human knowledge for action
must remain in indirect proportion to man's immanent
intellectual assimilation of reality.

Even in the application of theoretical knowledge to life

[38] 1a, 2ae, q. 24, a. 9.
[39] *Cf. De Malo*, 16, 5 and parallel passages in the *Summa's*.

man's intellectual inability in regard to the knowledge of concrete individuals implies, as we have said, a large dose of uncertainty and obscurity. The universal is the favoured object of the human mind, and the universal represents rather a fictitious condition of individual concrete realities ; it merely simulates what is the proper object of intelligence, the intelligible purity of the Separate Intelligences. Now, " those who seek only general propositions in the domain of human conduct deceive themselves." [40] " The subject-matter of moral science is diverse and varied and does not allow of perfect certitude." [41] " The practical sciences enjoy only the smallest degree of certainty because of the many circumstances that must be taken into consideration." [42] Accordingly St. Thomas goes so far as to say that moral theory, even in its abstract form, fashions a new kind of " truth " which differs from the speculative kind in virtue of its flexibility and relativity. *In speculativis est eadem veritas apud omnes tam in principiis et in conclusionibus. . . . In operativis autem non est eadem veritas vel rectitudo practica apud omnes quantum ad propria.* Elsewhere [43] he points out that what this new kind of truth loses in speculative value it gains in subjective tranquillity. For while it is possible in speculative matters to reach a definitive stage of doubt this possibility is excluded in moral matters : one cannot remain suspended in indecision (*perplexus*), a moral law is inexistent for him who knows nothing of it,[44] and it is possible to be in harmony with the divine Will while wishing materially what is contrary to it, etc. These examples go to show that the intellectual grasp of reality *as it is in itself* may be *per accidens*, a matter of indifference to good moral apprehension : some forms of ignorance and error exist which are not evil for the mind.

What is true of abstract moral knowledge and of its

[40] In 1 *Pol.*, l. 10.
[41] In 1 *Eth.*, l. 3.
[42] In 1 *Met.*, l. 2.
[43] 1a, 2ae, q. 94, a. 4.
[44] *Ver.*, 17, 3. *Nullus ligatur per praeceptum aliquod nisi mediante scientia alicujus praecepti. Cf.* solutions of particular cases : 2a, 2ae, q. 64, a. 6 ad 3 ; q. 88, a. 12 ad 2 ; and the more general principle in 1 d. 48, a. 4 : *Nullus appetitus tenetur tendere in illud bonum cujus rationem non apprehendit*.

necessary condition, the idea which enlightens, is still more true of the idea which is a force for action. By definition it is obtained not only from the data of the senses but belongs properly to sensitive faculties ; it signifies a certain informing of the organism and something that affects the imagination. Accordingly it will be coloured by the uncertainty and sub-jectivity of sense-knowledge. In proportion as it is efficacious for action it is always equally possible that it will be an inadequate rendering of reality. Rhetoric and poetry which give rise to practical ideas are equally potent in their order either in the cause of truth or error. Obscurity, absence of conscious limpidity, the possession of reality as it is in itself, always accompany the practically efficacious idea. In all this there is simply that fundamental conflict with the natural limpidity of intelligence which is the paradox of the human composition of intelligence and matter. Man ought to act uniquely *according* to reason and yet he cannot act *by* reason alone. Corresponding to reason's exclusive right to command in human affairs there is no " despotic power " on its part to enforce its injunctions ; such would have been the case only if virtue and knowledge were equivalent.[45]

Here indeed it must be said that practical value and theoretical truth, in so far as it can be possessed by a purely sensitive nature, resemble one another without any inferiority on the part of practical value. When passed on to the proper domain of mind and truth this equilibrium is broken and the intellectual possession of reality diminishes. *Veritas primo et per se in immaterialibus consistit et in universalibus.* For if here the idea is to become a force for action, then a complete transposition becomes necessary seeing that reality as it is in itself absolutely transcends the powers of imagination. Immaterial reality becomes dependent on what is sensible and tangible, and here the only form that " practical truth " can assume is that of a symbol. A symbol will be *true* to the extent of its influence over the irrational elements of man, making them subserve the end indicated for human action by mind, an end that entirely goes beyond their

---

[45] 1a, 2ae, q. 58, a. 2.

reach. The " lion of Juda " exists nowhere in reality, but its image in my imagination is justified when I think of God because it has the effect of persuading my emotional system to serve my will which fears God. The moral and religious symbol then, besides its value for action, has a certain subordinate speculative significance.[46]

When we come finally to the idea which is *immediately* practical and which directly suggests the action to be performed, whether that action takes the form of movement or of words uttered or of " making " and construction, we reach the peak-point where the maximum of force for action coincides with the maximum of intellectual grasp of reality as it is in itself. This practical idea is the indispensable and efficacious instrument of action, it represents the mind itself leaping into action, and, on the other hand, it corresponds to nothing already in reality ; nor does it pretend to do so. As the source of such exemplary ideas intelligence ranks as that " practical reason " which is so typical of the human mind,[47] and which St. Thomas always regards as in constant opposition to speculative intelligence, the function of which is to grasp reality as it is in itself. " The intellectual substance subordinates all things to itself, either to realise its own intelligible perfection by the contemplation of truth in them, or for the realisation of itself as an active power in the unfolding of its knowledge much like the artist who

---

[46] *Cf. Sent.*, 4 d. 10, q. 1, a. 4, sol. 2. If Christ is seen in the Host, there is no deception even though God has only miraculously modified the visual organ of the person who sees Him, *quia non fit nisi ad instructionem Fidei, et devotionem excitandam.*

[47] *Ratio practica, quae est hominis propria secundum suum gradum* (*Virt. Card.*, 1). It is unnecessary to point out that the term " practical reason " refers to intelligence as directed towards external action. *Cf. Ver.*, 7, 7 : Scientia operabilium ad prudentiam pertinens est homini naturalior quam scientia speculabilium. 1 q. 33, a. 7 ad 3 : Bonum proportionatum communi statui naturae accidit ut in pluribus, et deficit ut in paucioribus. Sed bonum quod excedit communem statum naturae, invenitur ut in paucioribus, et deficit ut in pluribus. Sicut patet quod plures hominum sunt qui habent sufficientem scientiam ad regimen vitae suae, pauciores autem qui hac scientia carent, qui moriones vel stulti dicuntur ; sed paucissimi sunt respectu aliorum qui attingunt ad habendam profundam scientiam intelligibilium rerum. It would seem that man was made to " work up " matter in an intelligent manner. *Cf.* In *Caus.*, l. 14 : intelligible realities which in themselves are undivided, unified and unchangeable " sunt in anima divisibiliter, multipliciter et mobiliter per comparationem ad intelligentiam. Sunt enim ad hoc proportionatae, ut sint causa multitudinis et divisionis et motus rerum sensibilium."

realises and expresses his own ideal in matter." [48] When we recall what was said at the outset of this volume in regard to the intellectual process as such, it is easy to see in this conception of the human mind as " artistic " the whole doctrine of its imperfect immanence and of its inherent capacity for pure intellectual activity. For us the capacity to modify reality by means of our organs is one way of "grasping" things, and, in a sense, a more real way than that which takes place in knowledge where reality is taken up by mind into its own life. [49] This necessary bifurcation of human action marks precisely man's position in the hierarchy of intelligences. He is lower than those pure intelligences whose intellectual activity is intuitive, since in their regard matter is incapable either of embodying their ideas or of helping them in their intellectual development. [50] Especially is man inferior to the infinite Intelligence Whose knowledge is the active cause of all there is : *Scientia Dei est causa rerum.*

[48] 3 *Contra Gentes*, 112, 6.

[49] *Ver.*, 18, 8, 3. Vel dicendum quod inferiores vires quantum ad aliquid superiores sunt, maxime in virtute agendi et causandi, ex hoc ipso quod sunt propinquiores rebus exterioribus, quae sunt causa et mensura cognitionis nostrae.

[50] 3 *Contra Gentes*, 80. Superiores quidem inter intellectuales substantias habent virtutem non explicabiles per aliquam virtutem corpoream . . .

CONCLUSION

INTELLECTUALISM AS A RELIGIOUS PHILOSOPHY

I

SPEAKING of Auguste Comte a positivist has recently penned the following lines : " The awe inspired by some of his words results on last analysis from the difficulty we experience in representing to ourselves the vivid intersection of thought by emotion, of a purely theoretical formula by action." Something similar is suggested by St. Thomas. How is it that his synthesis, which is a masterpiece of rational systematisation, has been for some the very ideal of religious philosophy ? To have an understanding of that it would be necessary to penetrate to the very depths of his thought and to realise as vividly as possible that for St. Thomas intellectualism implied a form of life the most intense and that for him mysticism was synonymous with an integral intellectualism.

A first acquaintance with Thomism does not give the impression of this depth of spiritual life which his system contains. What strikes one at first is his imperturbable confidence in reason and his absolute contempt in matters philosophical for irrational factors ; what may well be called the logical form of his intellectualism is very much in evidence. Thereby he stands in opposition to all philosophers who subordinate knowledge to the heart and will. " The really decisive factor for intellect is infallible truth ; every time it allows itself to be carried away by a sign that could deceive there is disorder."

As his requirements in the matter of certain knowledge are examined more closely it is found that his damaging critique of human knowledge forms an essential part of his system. And then his intellectualism is found to be indirectly opposed to " rationalism." " The soul of man is last in the series of beings endowed with intelligence and of all possesses the least share of intellectual power."

By then, however, he has abandoned nothing of what has been already acquired in his study of intellectualism, and it becomes necessary to relate the low opinion he entertains of man's intellectual capacity with his ideas on the absolute exigencies of intellectual knowledge in the abstract. Mind sees in itself a subject capable of dictating laws to which reality must conform. And here the affirmation of an infinite Intelligence becomes an absolute necessity. Many things surpass the power of man to understand, but there is nothing which, absolutely speaking, is not somewhere understood. If the owl does not see the sun, there is an eagle.[1] *There exists a form of intellectual activity, which is infinite in its efficacy, and which we call God.* In this thesis lies the very essence of ontological and moral intellectualism. It throws light on all those facts which pointed to the primacy of mind. It excludes all contrary objections by tracing them to their source in man's present defective and opaque mode of knowledge. It places the end of man in an intellectual acquisition of that transcendent Reality, Truth, and of that spiritual Personality whose nature is totally and identically speculative Idea. A definition of intellectualism results which places it in marked opposition to all doctrines which seek the ultimate nature of things in some form of dynamism or other as well as to that form of anthropomorphic Moralism which would suppress a " Being " over and above humanity and find a substitute for such a " Being " in abstract " Laws."

II

It was necessary to have been led thus far by the natural movement of thought before we could have hoped to recognise the exact antithesis of Thomism, and before the inner essence of a radical and consistent voluntarism could have been laid bare.

---

[1] *Sicut solem etsi non videat oculus nycticoracis, videt tamen eum oculus aquilae.* In 2 *Met.*, l. 111.

It is impossible to stop short at such conceptions as are covered by the terms " action," " heart " or " life." Nothing really characteristic, from a philosophic point of view, is afforded by the development of such ideas, and the most convinced Thomist could not object to them, except to say that they express too vaguely the " imperishable soul " of truth which he recognises in them. The real trouble does not lie there.

An approach is made to the really vital issue when voluntarism undertakes to determine more exactly the relations that hold between knowing and willing, and, fearing lest it might subordinate one to the other, prefers rather to accept the idea of a rupture between them and is satisfied to subject moral life to the rule of an irrational imperative. A further advance is made once it becomes possible to pick out the underlying postulate, generally an implicit one, which would identify all knowledge with human knowledge.

The really decisive stage, however, is reached, and the strict formula which expresses the primacy of appetite over reason appears, only when voluntarism is led to the denial of those very characteristic attributes which mark off reason from appetite. By nature mind is led to affirm an immutable order of things which is independent of movement, outside time, and above the realm of progress. To seek the ultimate nature of the real in desire or *tendency* would be to subscribe to an absolute dynamism. Just as intellectualism, at first impressed by judgments that are certain and then by direct intuition, only gradually finds itself when it is led on to the affirmation of subsisting Truth, so also does voluntarism pass from its initial contempt for knowledge, which it identifies with human reasoning, to discover its full ideal in the concept of movement as such. Intellectualism finds apt expression in the ancient formula : γένεσις ἕνεχα οὐσίας, and likewise voluntarism will recognise itself in this other one : γένεσις ἕνεχα γενέσεως. It will be seen that voluntarism substitutes becoming as the supreme good for the older idea of a subsisting absolute, the immutable God.

This reduction of pure and unconditioned intelligibility to the conditioned, limited and restrained conditions of practical life stands at the very antipodes of the thought of Aquinas, and would constitute, in his eyes, the most unmitigated and radical form of anthropomorphism.

III

In the light of the generalisation just given we may now obtain a brief and rapid survey of the Thomist system of intellectualism in which there is such an intimate co-mingling of religion and philosophy.

It is true that the central and pivotal thesis may be aptly expressed by the ancient formula : γένεσις ἔνεκα οὐσίας.

But since Revelation has brought such light to Nature and indicated the ideal of a personal possession of God as the destiny of all finite minds, the old Greek formula now becomes convertible with the love-inspired dictum of the Apostle : *non estis vestri.* The whole movement of our opening pages, which were devoted to an exposition of ontological Platonism, converged towards the affirmation of the infinite, pure and divine Idea to " gain " which was the ideal for all finite minds and in the possession of which the finite would " gain " itself ; here we see that the doctrine of the intellectual possession of God coincides with the doctrine of the primacy of love over all. A profound harmony, and indeed a certain continuity, reigns between religion and philosophy and between the orders of nature and grace : *gratia non tollit naturam, sed perficit.*

In other words, if the Middle Ages, which mark the classical epoch in which impersonal Reason held sway,[2] are also the ages in which Intelligence was worshipped as a personal Reality, we must look for the very quintessence of the mediæval mind in the writings of St. Thomas ; in him these two enthusiasms form one and the same thing. When, therefore, his intellectualism is attacked as irreconcilable with intensity of moral life on the pleas that there exists an

[2] In the Middle Ages there was no copyright for ideas, and the personality of the author counted for nothing. The pertinacity of the Scholastics in refusing either to give the names of their adversaries or to cite contemporary sources is only one of the proofs that then more than at any other time truth was considered the rightful possession of all.

opposition between the inner Master and the Supreme Cause or between the Word that illumines and the living God, this only goes to show what a meagre understanding the objector has of the fundamental principle of the Thomist system.

Absolute Life exists, so does infinite Reason and subsisting Truth : they are simply names for the existing God. On this unique principle are grounded the three undeniable traits of the Thomistic mentality : His religious dogmatism, his intellectual radicalism, and his " mystical " disdain of human reasoning.

A passionate love for the absolute Mind naturally engenders a love of dogma. The truth of Faith is the basis of our religion, and dogma serves to express the *object* of our religion. Were religion nothing more than a human product, and dogma merely the expression of human reactions to the facts of dogma, it would be the merest folly to sacrifice human happiness or human life for the sake of a dogma. But dogma has truth, it is more true even than science, and the object of dogma is above and beyond man. Likewise, sins against dogma are the most grievous of all,[3] and errors concerning ideas are more dangerous than those concerning men.[4] Take away dogma and you take God away ; to touch dogma is to touch God. To sin against dogma is to sin against God.

The exclusive and complete competency that we attribute to intelligence arises from our conviction that intellect is the faculty of the divine. This conviction leads us also to see in its exercise the highest and most lovable activity of which man is capable. All truth possesses pre-eminent

[3] See 4 d. 9, q. 1, a. 3, sol. 4 ; d. 13, q. 2, a. 2 ; 2a, 2ae, q. 94, a. 3, especially 2a, 2ae, q. 39, a. 2 : *Utrum schisma sit gravius peccatum quam infidelitas.* Of the two infidelity is the greater because it represents " peccatum contra ipsum Deum, secundum quod in se est veritas prima, cui fides innitur ; schisma autem est contra ecclesiasticam unitatem, quae est quoddam bonum participatum, et minus quam sit ipse Deus." Likewise, as appears from ad 2, the good of the multitude *est minus quam bonum extrinsecum, ad quod multitudo ordinatur.* Undoubtedly St. Thomas could say *dogma propter hominem,* understanding by dogma precisely the humanly deficient and conceptual expression of the ineffable reality corresponding to it, but he would have added immediately : *sed homo propter rem dogmatis.*

[4] In 1 *Cor.,* 4, 1 ; *Quodl.,* 12, 13 ; *Opusc.,* 1, p. 3, c. 1.

value, all truth is of God : *Omne verum, a quocumque dicatur, a Spiritu sancto est.*[5] Truth must then be sought after persistently, it must be accepted with avidity, and it must be possessed in all serenity of soul. Every proposition born of a reasoning that is certain must be considered as something acquired and as definitively justified : logical radicalism demands it. When speculative reason hearkening to the exigencies of being and reality affirms something, its affirmation must be accepted confidently : nothing less will satisfy the requirements of an intellectual objectivity.

It is only when we are in the presence of that Intelligence " which is identically its own act," however, that we possess the measure and ideal of all knowledge. The whole critique of knowledge finds its ultimate explanation in the theory of the divine knowledge. The decreasing perfections we discover in intuition, concept, judgment and reasoning must be computed in terms of the disparity that is seen to exist between them and the unique simplicity of knowledge to be found in God. A being is endowed with greater or less intellectual force according as its consciousness is more embracive in its unity or more dependent on a multiplicity of perceptions. The human soul comes last in the order of intellects because its power of knowledge is proportionate to the universe in which it lives, and because this present world is of a sensitive order whereas God cannot be sensed. This is a world of what is only mediately intelligible, roughly conceivable, and the truth of which is subject to variation, *regio dissimilitudinis.* Undoubtedly, the power of the human mind to judge and to generalise, though it ranks man lowest in the order of intelligences, endows him with the capacity for creating certain collections of notions such as the sciences, systems and symbolic poems which bring him in the direction of the pure idea without ever allowing him fully to reach its light or vehement unity. There is nothing entirely satisfying about such human creations, and since God has promised by His grace the vision of His Essence, wisdom itself encourages man to

[5] A maxim of St. Ambrose more than once cited by St. Thomas, who seems to make his own of it, as, for instance, In *Tit.*, l. 1, 3.

discount the present happiness of his earthly speculations in the favour of the divine promises. Happiness such as man may hope to enjoy on earth must come from the life of Faith.

Christian life seems to have developed in the soul of St. Thomas an enthusiasm for intelligence side by side with a disdain for mere human reasoning. In the last days of his life, therefore, he cannot be said to have abandoned his own theories, but rather to have made a practical application of them, when he prolonged his hours of contemplation and ceased to study *suspendit organa scriptionis*, as the rather untranslatable Latin of the Chronicler puts it. The *Summa* had not been completed and his companion pressed him to take up his pen again. " Impossible," St. Thomas told him, " all I have written now appears to me as so much straw." *Raynalde, non possum : quia omnia quae scripsi, videntur mihi paleae.* In these words, one may say without fear of paradox, we possess an exact formula in which to express the intellectualism of St. Thomas.

APPENDIX

INTELLIGENCE AND SOCIETY

In this Appendix an effort is made to delineate what may be called the social and political Intellectualism of St. Thomas. *Omnes homines participatione speciei sunt quasi unus homo.* In his theory of society the general principles that govern his outlook on intelligence in the life of the individual make their appearance again, and the present account may be looked upon as a kind of check on the general doctrine already given as well as perhaps a verification of it. His doctrine of society, however, remains rather too general in his outlines, and he has scarcely modified the views of his predecessors (Aristotle, Augustine, Maimonides) sufficiently to allow us to carry it with any success into matters of detail. We have accordingly confined ourselves to the chief headings under which his doctrine may be placed and have followed somewhat the same order as in the body of the text.

I. THE PRIMACY OF INTELLIGENCE

The ultimate end of humanity, as of the individual, is contemplation. This is true of man's existence on earth, in so far as such a life is feasible, *secundum quod contingit multitudinem contemplationi vacare.*[1] For if intelligence constitutes man's " most precious possession," then the doctors and thinkers occupy the first place in the ranks of men. Amongst these individuals themselves primacy belongs to those who, out of the superabundance of their own contemplative life, are in a position to pass on their light to others, to be " illuminators " of humanity. Bishops, doctors, preachers are in this exalted position.[2] St. Thomas too seeks the most imposing words to convey the prestige and authority of those whose rôle it is to teach in the name of God. *Respectu Dei sunt homines et respectu hominum sunt dii.*[3] He has little difficulty in linking up this doctrine of their pre-eminence with his metaphysic. For if the doctors of intellectual warfare are in

---

[1] 3 *Sent.*, d. 35, q. 1, a. 4, sol. 1 ad 2.
[2] 2a, 2ae, q. 188, a. 6 ; *Opusc. de Perf. vitae spir.*, c. 19 and 20. Teaching as such belongs to the active life (2a, 2ae, q. 181, a. 3 ; *Opusc. Contra Retrahentes*, c. 7). But for the real " Illuminators " teaching is the natural result of their lives of contemplation.
[3] 3 *Sent.*, d. 25, q. 2, a. 1, sol. 4.

a position to win a crown (*aureola*) more glorious than any other, it is because such battles are waged *circa bona intelligibilia, aliae vero pugnae circa sensibiles passiones.*[4] Filled with admiration for this type of " illuminative " life, the realisation of which he sees both in the Episcopate and in the Dominican family, St. Thomas is less impressed by the humble devotedness of the race of parish priests : *In aedificio autem spirituali sunt quasi manuales operarii, qui particulariter insistunt curae animarum, puta sacramenta ministrando, vel aliquod hujus modi particulariter agendo.* The bishop and the masters in theology, whose sphere of influence is more extensive, are endowed with knowledge that is " architectonic."[5] Political power ranks lower in his hierarchy of values since the end of civil society is terrestrial whereas that of the Church is celestial. Besides, granting that the " State may be looked upon as the greatest achievement of the practical reason,"[6] yet the human spirit is not completely imprisoned within its confines : " political society is not the ultimate end of man from every point of view."[7] And since the end envisaged by civil power, that of a socially virtuous life, is itself subordinate to the ultimate possession of God, civil power itself in the entire context of the universe where all must subserve divine ends is subordinate to spiritual authority.[8] We have here a current theory in the Middle Ages which has been rightly compared to the Platonic theory of the reign of the Idea in the State by concentrating power in the hands of philosophers. This *rapprochement* is doubly justified in the case of St. Thomas, who favours, even in the temporal order, the predominance of intellectuals in the matter of governing : *Illi homines qui excedunt in virtute operativa oportet quod dirigantur ab illis qui in virtute intellectiva excedunt.*[9] *Sicut autem in operibus unius hominis, ex hoc inordinatio provenit quod intellectus sensualem virtutem sequitur . . . , ita et in regimine humano inordinatio provenit ex eo quod non propter intellectus praeeminentiam aliquid praest.*[10] This conclusion, which he supports with the authority of Aristotle and of one " Salomon," may seem rather out of joint with the ideas of political traditionalism elsewhere defended, but it is explained in the light of the reflections which follow. Even when the governing power is not outstanding for intellectual capacity, yet it is Intelligence which governs when such an individual takes guidance from wise advisors : *servus sapiens dominabitur filiis stultis.*[11]

[4] 4 *Sent.*, d. 49, q. 5, a. 5, sol. 2.
[5] *Quodl.*, l. 14.
[6] In *Politic. Prol.*
[7] 1a, 2ae, q. 21, a. 4 ad 3.
[8] *Opusc.*, 16, c. 1, 14.
[9] 3 *Contra Gentes*, 78, 3.
[10] 3 *Contra Gentes*, 81.
[11] 3 *Contra Gentes*, 81.

II. THE INTELLIGENCE OF HUMANITY

Humanity is composed of a number of individual intelligences wedded to matter. This deep-seated composition of intelligence and matter in the nature of humanity brings the necessity of progress into relief as the primordial condition of man. Progress will mean a triumph over the opaque conditions of matter, represented by man's dependency on the senses for his knowledge, and the realisation of the kingdom of mind. In the life of the individual we have seen that by the *simultaneous* collaboration of his lower powers of knowledge man endeavours to find a substitute for the pure idea. In his doctrine of the intelligence of the race what strikes us is rather his view of the successive triumphs by which the mass of men is led on towards an increasingly purer vision of things. The history of philosophy (a rather rudimentary one) which he takes from Aristotle suggests to him a constant progress in this direction. From a rather crude perception of things to a closer appreciation of them, in which there is an increasing appreciation of the complexity of reality and its interrelations, he sees a progress which, while it consists in overcoming mere subjectivity, is also at the same time a step towards a more intellectual knowledge of things.[12] But the

[12] The primitive thing in intellectual knowledge is a certain transparent identifying of the mind with reality. Consequently progress for reflective or philosophic thought is twofold. On the one hand, it will consist in the ability to distinguish between the thing in itself and the conditions of its perception. On the other, it will mean distinguishing intelligence itself from material essences the conception of which actualises it. These two forms of progress are correlative. *Hoc enim animis omnium communiter inditum fuit, quod simile simili cognoscitur. Existimabant autem (antiqui philosophi), quod forma cogniti sit in cognoscente eo modo quo est in re cognita. . . . Priores vero naturales quia considerabant res cognitas esse corporeas et materiales, posuerunt oportere res cognitas etiam in anima cognoscente materialiter esse. Et ideo, ut animae attribuerent omnium cognitionem, posuerunt eam habere naturam communem cum omnibus . . . ; ita quod qui dixit principium omnium esse ignem, posuit animam esse de natura ignis ; et similiter de aere et aqua* (1 q. 84, a. 2). *Existimabant autem antiqui philosophi quod res responderent apprehensioni intellectus et sensus ; unde dicebant quod omne quod videtur est verum, ut in* 4° *Metaph. dicitur : et propter hoc credebant, quod etiam in rebus esset infinitum* ... *eadem ratione videtur esse extra caelum quoddam spatium infinitum : quia possumus imaginari extra caelum in infinitum quasdam dimensiones* (In 3 *Phys.*, l. 6, 406, a. ; cf. *Ar. Phys.*, 4). They have then, according to St. Thomas (he probably places Pythagoras among the πρῶτοι θεολογοῦντες), united naïve realism with absolute relativism. *Primi philosophi, qui de naturis rerum inquisiverunt, putaverunt nihil esse in mundo praeter corpus. Et quia videbant omnia corpora mobilia esse et putabant ea in continuo fluxu esse, existimaverunt, quod nulla certitudo de rerum veritate haberi possit a nobis* (1 q. 84, a. 2). The theory of the absolute " flux " of things and of the impossibility of affirming unchanging truth was a necessary consequence of their materialism : *Cum res materialiter in anima ponerent, posuerunt omnem cognitionem animae materialem esse, non discernentes inter intellectum et sensum* (1 q. 48, a. 2). Plato, coming later, did have the idea of immutable truth, but, unable as yet to give a critique of knowledge, he fell into a kind of realism or inverted subjectivism. *Patet autem diligenter intuenti rationes Platonis, quod ex hoc in sua*

development of revealed truth is still more instructive than that
of philosophy. Following the dictum of St. Gregory, *secundum
incrementa temporum crevit divinae cognitionis augmentum*, St. Thomas
in reality does not extend this development beyond the Apostolic
Age ; but the comparison which he institutes between the present
era and those which preceded it (there are three great epochs :
ante legem, sub lege, sub gratia [13]) brings out notable differences
between the increasingly perfect acquisition of truth and suffices
to suggest the progress towards a more and more enlightened
intellectuality. The Jews, according to the doctrine of the
Apostle, were " slaves of sordid elements " and were confined to
parables. *Omnia quae credenda traduntur in Novo Testamento
explicite et aperte, traduntur credenda in Veteri Testamento, sed implicite
et sub figura . . . etiam quantum ad credenda lex nova continetur in
vetere.* [14] Though everything contained in the Law was true,
yet " the Law made no mention of external life." [15] The principle to be constantly invoked for the interpretation of Genesis
is the following : *Moyses rudi populo loquebatur, quorum imbecillitati
condescendens, illa solum eis proposuit quae manifeste sensui apparent.* [16]
To maintain *the truth* of all this figurative expression and at the
same time to see in it the " shadow " and the " night " of
Christian revelation (*Umbram fugat veritas, noctem lux eliminat*)
is to admit in a very real way that all truth is not definitive and
that humanity in its assimilation of the most vital truths has
made progress.

So much for what may be called *successive* approximations to
truth. But if we consider the intelligence of the human race at
any given moment, we shall also see that the multitude of
individual intelligences may be said to come together and,
united, give birth to one unique idea which is the particular
possession of no individual man but is shared by all. In the
chapter dealing with Science we have seen something similar

positione erravit, quia credidit, quod modus rei intellectae in suo esse sit sicut modus
intelligendi rem . . . utrique abstractioni intellectus posuit respondere abstractionem in
essentiis rerum . . ." (in I *Met.*, l. 8). To repeat a comparison dear to St.
Thomas, it may be said that Plato erred because in philosophy he took up the
attitude of the mathematician or geometrician. He looked upon things as
abstractions of mind and did not grasp the unreality that characterises the
abstractive activity of our reason. The opposite error, though analogous to
that of Plato, is found in those who regard " forms " as substances because
they cannot rise above imagination (*V.i.C.*, a. 11) and look upon the Angels as
individuals *in concretione*. Progress in philosophy can only come from the
strictest criticism of the human conditions of knowledge with a view to affirming ever more convincingly the inconceivable purity of spiritual Realities
(*cf.*, Part 11, a. 2).

[13] 2a, 2ae, q. 174, a. 6.
[14] 1a, 2ae, q. 107, a. 3, ad 1.
[15] In *Rom.*, x, 1.
[16] 1 q. 68, a. 3. *Cf.* q. 61, a. 1 ad 1, etc.

where the integral knowledge of any period may be said to exist in a coherent and articulated form outside and above the intelligences of individuals who for themselves possess merely an isolated piece of the whole. Belief, which is so absolutely necessary for human kind in the domain of *facts*, suggests analogous reflections. The rational certitude possessed by one man is not the direct result of his intuition of the intelligible object in such matters, nor is it based upon a rational analysis of it into its fundamental principles. Rather is it something linked up with the knowledge of his neighbour and his neighbour's testimony, for only in that way can the world progress.[17]

Regarding religious and moral truth, must a similar dependence be admitted? Every man who has correct ideas on God, the soul, the Church, ideas sufficiently clear to guide him to his destiny, is he in a position personally to verify them and justify them for himself? St. Thomas found himself here in a difficult position. The nature of mind, on his principles, was such that by the exercise of its powers a man should arrive at his perfection : any assent given which is not accountable to reason is a disorder. On the other hand, he could not blind himself to facts, the intellectual incapacity of many men, the urgent necessities of life which demanded constant attention to temporal affairs, a certain laziness in some and passions in others, not to speak of divergencies amongst philosophers. These reasons compelled him to conclude, following Maimonides, to a certain moral necessity of Revelation.[18] On the hypothesis of a God-given Revelation assent to the necessary truths for life is greatly facilitated. Yet the problem is not thereby wholly removed. It is true that divine things, shrouded in Scriptural symbols, are placed within the reach of all ; the Eternal is brought into time by the Incarnation of the Word and the Invisible is rendered tangible. But God has not chosen to speak directly and to the same extent to all men. *Reasons* must be found for belief. That being so, the rustic and the busy man, individuals who, morally speaking, would not be in a position to find their God in a rational way, will they have less trouble in discerning the true Religion?

At first sight it is difficult to reconcile certain passages which seem to introduce the irreparable breach of traditionalism into his theory of the sovereignty of personal reason. St. Thomas seems to accept on his own account the old distinction of those who know and the πιστοί and to regard the faith of the latter as reasonable only in so far as it may be said to be continuous with that of the former. But this difficulty is diminished if we remember that in the passages in question he is studying the

---

[17] In *Trin.*, 3, 1 ; 2a, 2ae, q. 109, a. 3, etc.
[18] 1 *Contra Gentes*, 4 ; In *Trin.*, 3, 1 ; 2a, 2ae, q. 2, a. 4.

relations of minds to truth not merely from a static, but also from a dynamic and chronological point of view. The difficulty resolves itself much in the same way as the apparent vicious circle of prudence and the virtues. Man is essentially a potential being with capacities undeveloped. As with those luxuried acquisitions that go by the name of the Sciences, so it is with the knowledge of God and of duty necessary for all men : *oportet addiscentem credere*.[19] The child can only believe what the man knows. And while waiting until he comes into conscious possession of himself, how can he act as a distinct spiritual person ? " The son is naturally part of the father." Just as before his birth the child is imprisoned in his mother's womb, so before the use of reason he " remains under the care of his parents as in a spiritual womb," and quite naturally it is the parents' reason which directs him on the way to God since *naturally* it is they who are charged with the care of him.[20]

It would be an error, however, to generalise the theory of the *spiritualis uterus* and to read St. Thomas as explaining the faith of the multitude in the same way as he explains that of children. Assuredly, reflex, speculative and ordered knowledge, according to him, is the privilege only of the few. Despite his views, already referred to, regarding the intellectual progress of the race he seems to have thought that illiterate masses would be always with us, just as children will be. But the unlettered multitudes are not completely deprived, even in speculative matters, of a certain minimum of rational convictions. If the scientific knowledge of God presupposes that of all the sciences,[21] yet a general idea of God as supreme Intelligence appears comparatively early and naturally in the minds of all.[22] For all the reasons for belief in Christianity are easily grasped and convincing. Finally, subtle reflections upon the mysteries of religion are reserved for the learned, who act imprudently in indiscriminate manifestation of such theorisings to all,[23] yet the uncultured must know for themselves explicitly the principal

---

[19] See In *Trin.*, I, c. *Sed quia ex nullo horum quae ultimo cognoscimus, sunt nota ea quae primo cognoscimus, oportet nos etiam primo aliquam notitiam habere de illius quae sunt per se magis nota : quod fieri non potest nisi credendo.* Reference is explicitly made to rational sciences and to the knowledge of divine things : *ad quorum quaedam cognoscenda plene possibile est homini pervenire per viam rationis in statu viae . . .*

[20] *Quodl.*, 2, a. 7. *Filius enim naturaliter est aliquid patris . . . continetur sub parentum cura sicut sub quodam spirituali utero.* I b ad 4 : *Puer, antequam usum rationis habeat, naturali ordine ordinatur in Deum per rationem parentum, quorum curae naturaliter subiacet.* St. Thomas concludes from this that it is not lawful to baptise the children of Jews against the parents' will. He also recalls this theological doctrine of the Middle Ages : *De pueris antiquorum patrum dicitur quod salvebantur in fide parentum. Cf. Quodl.*, 3, 11, 2 and 4, 23.

[21] In *Trin.*, I, c.

[22] 3 *Contra Gentes*, 38.

[23] In *Trin.*, 2, 4.

mysteries of Salvation [24] ; on these points it will not suffice for them to have " a mere implicit faith or one that is contained in that of the more learned." [25]

In a word, granting that St. Thomas is not afraid to look upon *successive* conquests of reality by mind as moments in one great movement, yet he does not consider that humanity at any given moment of time is such a unity that the rational convictions of one individual can supply for those of another. As against Averrhoism he held that to each man belonged his own intelligence, and from this inferred for the individual a strict duty to direct his life according to his lights and to act only for such motives as he himself should have perceived. [26]

III. INTELLIGENCE AND ACTION IN SOCIETY

If the idea as *light*, which concentrates for individual intelligence surrounding reality, is all the more rich as it is the more deeply immanent and the more personally possessed, the power of the idea as *force* depends on its empire over what is not purely intellectual in man. This holds true of societies as well as of individuals. That is why custom, which is so forceful in giving a particular bent to the social organism and of fundamental interest in the practical direction of life, is devoid of any value in those disciplines that address themselves primarily to man's mind. Progress is the motto of science, whereas tradition is the important thing in politics. *Ea quae sunt artis, habet efficaciam ex sola ratione ; et ideo ubicumque melioratio occurrit, est mutandum quod prius tenebatur. Sed leges habent maximam virtutem ex consuetudine, ut Philosophus dicit in 2° Polit., et ideo non sunt de facili mutandae.* [27] " Changes are not to be lightly made " : all progress is not excluded. But in the matter of legislation, according to St. Thomas, progress is not to be effected by the sudden promulgation to-day of what was entirely unknown yesterday : such progress is rather the work of those slow transformations which modify profoundly our ways of viewing things. In the life of the individual a distinction has been made between vital, fundamental and intimate judgments and such propositions as affect

---

[24] 2a, 2ae, q. 2, a. 7, etc.

[25] *Ibid.*, a. 6 ; *De Ver.*, 14, 7, etc.

[26] This principle is very definitely stated in regard to religious obedience. *Subditus non habet indicare de praecepto praelati, sed de impletione praecepti, quae ad ipsum spectat. Unusquisque enim tenetur actus suos examinare ad scientiam quam a Deo habet, sive sit naturalis, sive acquisita, sive infusa : omnis homo debet secundum rationem agere. Ver.*, 17, 5, 4. In the article from which this reply is taken St. Thomas explains that if conscience clearly sees a sin in the command given by the superior, it is a sin to obey : *Conscientia ligabit praecepto praelati in contrarium existente.*

[27] 1a, 2ae, q. 97, a. 2 ad 1.

only the very outward, almost verbal, surface of consciousness.
Recall the example of the drunken man : *etsi ore proferat hoc non
esse faciendum, tamen interius hoc animo sentit quod sit faciendum.*[28] In
the consciousness of peoples an exactly similar phenomenon will
be found. *Custom prevails over the law because it is the expression of a
deeper and more deliberate judgment. Per actus maxime multiplicatos,
qui consuetudinem efficiunt, mutari potest lex, et exponi, et etiam aliquid
causari quod legis virtutem obtineat ; inquantum scilicet, per exteriores
actus multiplicatos, interior voluntatis motus, et rationis conceptus
efficacissime declaratur. Cum enim aliquid multoties fit, videtur ex
deliberato rationis judicio provenire.*[29] Thus it comes to pass that the
written law must cede to custom, being nothing better than an
" empty declaration " seeing that the law is intended entirely for
man's utility. It is quite the contrary for Dogma, which is truth
above reform. In this theory of custom we meet again the principle which has dominated our whole study, the principle of the
difference between practical reason as the function of human
action and of speculative intelligence as the supreme end of the
universe. Should it happen that we find ourselves in presence
of a people for whom the law absolutely dominated man, binding
him to its inflexible limits instead of accommodating itself to
human needs, that people is none other than the race whose
existence itself was a symbol and whose life as a consequence had
something in it of the rigour of things intellectual. That is how
St. Thomas understands the Law which was so inflexible and
inhuman—so typically unperipatetic, one should have liked to
whisper to him. These poor Israelites were scarcely σπουδαῖοι !
*facilius . . . dispensatur in nova quam in veteri lege ; quia figura
pertinet ad protestationem veritatis, quam nec in modico praeterire
oportet ; opera autem secundum se considerata immutari possunt pro loco
et tempore.*[30]

[28] 1a, 2ae, q. 77, a. 2 ad 5.
[29] 1a, 2ae, q. 97, a. 3.
[30] 2a, 2ae, q. 122, a. 4 ad 4.